Finding Everett Ruess

ALSO BY DAVID ROBERTS

The Mountain of My Fear

Deborah: A Wilderness Narrative

Great Exploration Hoaxes

Moments of Doubt

Jean Stafford: A Biography

Iceland: Land of the Sagas (with Jon Krakauer)

Mount McKinley: The Conquest of Denali
(with Bradford Washburn)

*Once They Moved Like the Wind: Cochise, Geronimo, and
the Apache Wars*

*In Search of the Old Ones: Exploring the Anasazi
World of the Southwest*

Escape Routes

The Lost Explorer: Finding Mallory on Mount Everest
(with Conrad Anker)

*A Newer World: Kit Carson, John C. Frémont, and the
Claiming of the American West*

*True Summit: What Really Happened on the Legendary
Ascent of Annapurna*

Escape from Lucania: An Epic Story of Survival

*Four Against the Arctic: Shipwrecked for Six Years at the Top
of the World*

*The Pueblo Revolt: The Secret Rebellion That Drove the
Spaniards Out of the Southwest*

*On the Ridge Between Life and Death:
A Climbing Life Reexamined*

Sandstone Spine: Seeking the Anasazi on the First Traverse of the Comb Ridge

No Shortcuts to the Top: Climbing the World's 14 Highest Peaks (with Ed Viesturs)

Devil's Gate: Brigham Young and the Great Mormon Handcart Tragedy

The Last of His Kind: The Life and Adventures of Bradford Washburn, America's Boldest Mountaineer

K2: Life and Death on the World's Most Dangerous Mountain (with Ed Viesturs)

Finding
Everett Ruess

The Life and Unsolved

Disappearance of a Legendary

Wilderness Explorer

David Roberts

Broadway Books
New York

Grateful acknowledgment is made to the Special Collections, J. Willard Marriott
Library, University of Utah, for permission to reprint text from the Ruess Family
Papers; excerpts from letters, diaries, and essays by Everett Ruess; excerpts from
correspondence, essays, and diary notations by Christopher, Stella, and Waldo Ruess;
and excerpts of correspondence from others to the Ruesses.

Grateful acknowledgment also to Michèle Ruess, for permission to quote from diaries,
essays, and letters belonging to the Ruess family.
The Utah State Historical Society kindly granted permission to quote
from the papers of Harry LeRoy Aleson.
The blockprints at the head of each chapter are reproduced
from originals by Everett Ruess.

Library of Congress Cataloging-in-Publication Data
Roberts, David.
Finding Everett Ruess/David Roberts.—1st ed.
p.   cm.
1. Ruess, Everett, b. 1914.   2. Poets, American—20th century—Biography.   I. Title.
PS3535.U26Z78 2011
811'.52—dc22
[B]   2011008379

ISBN 978-0-307-59176-0
eISBN 978-0-307-59178-4

Printed in the United States of America

Book design by Leonard W. Henderson
Maps by Jeffrey L. Ward
Jacket design by David Tran
Front cover photograph courtesy of
the University of Utah, J. Willard Marriott Library,
Special Collections Department

1 3 5 7 9 10 8 6 4 2

First Edition

To the memory of Stella, Christopher, and Waldo Ruess—
Who loved Everett without qualification,
And who spent the rest of their days keeping his flame alive

Wherever poets, adventurers and wanderers of the Southwest gather, the story of Everett Ruess will be told. His name, like woodsmoke, conjures far horizons.

—*Hugh Lacy, 1938*

CONTENTS

In the spring of 1992, a twenty-four-year-old man from suburban Washington, D.C., seeking self-knowledge and a meaningful challenge, hitchhiked to Alaska and walked into the wilderness to live off the land. His name was Chris McCandless. As one of his last acts before heading into the bush alone, he mailed a postcard to a friend that cheerfully declared,

> Greetings from Fairbanks! This is the last you shall hear from me Wayne. . . . Please return all mail I receive to the sender. It might be a very long time before I return South. If this adventure proves fatal and you don't ever hear from me again, I want you to know you're a great man. I now walk into the wild.

Four months later, when McCandless's emaciated remains were discovered by moose hunters near the northern boundary of Denali National Park, *Outside* magazine assigned me to write an article about the tragedy, which I subsequently expanded into a book that was published in 1996 as *Into the Wild*. In the summer of 1993, while immersed in the research for the book, I was chatting about the project with David Roberts when he remarked, "You know, McCandless sounds a lot like Everett Ruess . . ."

"Uh, who's Everett Ruess?" I sheepishly inquired. Appalled at my ignorance, Roberts commanded me to get my hands on a copy of *Everett Ruess: A Vagabond for Beauty,* a collection of Ruess's letters and diary entries edited by W. L. Rusho, which had been published ten years earlier. As soon as I hung up the phone, I hurried out to my local bookstore and bought a copy, then stayed up the rest of the night reading it. By the time the sun came up I realized that Roberts was absolutely right: A number of the parallels between Ruess and McCandless were extraordinary.

Ruess disappeared in 1934, at the age of twenty, while on a solo trek through the red-rock canyon country of southern Utah—at the time a daunting expanse of wilderness imbued with a mystique comparable to that of present-day Alaska. Like McCandless, he was an idealist and a romantic. Both men felt a passionate attraction to risky endeavors in untrammeled landscapes. Here, for example, are two sentences from a postcard McCandless wrote while paddling alone down the Colorado River, sixteen months before embarking on his fatal Alaskan adventure:

> I've decided that I'm going to live this life for some time to come. The freedom and simple beauty of it is just too good to pass up.

And here are a couple of lines from a letter Ruess sent in November 1934, shortly before he vanished without a trace:

> As to when I shall visit civilization, it will not be soon, I think. I have not tired of wilderness; rather I enjoy its beauty and the vagrant life I lead, more keenly all the time.

The uncanny resonance between these and other bits of writing by the two young adventurers was so arresting that a week after learning about Ruess from Roberts, I drove 1,200 miles from my home in Seattle to the headwaters of an obscure ravine called Davis Gulch, the site of Ruess's last known camp. For most of its four-mile length, as I later described the defile in *Into the Wild*, it

> exists as a deep, twisting gash in the slickrock, narrow enough in places to spit across, lined by overhanging sandstone walls that bar access to the canyon floor. . . . The country surrounding Davis Gulch is a desiccated expanse of bald rock and brick-red sand. Vegetation is lean. Shade from the withering sun is virtually non-existent. To descend into the confines of the canyon, however, is to arrive in another world. Cottonwoods lean gracefully over drifts of flowering prickly pear. Tall grasses sway in the breeze. The ephemeral bloom of a sego lily peeks from the toe of a ninety-foot stone arch, and canyon wrens call back and forth in plaintive tones from a thatch of scrub oak. High above the creek a spring seeps from the cliff face, irrigating a growth of moss and maidenhair fern that hangs from the rock in lush green mats.

Standing on the canyon floor, pondering the precise spot where Ruess cooked his beans and grazed his burros and slept under the stars, I hoped to divine something from the particulars of the setting—some clue about his essence—that would by extension shed some light, however obliquely, on McCandless. I was not disappointed. My visit to Davis Gulch motivated me to learn as much as I could about Ruess, and ultimately led me to include a chapter describing his abbreviated life and baffling disappearance in *Into the Wild*.

At the time, the best source of published information was *Everett Ruess: A Vagabond for Beauty*. Now, twenty-eight years after the publication of Rusho's compilation, David Roberts has written the first comprehensive biography of Ruess. An irresistible read, *Finding Everett Ruess* is a remarkable book, the best thing Roberts has ever written. Although he doesn't claim to solve the riddle of his subject's death, Roberts presents an abundance of provocative new evidence that makes the mystery of Ruess's evanescent existence more compelling than ever.

Anyone who was intrigued by the story of Chris McCandless is likely to find *Finding Everett Ruess* utterly fascinating.

Jon Krakauer

AUTHOR'S NOTE

The title of this book carries a deliberate double meaning. Since 1998, when I first visited the Escalante country in a concerted effort to see if there was anything new that could be learned about the fate of Everett Ruess, I have cherished the hope that the passionate wilderness wanderer who disappeared so enigmatically in 1934, at the age of twenty, might actually be found. Or if the remains of his body could not be discovered, that enough clues could be ferreted out of the desert and the canyons so that we might be able to determine just how and where the young man met his untimely end.

I was hardly alone in that quest. During the more than seven decades that have elapsed since Everett vanished, all kinds of dedicated sleuths (and not a few mystical wackos) have made it a personal goal to solve the riddle of the vagabond's disappearance. The cult of Everett Ruess, which has steadily grown over the years, centers on that riddle. Every devotee who responds to the romantic intensity of Everett's writing or the visionary rapture of his paintings and blockprints wants to know what happened to him after he headed into Davis Gulch in November 1934.

Yet at the same time, steeping myself in the writings and artwork served another purpose, which was to "find" Everett Ruess in the maze of his moods and contradictions. What made him tick? What was he ultimately after? Why did he need such unrelenting solo adventures in the wilderness to test himself? And if he had a goal beyond endless wandering, how close did he come to fulfilling it?

Then, for more than a year, between the summer of 2008 and the autumn of 2009, along with a small group of friends and associates in southeastern Utah, I thought that we might have actually found Everett's body, wedged awkwardly inside a rock crevice in the sandstone monocline of the Comb Ridge. The ins and outs and ups and downs of that bizarre discovery and its aftermath took all of us on an extended emotional roller-coaster ride, and provoked a public response reaching as far as Russia and Japan.

It may be that the mystery of Everett's disappearance will never be solved. But thanks to the controversy that swirled around Comb Ridge, we have more hints and clues about the wanderer's fate—and about his character—than we have ever had before. In that sense, *Finding Everett Ruess* may form the appropriate rubric for a collective quest to solve a riddle that has no parallel in the history of the American West.

Opposite page: The first page of a letter from Everett Ruess to his brother, Waldo, the last he wrote before his disappearance. *Special Collections Dept. J. Willard Marriott Library, University of Utah*

UNITED STATES
DEPARTMENT OF THE INTERIOR
OFFICE OF INDIAN AFFAIRS
FIELD SERVICE

November the 8. 1934
Escalante Rim, Utah

Dear Waldo, Your letter of October 12th reached me a week ago
at Bryce Canyon. Since I left Desert View, a riot of adventures
and curious experiences have befallen me. To remember back, I
have to think of hundreds of miles of trails, thru deserts and canyons,
under vermilion cliffs and thru dense, nearly impenetrable forests.
As my mind traverses that distance, it goes thru a long list of
personalities too.

But I think I have not written you since I was in the Navajo
country, and the strange times I had there and in the sunswept mesas
of the Hopis, would stagger me if I tried to convey them. I think
there is much in everyones life that no one else can ever understand
or appreciate, without living thru the same experiences, and most
could not do that.

I have had a few narrow escapes from rattlers and crumbling cliffs. The
last misadventure occurred when Chocolatero stirred up some wild bees.
A few more stings might have been too much for me. I was three or four
days getting my eyes open and recovering the use of my hands.

I stopped a few days in a little Mormon town and indulged myself
in family life, church going and dances. If I had stayed any longer
I would have fallen in love with a Mormon girl, but I think its a
good thing I didn't. I've become a little too different from most
of the rest of the world.

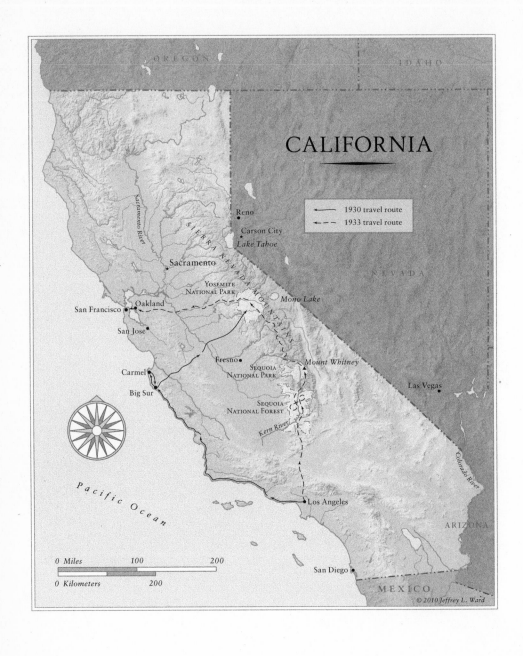

CALIFORNIA

— 1930 travel route
-- 1933 travel route

OREGON

IDAHO

Reno

Carson City
Lake Tahoe

NEVADA

Sacramento

Sacramento River

SIERRA NEVADA MOUNTAINS

YOSEMITE
NATIONAL PARK

Mono Lake

San Francisco
Oakland

San Jose

Fresno

SEQUOIA
NATIONAL PARK

Mount Whitney

Carmel

Big Sur

SEQUOIA
NATIONAL FOREST

Las Vegas

Kern River

Pacific Ocean

Colorado River

Los Angeles

ARIZONA

0 Miles   100   200

0 Kilometers   200

San Diego

MEXICO

© 2010 Jeffrey L. Ward

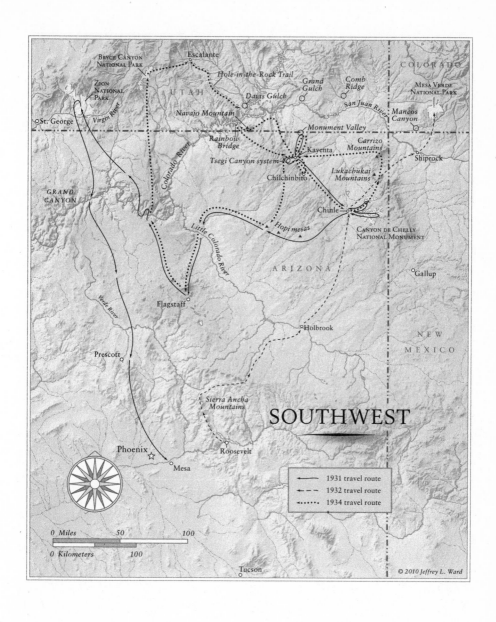

BRYCE CANYON
NATIONAL PARK
ZION
NATIONAL
PARK
St. George
Virgin River

Escalante
Hole-in-the-Rock Trail
Davis Gulch
Navajo Mountain
Rainbow
Bridge
Colorado River

U T A H

Grand
Gulch
Comb
Ridge
San Juan River

COLORADO

MESA VERDE
NATIONAL PARK
Mancos
Canyon

Monument Valley
Kayenta
Tsegi Canyon system
Chilchinbito
Carrizo
Mountains
Lukachukai
Mountains
Shiprock

GRAND
CANYON

Little Colorado River

Chinle

CANYON DE CHELLY
NATIONAL MONUMENT

Hopi mesas

A R I Z O N A

Gallup

Flagstaff

Verde River

Holbrook

N E W
M E X I C O

Prescott

Sierra Ancha
Mountains

SOUTHWEST

Phoenix
Mesa
Roosevelt

⟶ 1931 travel route
--- 1932 travel route
••• 1934 travel route

0 Miles   50   100
0 Kilometers   100

Tucson

© 2010 Jeffrey L. Ward

Finding Everett Ruess

PROLOGUE

I T WAS A CHILLY DAY in November 1934. The country had been mired in the Great Depression for over five years, and no town felt the pinch of poverty more acutely than Escalante. Founded by Mormon pioneers fifty-nine years earlier, the small settlement in southern Utah—then one of the remotest towns in the United States—had been stricken in successive summers by a plague of grasshoppers that ruined the crops and by the worst drought in nearly eight decades.

In late autumn, the arrival of any visitor in Escalante was a rare occurrence. It was all the more surprising, then, when the thin, sandy-haired stranger rode into town from the west, saddled on one undersized burro, leading another that was packed with camping gear. His name, he told the locals, was Everett Ruess. He was from California. And although he was only twenty, he had been wandering all over the West and Southwest for the better part of the last five years.

The young boys of Escalante took an instant liking to the vagabond. During the next several days they rode horseback with him along the nearby ridges, hunted for arrowheads, and shared his campfire dinner of venison and potatoes. One of those boys, ten years old at the time, was Norm Christensen. "He told us all about his family,"

3

Christensen remembers. "Showed us how the Indians could make fire using sticks. We hiked the hills, showed him the Indian writings"— petroglyphs etched on the sandstone walls by Anasazi and Fremont people more than six hundred years earlier. "He didn't brag on himself. Wasn't a show-off. He said he'd come out to look the country over and make his paintings. Showed us some."

Another Escalante native, Melvin Alvey, was twenty-six years old that autumn. Decades later, standing in the front room of the house in which he had lived all his life, Alvey pointed out the window. "I talked to Everett over there in the street as he was leavin' town," he recalled. "He had these two little burros. They didn't stand that high." Alvey flattened his palm four feet above the rug. "I don't think either of 'em had fifty pounds [loaded] on 'em. I looked at those two little burros, goin' out in November. He never even had a tent. Didn't have a good camp stove."

Alvey tilted his head back, summoning memories. "He said he was goin' to go down in the Desert and stay six weeks. Claimed he was goin' to be an artist and write stories. He didn't have enough for one week, let alone six. I said, 'It looks like you're travelin' pretty light.' 'Yes,' he said, 'I don't need much.' "

According to Norm Christensen, "Everett had a lot of spotted dog in his pack bags—rice and raisins with condensed milk. We gave him a bunch of potatoes. Offered him bottled fruit, but he just didn't have room for it."

Arnold Alvey, Melvin's nephew, six years old in 1934, recalls, "He came to our place on the outskirts of town. I was standin' out there by the well, here come this young guy with a coupla little gray burros. I'd never seen burros before.

"He said, 'Could I water my burros in your trough?' I said, 'Sure.' He had on a floppy hat. A light-colored orange shirt that fluttered in the breeze. He had quite high cheekbones. Quite a nice-lookin' guy.

Said he was goin' down in the Desert to spend the winter. I can see it like it was yesterday."

"Last night he was here," Norm Christensen recounted, "he took some of us kids to the picture show. It was called *Death Takes a Holiday*. Probably cost ten cents. Everett treated us."

Christensen shook his head. "I still remember him wavin' next morning as he passed on down the river."

"I've thought about him quite a bit over the years," Melvin Alvey confessed. "Whenever it gets cold. To go down there and draw as an artist, in November, when you only got three–four hours of decent weather in the day . . . I think he had some plans that nobody knew."

From Escalante that November, Everett set out southeast down the Hole-in-the-Rock Trail. The path had been blazed during the winter of 1879–80 by a remarkable band of Mormon pioneers, as they crossed the Colorado River, forged their way through labyrinthine canyons and mesas, and finally established the town of Bluff on the San Juan River, the first Mormon stronghold in southeast Utah. Fifty-four years after the pioneers, Everett gradually left behind the piñon-juniper forest that sheltered Escalante and its outskirts, as he passed through an increasingly barren landscape of slickrock and drifting orange sand—the badlands that the locals simply called the Desert.

A week down the trail, more than fifty miles out of Escalante, Everett ran into a pair of sheepherders at the head of Soda Gulch, a short, dry tributary of the Escalante River. Addlin Lay and Clayton Porter invited the young man to share their campfire. He stayed two nights, during which he quizzed the sheepherders about the canyons, trails, and prehistoric ruins to the east. Lay and Porter offered Everett a quarter of mutton, but the young man said he didn't have room for it in his burros' saddlebags. He had plenty of food of his own, he insisted.

On the morning of November 21, Everett parted ways with the sheepherders. They watched him as he ambled with his burros farther southeast, headed for the Hole-in-the-Rock, the steep cleft in the nine-hundred-foot precipice down which the Mormon pioneers, with painstaking care, had lowered their eighty-three wagons in January and February of 1880 before ferrying them across the Colorado River.

And then Everett Ruess vanished from the face of the earth.

*   *   *

At the time of his disappearance, Ruess was unknown in the larger world. Seventy-seven years later, he is the object of an intense and romantic cult that has no parallel in the long annals of the American Southwest.

Beginning in March 1935, a series of search parties scoured the wilderness, looking for clues to the wanderer's whereabouts—or, as seemed increasingly likely, to his demise. The first of those parties quickly discovered what has been regarded ever since as Everett's last known campsite, in Davis Gulch, a far-eastern tributary of the Escalante River. But the odd assemblage of objects those searchers found on the ground remains tantalizing and ambiguous today. In the end, none of the parties came close to solving the mystery of the young man's disappearance. And in the absence of a definitive answer, all kinds of theories about what happened to Everett after November 1934 were thrust onto the stage—theories that are still fiercely debated by Ruess devotees today.

The cult of Everett Ruess owes much to the mystery of his vanishing. Yet in the long run, it is the writings, paintings, and engravings the young man produced before his twenty-first birthday that anchor and validate his lasting fame—the very fame he longed so passionately to achieve. Whether or not Everett Ruess, had he lived, might have become a major writer or artist is another question that his partisans debate endlessly. But in a sense, it is beside the point. The Ruess cult ultimately springs from the young man's ecstatic vision of the wilderness, tied to an insatiable wanderlust that drove him to one solitary challenge and ordeal after another, as he traversed the deserts and canyons of what in the 1930s was the wildest landscape in the United States. Although other writers and artists profoundly influenced Everett—he was a voracious reader and a habitué of art galleries and museums—the vision that transfixed him was uniquely of his own making.

Not every aficionado of the Southwest subscribes to the Ruess mystique. Skeptics and realists tend to hold his effusions at arm's length, as the fevered strivings of a precocious but self-conscious idealist. Yet for the thousands of lovers of the outdoors who hold up Everett as a poet-saint, his utterings have an aphoristic glory. Quotations from his letters and diaries are recited today with all the reverence accorded to Henry David Thoreau's apothegms or Mark Twain's *bons mots*. Everett's blockprint engravings have been stenciled onto T-shirts, printed on the covers of blank notebooks, and embossed onto refrigerator magnets. The world of his devotees has expanded beyond the borders of the Southwest, even beyond the boundaries of the United States. Today, Everett counts among his acolytes men and women as far away as Russia and Japan, few of whom have ever visited the canyons and mesas where the young adventurer walked and rode with his burros into the mystical wild that cost him his life.

* * *

Grief-stricken at the loss of their son, Everett's parents, Christopher and Stella, determined to keep alive his memory. Since childhood, the boy had written letters to his parents and to his brother, Waldo, every time they were apart for as short a stretch as a day or two. During the years of his vagabondage, from 1930 to 1934, those letters steadily deepened in thought and feeling. His family kept every page, and later collected many of the letters Everett had written to his best friends back home.

Those letters are no mere newsy bulletins: instead, Everett strove for oracular declarations to capture the transport that wilderness brought him. "Once more I am roaring drunk with the lust of life and adventure and unbearable beauty," he wrote to one friend his own age. And to another, "I am overwhelmed by the appalling strangeness and intricacy of the curiously tangled knot of life."

At his jauntiest, Everett struck a Nietzschean pose: "Alone I shoulder the sky and hurl my defiance and shout the song of the conqueror to the four winds, earth, sea, sun, moon, and stars." Yet those vaulting flights were counterbalanced by passages that dwelt on hardship and agony, tinged with a premonition of doom: "Bitter pain is in store for me, but I shall bear it. . . . Death may await me; with vitality, impetuosity and confidence I will combat it."

As a poet, Everett also aimed at the oracular, writing about himself often in the past or perfect tense, as if his life were already over. Thus, in "Wilderness Song":

> *Say that I starved; that I was lost and weary;*
> *That I was burned and blinded by the desert sun;*
> *Footsore, thirsty, sick with strange diseases;*
> *Lonely and wet and cold . . . but that I kept my dream!*

As well as encouraging Everett to write poems and essays, Christopher and Stella had taught both their sons to keep diaries from an early age. Diary-writing was, in fact, such a family compulsion that all four members routinely transcribed passages from their daily entries to share in their letters to one another.

An artist herself, as well as a patroness of the arts, Stella had taught Everett how to paint with watercolors and how to carve the linoleum blocks that he used to make black-and-white prints. Especially in his blockprints, well before the age of twenty Everett had achieved a certain mastery. He reduced the ruin called Square Tower

House at Mesa Verde to an almost abstract design of oblong room-blocks, black squares for windows, and horizontal streaks intimating the arching sandstone alcove that guarded the prehistoric village. He rendered a California seacoast as a single storm-tossed cypress floating over an adamantine granite boulder.

For years after 1935, Christopher and Stella tried to interest publishers in a small volume collecting Everett's poems, passages from his essays and letters and diaries, and specimens of his artwork. Their efforts bore fruit in 1940, when a small California press brought out a slender miscellany titled *On Desert Trails with Everett Ruess.* Though the book sold only modestly, it attracted the attention of Wallace Stegner, who devoted a chapter to Ruess in his 1942 book, *Mormon Country.* Stegner held Everett's soaring idealism, his intense quest for beauty for its own sake, at arm's length. But he concluded memorably, "If we laugh at Everett Ruess we shall have to laugh at John Muir, because there was little difference between them except age."

Slowly over the decades the Ruess cult gathered momentum. But it was not until 1983, when W. L. (Bud) Rusho published *Everett Ruess: A Vagabond for Beauty,* that a rich anthology of Everett's writings gained a wider audience than that of friends and family. Though not a true biography, *Vagabond* laid out the essential facts of the adventurer's short life, and pondered at some length the mystery of his disappearance.

Rusho's book in turn caught the eye of Jon Krakauer, who saw in Ruess a striking parallel to Chris McCandless, the equally passionate loner who died in the wilderness north of Denali in Alaska in a prolonged effort to live off the land. In his 1996 bestseller, *Into the Wild,* Krakauer devoted eleven pages to Ruess. Tens of thousands of readers who had never before heard of Everett intertwined their fascination with Chris McCandless with the puzzle of the romantic wanderer who had vanished in Utah back in 1934. The Ruess cult soared to a new level.

Then, in 2008, an entirely new twist to the seventy-four-year-old mystery came like a zigzag of lightning cleaving a blue sky. It sprang from the most unlikely of sources: an eerie tale guarded secretly for decades by a Navajo man, who eventually handed it down to his granddaughter, who in turn told it to her brother, who went out to search in the Utah wilderness. . . .

The controversy spawned by this strange discovery smolders on. Thanks to the intensity of feeling that it stirred up, the Ruess cult has gained a new dimension, in which fervent admiration clashes with partisan polemic, and the believers in one theory of how he met his end raise their rhetorical rifles to fire at the opponents who cling to another.

In the words of more than one graffito scrawled in trailhead registers in recent years:

Everett lives!

PART ONE

The Desire to Live

ONE

"I Have Given the Wind My Pledge"

EVERETT RUESS* WAS BORN on March 28, 1914, in Oakland, California. For his mother, Stella, his arrival was a mixed blessing.

The family was an intensely intellectual and bohemian one. Everett's father, Christopher, had graduated summa cum laude from Harvard, then attended the Harvard Divinity School. In Oakland he served as a Unitarian minister, though later, to support his family, he would take a series of secular jobs.

Stella was a dancer, an aesthete, and an accomplished artist. Her father, William Henry Knight, had been a Civil War veteran from New York State who migrated to California, where he gained prominence in publishing, music, and science, serving twice as president of the Southern California Academy of Sciences. He also wrote editorials for the *Los Angeles Times*.

*Curiously, we cannot be sure how Everett Ruess pronounced his last name. Over the decades of the twentieth century, various family members pronounced the patronymic either as "Roo-iss" (rhyming with "Lewis") or as a single-syllable "Roos." As recently as 1960, Everett's brother used the two-syllable version, but today most of Everett's closest surviving family members prefer the Germanic "Roos." The reason for the variation is itself obscure, but may derive from Everett's mother's feeling that "Roo-iss" was a more poetic pronunciation. The cultural origins of the name are also uncertain: it could be Russian, as in *Russland,* or German (*Ruß* is German for "soot," and may allude to the profession of chimney sweep), but the name "Ruess" is exceedingly rare in Germany today.

Under Stella's guidance, the close-knit family produced a constant stream of art and poetry, even while Waldo and Everett were still very young. At regular intervals, Stella home-published collections of this work, under the rubric *Ruess Quartette*. These miscellanies bore the imprint of the family seal, a sundial inscribed with the motto "Glorify the Hour"—an injunction Everett would live by during his wandering years.

Christopher and Stella had married on April 2, 1905. They would share forty-nine years together before Christopher's death in 1954, a half-century filled with undimmed love and mutual respect.

The great tragedy of the couple's life before the disappearance of Everett was the death at the age of six weeks of their firstborn, Christella, in 1908. The girl's name, of course, was an amalgamation of her parents'. In her journal, Stella later wrote, "Christella was as beautiful as a rosebud, with long dark hair and I thought she was perfect. But after two weeks Dr. Shuey told me that she could not live, her spine was not right."

Spina bifida, from which Christella suffered, is a birth defect in which the fetus's spine forms incorrectly. Some of the vertebrae that normally enclose the spinal cord do not close correctly, leaving a hole through which the cord may protrude. Today the defect can usually be surgically repaired, but in 1908 it was often fatal.

On April 2, 1909, on their fourth wedding anniversary, Christopher and Stella scattered Christella's ashes over San Francisco Bay from a ferry, just as it passed opposite the Golden Gate. Thus was launched a family tradition that would still hold sway a century later.

At the time, Stella was four months pregnant with her second child. Since spina bifida is in part genetic, the parents knew there was a higher than average chance that their second child would also have the defect. But on September 5, 1909, Waldo was born, a completely healthy infant. He was named for Ralph Waldo Emerson, a poet and philosopher whom Christopher held (as Everett later would) in high esteem.

Four years later, Stella got pregnant again. Still mourning Chris-tella, she wished fervently for a girl. She had, in fact, already named her unborn daughter.

On April 2, 1914, Stella wrote in her anniversary record:

> Dear Kathleen—Little Dream-daughter—
> You were invited here for our Wedding Anniversary, but did
> not come. But you sent a substitute—a dear brother to make
> one more of the family to watch for you later. . . . His name,
> Everett, will endow him with the attributes of kindness and
> the helping hand for which Edward Everett Hale was noted,
> the beloved preacher whom Christopher knew in Boston.

Edward Everett Hale, who died in 1909, is best known today for his scarifying patriotic allegory, "The Man Without a Country."

It was the family's compulsively literary bent that led the parents to encourage Waldo and Everett to keep regular diaries from an early age on, as well as to copy long passages from those diaries into the letters they wrote to their parents whenever they were separated from them, no matter how briefly. Some observers of the Ruess ménage have seen Christopher and Stella as overly involved with their sons' private lives, to the point of intrusiveness. According to this view, Everett's vagabondage was motivated in large part by a need to flee the family's stifling intimacy. In his early twenties, Waldo moved to China, where he took a job as secretary for a religious mission. Other jobs followed, as he stayed in China for several years. In the volu-minous correspondence between father and son during this period, Waldo occasionally bridles at his father's neediness and insistence on giving advice about everything from marriage to career.

But in the surviving letters from Everett to his parents, there is scarcely a hint of annoyance at Christopher and Stella's involvement in his life. In a few instances he explicitly seeks out their guidance,

notably in a by-now-famous letter from December 1933, in which
Everett wrote out a list of eighteen deep philosophical questions that
he posed to his father. They include "Are pain and pleasure equally
desirable and necessary?" and "Can one make great sacrifices without
submerging oneself?" Taken as a whole, this exchange between Everett and Christopher (who answered each question in heartfelt detail)
amounts to a parental catechism in how to lead a moral life.

In 1928, Stella wrote a brief synopsis of Everett's life to the age of
fourteen, detailing the frequent moves around the country the family
had to make as Christopher changed jobs. This lovingly indulgent
sketch begins with a mock first-person epistle that Stella pretended
Everett had written to his grandmother on his third birthday. De-
signed to be cute and charming, this semi-nonsensical soliloquy nonetheless gives a vivid glimpse of Everett as a child, with an emphasis on
his precocious curiosity.

> Dear Grandma—
> Today I am three years old, and 38–1/2 inches tall, and 32
> pounds heavy. Papa often says he wishes he had a phonograph
> record of my prattle, so Mother decided to write down some
> of my remarks today, just to smile over when I'm big. . . .
> I had a ride on Pegasus, too. That's my velocipede. I
> couldn't play with my Astronomy Game, because we lost
> it one day. Mama says I knew about 25 names like Leo
> and Lepus, Cassiopeia, Hercules, Persus [sic], Virgo, Aries,
> Cygnus and Delphinus. She thought it was funny when I
> named her Indian clubs Pollux and Castor, but it's because
> they were twin brothers.

Fourteen years later, Everett would name one of his burros Pegasus.
Prattle, indeed, must have been the three-year-old's forte, if Stella's
rendering of it does it justice:

While I was eating lunch, I asked—"How do you spell sandwich? How do you spell boxes? How do you spell one box? How do you spell tocolate? How do you spell hankshadiff? How do you spell tree? How do you spell milk? How do you spell spoon? How do you spell egg? How do you spell sky?" . . . One day Waldo said, "Everett is a b-a-d b-o-y," but I said, "No, I'm a *good* b-o-y!" Mama counted up about 1200 words that I use. That is 200 more than Waldo knew, but you see he didn't have a big brother to teach him.

Stella's affectionate impersonation of her hyperactive three-year-old contains a strange scene that suggests that the urge to take off and wander was already part of Everett's nature:

[Mama] put me in bed after lunch with some books because she thought I wouldn't be sleepy after my long nap yesterday, but I surprised her. Jerry was tied to the corner post, and I just got quiet and forgot the books—books to the right of me, books under me and books on top of me. Jerry is my left foot. When Mama says, "You *must* go to sleep today," she ties Jerry and Jupiter too, but she tells them to kick very hard first so they'll be tired. When she thinks I'm not very sleepy but she wants to be sure *where I am,* and that I'm not playing in a mud puddle, she ties only Jerry. When I *must* go to sleep, she tells Sparkle and Twinkle to pull down the curtains. Those are my eyes, of course.

Such confinement was not limited to bedtime. After six paragraphs of "prattle," Stella returns Everett to the third person, but reports:

The small "Duck Bab" was always finding every wet and muddy spot in the neighborhood. Several times he ran away so that I came to rope him to the porch. Once he went a mile, over the bridge and the railroad tracks. I telephoned the police station and found he had been reported.

An entry in Stella's journal further confirms the bondage: "Waldo did some lessons every morning, and every afternoon we went swimming in the Creek. Everett was tied to a tree for Safety First."

In Everett's baby book, his mother recorded no fewer than thirty-three "pet names" by which the boy was called by his parents and their close friends. They include Little Contentment, Honeybunch, and Babykin Bye-o, but also Whirligig, Tumble-bug, Bounceritis, and Lord of Misrule.

In September 1918, the family moved all the way across the country, to Brookline, Massachusetts. Christopher felt the obligation to support not only his family of four, but his ailing parents, and so he had given up the impecunious profession of pastor to take a job with the Chautauqua Industrial Art Desk Company. The device the firm manufactured was indeed a desk, but it was festooned with all sorts of doodads, from a color wheel to piano keys to "telegraphic codes," required to carry out, in the company's ambitious claim, "a plan to promote the culture of work and play among children in the home."

In Brookline, Everett started school. Stella later wrote, "During his fifth year summer Everett was so eager to learn that I taught him to add and subtract with sea-beans on the floor, and he filled a copybook with little problems up to ten, including multiplication & division."

Despite the gap of more than four years in their ages, Waldo and Everett were inseparable chums. Yet they were boys of significantly different temperaments. It is not surprising that when Stella attempted to capture her sons' characters, she did so in verse. About Waldo, she wrote,

The spirit of adventure leads you far.
We joy to know that Loyalty,
And Purity, and Courtesy
Your true and ever faithful comrades are.

And about Everett,

The God of Poesy has smiled
On you, my nature-loving child.
May you look deep and wide and high;
Your art all nature glorify.

Such verses suggest that Everett was Stella's favorite. It is hard to imagine Waldo, praised for his purity and courtesy, not holding a grudge against the impulsive younger brother in whom their mother saw a nature-loving poet.

On rare automobile rides from Brookline, the whole family set out on literary tours of eastern Massachusetts, visiting Walden Pond and the homes of Emerson, Nathaniel Hawthorne, and Louisa May Alcott; the House of the Seven Gables in Salem, which had inspired Hawthorne's novel; and the Revolutionary War sites in Lexington and Concord, including the "rude bridge that arched the flood" of Emerson's poem. Everett's penchant for wandering off came to the surface on these outings. As Stella wrote in her journal,

One Sunday Christopher took the boys on an historical jaunt to the old North Church, and some way lost his small son. Everett proceeded to hunt up a policeman and journeyed to the police station, there to eat chocolates in perfect confidence that his father would find him. His father did, but it was after several hours of distraction!

In 1920, Christopher was reassigned by the Chautauqua Art Desk Company to a post in New York City. The family spent two years in Bay Ridge, Brooklyn, then two years in Palisades Park, New Jersey. Taking advantage of the proximity of highbrow culture, Stella enrolled her gifted younger son in classes at Brooklyn's Pratt Institute. From a home in New Jersey that the Ruesses named Cherry Croft, mother and son made frequent trips to Greenwich Village for classes in wood-carving and pottery-making. After class, the pair of aesthetes would head off to New York's famous museums, or to such bookstores as Scribner's and Brentano's, or to poetry readings by the likes of Edward Markham (remembered today, if at all, for "The Man with a Hoe").

In 1923, after her father fell ill, Stella and Everett took a cross-country journey by train to Los Angeles to care for him. They turned the trip into a sightseeing excursion, making a brief but memorable stop at the Grand Canyon. Then, during her father's convalescence, Stella and her nine-year-old son visited Yosemite Valley, where they went on several long hikes. In the middle of one, while they bathed in the Merced River, as Stella recalled five years later, "E was nearly drowned in the pool, choosing just the moment when I happened to be swimming under water!"

Everett kept a diary during this long detour into the West. It may be the earliest of his writings to survive. The entries are short and often perfunctory, but they nonetheless reflect the nine-year-old's wide-eyed curiosity about everything he saw in the countryside, and they presage the voracious wanderlust of Everett's late adolescence.

The boy's first reaction to the Grand Canyon is surprising, given the fascination the place would come to have for him in his late teens.

> April 4. Saw the Grand Canyon of Colorado. When I first
> looked over I was scared, but the next time I could see better.
> There are red and grey stone turrets rising up. The canyon is
> a mile deep, and I couldn't even see the river.

I looked at it through a spy glass in the lookout tower. Mother went down to the bottom on a horse. I saw a silly woman on a rock waving her arms. She would have fallen over if another woman hadn't caught her.

Stella's ride on the back of a mule (not a horse), while, as she put it, "E's impressions were all from the rim where he stayed with our English traveling acquaintances," probably marked the last occasion on which the mother proved more adventurous than her son.

The longest entry in Everett's 1923 diary is devoted to the several-day trip to Yosemite, where mother and son slept outdoors at Camp Curry. (Everett makes no mention of nearly drowning in the Merced River.) The young diarist briefly notes his first view of El Capitan, the nearly vertical 2,700-foot precipice of sheer granite that commands the valley, but he was more interested in the wildlife. "On the way [to Camp Curry] we saw chipmunks, as numerous as the falling leaves almost, peering at us from every nook and cranny, we saw a fawn and some deer."

Several days later:

After supper I fed a deer whose name was Jenny. She was a female, but the males would not come near you. The males have horns, but the females do not. I tried to pet Jenny but she balked, and would not let me. Jenny was very greedy and took large bites of biscuits, and I was soon back for more. One lady put a biscuit in her mouth and Jenny walked up and took it out.

For the nine-year-old, the high point of the trip was the nightly tourist stunt performed by Park Service officials well into the 1960s, before it was terminated as an ecological atrocity. Everett describes it with unfeigned awe:

> There was a great camp fire, and moving pictures were shown.
> Then there was a signal from the top of Glacier Point, and
> every one craned their necks upward. Someone whispered—
> "The firefall." Then a stream of dazzling brightness issued
> from out the sky it seemed. One could not distinguish the
> outline of Glacier Point from the Darkness. Then it ended.

The spectacle was concocted by setting a huge red fir tree trunk
on fire, then pushing it off Yosemite Falls. As it fell, the tree blazed a
glowing path, spangled with water-spray, through the night.

By the end of the summer, Stella and Everett were back in New
Jersey. The next year, Christopher was once again reassigned by the
Chautauqua Art Desk Company, this time to a job in Chicago. The
family packed up and moved to Valparaiso, Indiana, from which town
Christopher commuted fifty miles to work. He was hardly an absent
father, however. On August 5, 1924, already installed in his Chicago
office but awaiting the arrival of his wife and sons, Christopher wrote
to Everett:

> Will you not send me a postal card every day as Waldo
> does, and on it write your diary entry for the previous day?
> I would enjoy it. I don't like to have people feel that one
> of my sons does this, but that the other laddie forgets his
> daddy, do I?

At the time, fourteen-year-old Waldo was spending his summer
on a ranch in Montana, where he unabashedly bragged about a
"little girl" who had become his constant companion. Perhaps this
spurred Everett to envy, for in the same letter, Christopher reassured
his younger son:

> You will also love many little girls as you grow up in that
> way, and some day when you are older and more of a man

and able to earn money and build a home, you will marry
as Mother and I did and have beautiful sons and daughters,
of whom you will be as proud as I am of you and of Waldo,
and as Mother is.

Christopher's letters to his sons were always loving, but they carry
an undertone of stern demand that the boys live up to the highest
moral and intellectual standards. "Dear Leonardo da Vinci Everett,"
Christopher saluted his son in another 1924 letter. "If you were like
him and Waldo were like Ben Franklin, than [sic] would make a great
pair of great men from our little family." A year earlier, while Everett
was still only nine, Christopher admonished the "laddie":

> You may let Mother read this letter, too, if she will promise to
> hug you for me, or spank you, as the occasion may suggest. . . .
>   You know President Coolidge has two boys now, and
> the whole world is watching those boys. They are regular
> fellows too. They know how to work and how to play.

All this enforced intimacy, combined with such rigorous injunc-
tions to behave as what his father called a "PG" ("Perfect Gentle-
man"), could have easily turned Everett into a mama's boy or a
precocious show-off at school, or a sullen rebel. Yet Everett seems
to have bent in none of these directions. From the Valparaiso years
emerge several other examples of the earliest of Everett's writings to
have survived. One of his most beguiling youthful works he titled "All
Boy, Age 11, Secret Diary." The diary was evidently not secret, for the
surviving copy has been typed, probably by Everett's proud father.

The entries reveal an active boy with the normal eleven-year-old's
penchant for both mischief and adventure, and they also demonstrate
that Everett had developed a sly sense of humor. There is surprisingly
little of the show-off in them. Excerpts:

Jan. 10: Waldo, Mother, Sheldon and I went ice-skating and I found out that I had weak ankles. . . . I read a book at Sheldon's house about the land of Oz and I think that it is an awful good book.

Jan. 26: . . .

> Here I go
> On my toe
> Through the Snow.
> The Ice it's slippery
> And the Mud, it's mickery.
> So it's quite a job
> To catch a Bob. . . .

Feb. 29: There is no February 29th in this year.

March 20: Today I was all happy inside and could hardly keep from yelling for tomorrow I am going to Chicago. I don't like to do homework. It never does you any good anyhow.

May 11: My turtle has got the crawling fever. He is crawling all over. Mine is named Prince Crawlaway II and Harold's is Prince Crawlaway I.

Sept. 10: Today I and Harold and Sheldon went out tonight. I honked horns of autos and rang doorbells. We set water traps too.

Oct. 8: I got copped by Mrs. Taylor for shooting a match up to the ceiling and I was told to stay in, but I forgot all about it.

To sharpen his artistic talents, Stella enrolled Everett in classes at the Art Institute of Chicago. But the great discovery of his Valparaiso

years—1924 through 1928, from age ten to age fourteen—was nature. The countryside was lush with woods, into which Everett wandered at will. An old Indian trail, perhaps blazed by the Miami tribe,
passed very close to the town. The kinds of outdoor stimulation that
were hard to come by in Brookline, Brooklyn, or Palisades Park now
cast their spell over Everett. His passions focused on creatures of all
kinds, ranging from insects to mammals, and on all things Indian.

A number of Everett's school essays from this time survive. These
two- or three-page exercises deal with rats and mice, flies, crows,
skunks, coyotes, and birds. One is titled "The mt. lion as the friend
of the deer."

During this period, Christopher apparently worried that Everett
was becoming too interested in nature, at the expense of human beings. On September 30, 1926, he wrote to his son:

> You have a good mind. Now you need to observe *people* as
> you observe *things* and learn to make many *friends*. Try to
> please people. You are a little like your daddy, who gets so
> interested in ideas at times that he is absent-minded about
> people. That is bad. Because people have feelings.

A paradox that would lie at the core of Everett's being during the
wandering years of his late adolescence may have had its genesis in
Valparaiso. The boy was by nature gregarious and outgoing, so much
so that in California in his late teens he would think nothing of going
up to the homes of such famous artists as the photographers Edward
Weston and Ansel Adams, knocking on the front door, and introducing
himself as a fledgling protégé. Yet on his extended journeys with pack
animals across the Southwest, Everett would conclude, "After all the
lone trail is best"—partly, as he put it, "because I'm a freakish person."

In Indians, Everett found what for a while seemed the perfect solution to those contradictory tensions. Indians were people, but around

Valparaiso it was not living natives that caught the lad's fancy, but the prehistoric relics they had left behind. In those Indiana forests, Everett found his first arrowheads.

In Valparaiso, he wrote a pair of poems about arrowhead discoveries that are remarkably accomplished for his age. The better of the two, written in November 1927 at the age of thirteen, was titled "The Relic."

> *In a deserted field I found an arrowhead.*
> *Worn by the rains and snows of many a year,*
> *It had survived its maker, buried here,*
> *For he who shot the arrow from his bow was dead.*
>
> *How far this chiseled piece of stone leads back the mind!*
> *By careful Indian craftsman it was wrought,*
> *For many purposes had it been sought.*
> *To me it was a very precious treasure find.*

Throughout his later wanderings in the Southwest, Everett would continue to delight in "precious treasure finds," mailing or bringing home arrowheads, Anasazi pots, and even an intact necklace he found in a burial site. Modern readers of Everett's letters and diaries, in which he brags about keeping ancient artifacts, are often disturbed by his acquisitiveness, but it is worth remembering that in the 1930s there was no prevailing ethic to discourage the looting of prehistoric ruins. Every country store and saloon had framed arrowhead collections hung on the wall, the points arranged in pleasing designs, and the metates (stone basins) on which the ancients had ground their corn were routinely used as yard ornaments and doorstops.

The school essays from Everett's Valparaiso years are mostly short and dryly matter-of-fact pieces, but several hint at higher strivings. The most interesting of them is an eerily prescient short story called "Vultures." It begins:

A man lay sprawled on the stinging hot sand beneath a twisted Joshua tree in the desert. Its crooked shade made a fantastic pattern, and fell in sultry stripes across his weary body. The shadow moved, and with a tired lurch, the man moved his head into a band of shade.

This dramatic beginning is clarified only in the third paragraph:

The man was an artist. He had come here to die—or to recover his lost ambitions. His sensitive eyes roved over the unreal landscape; the barren wastes of sand, the desert cliffs, the bleak, bent cactus trees darkly outlined against the moon, over which there passed a ghostly wraith of cloud. But the artist's soul was dead within him; the weird beauty was not reflected in his face, stoical and hopeless.

The story is only two and a half typed pages long, but the prose vividly evokes the desert landscape that would become Everett's chosen wilderness. The unnamed artist's mission is a three-day stagger in search of an epiphany. At last it comes:

Though he had not found the inspiration he sought, the desire to live was suddenly reawakened. Tortured flesh complained insistently and would not be denied. In sudden frenzy he turned about and began in tottering haste to retrace his way.

But the turnaround comes too late. Out of water on the third day, the man crawls atop a lonely butte to die. A torrential rainstorm sweeps the landscape.

The rain passed, leaving the desert glorious and cool. As the vultures poised in the air and came to tear him to pieces, he looked toward the horizon. All that was left of his anguish now vanished, and a light shone in his eyes, as he saw the dying sun flood the waste lands with splendor. The last thing he saw was the burnished bronze of a vulture's wings, glinting in the sunlight, as it snatched his eyes out.

He did not feel the pain. A moment later, the blood-hued sunset passed swiftly to night.

In the summer of 1928, after the Chautauqua Art Desk Company had folded, Christopher found a new job in California. The family moved from Valparaiso to Los Angeles, where Christopher started work as a county probation officer.

Less than two years later, Everett would begin the serious vagabondage that became the true mission of his short life, and that would, against all odds, make him posthumously famous.

*   *   *

In June 1930, at the age of sixteen, while still a student at Hollywood High School, Everett set out on the first of his five annual expeditions, as he hitchhiked up the coastal highway from Los Angeles to Carmel. The diary that Everett kept during that first rambling trip may be irrevocably lost. What we know of the 1930 outing (the least ambitious of the five that Everett would undertake) comes from some sixteen letters he wrote to his parents and to Waldo, and a single letter to his high-school friend Bill Jacobs.

In Carmel, one of the first things Everett did was to find the studio of the famous photographer Edward Weston, knock on the door, and introduce himself. "A man who gave me a ride near Morro Bay had told me about him," Everett wrote to his mother.

Weston was forty-four years old that summer. He had already taken some of his most celebrated photographs, including many of the nudes and still lifes that would become his hallmark achievements.

Solo exhibitions in New York City had been devoted to his work. Two years after Everett's visit, in 1932, Weston would cofound Group f/64 with Ansel Adams and others.

The brazen confidence it took for Everett to thrust himself upon such a distinguished artist may have originated in his upbringing. The boosterism of his parents ("Leonardo da Vinci Everett") may well have instilled a sense of entitlement in the aspiring poet and painter. But the fact that Weston did not simply turn away the uninvited guest testifies to Everett's charm, and perhaps to the notion that Weston saw real talent in the lad. During the next several days, Everett palled up with Weston's teenage sons, Neil and Cole (both younger than he), for fishing and swimming excursions. Weston himself invited Everett to eat dinner with the family and to sleep in his garage.

In view of Everett's later obsession with the desert Southwest, it is interesting that on this first journey, it was the ocean and the seashore that captivated him. During the days spent in the Westons' orbit, Everett sometimes camped out on the beach. Writing home about these solo bivouacs, he could not suppress a gleeful pride in his newfound self-sufficiency.

> First I chopped plenty of firewood. Then I made my bed, and cooked supper. A short time after supper, I went swimming. After the swim, I went to bed, and enjoyed the extra blanket.
>
> Wednesday morning, I had Cornflakes and condensed milk for breakfast. . . .

All his life, Everett would suffer agonizingly from poison oak and poison ivy. In one letter home, he admits, "The poison oak is nearly over on my face, but it is still flaming on my legs and hands." Given how sensitive he was to the oily resin that caused his outbreaks—the rashes forced him to be hospitalized more than once—it is a puzzle that in both California and the Southwest, Everett never seemed to learn how to avoid coming in contact with the three-leaved plants. Instead, Everett seemed to accept the itchy rashes as a medical condition like asthma or anemia.

Whether Edward Weston made any appraisal of the young artist's paintings, Everett's letters do not reveal. Those epistles home, some as long as five pages, only rarely strive for rhetorical or poetic effects, as they would increasingly over the following years. They are still closer in style to the reportage of Everett's Valparaiso years, as he simply summarizes his adventures. But some of the poems and essays Everett was writing at the time already struggle to express in words the transports that landscape brought to his spirit.

> I awoke with a quiver, nerves tautly on edge. It came again, what had wakened me—the harsh, weird scream of a grey gull swooping low above me in the darkness. A heavy, clinging fog had set in, making the place indescribably desolate. Nothing was visible.

After hanging around Carmel for more than three weeks, Everett decided to strike out for wilder country, setting his sights on Big Sur, which in 1930 was still little traveled. A combination of hitchhiking and walking brought him to the rugged seacoast, where he camped out, climbed the hills, explored the shore, and painted. For the first time, Everett carried his belongings and food in a backpack. Even the tribulations of this first foray into semi-wilderness added zest to the outing. As he wrote his family on July 24:

> I made a watercolor under the most difficult conditions I have yet endured. The wind blew sand into my paint and on my picture all the time I was painting. The sand is still stuck to the picture, and produced an interesting effect, but I don't think there will be much color left on the picture when the sand comes off.

As the days flew past, Everett took an odd job here and there to earn a little cash to pay for his groceries. While still in Carmel, he spent several days caddying at a local golf course. To picture the future desert wanderer lugging gentlemen's clubs around a manicured eighteen-hole layout requires an imaginative stretch, and in fact, Everett hated the routine that required him to show up at the caddymaster's shack and hope to be assigned to a foursome.

One of Everett's best poems, which he called "Pledge to the Wind," evokes a landscape like Big Sur. It closes,

> *Here in the utter stillness,*
> *High on a lonely cliff-ledge,*
> *Where the air is trembling with lightning,*
> *I have given the wind my pledge.*

Yet even Big Sur was not wild enough for Everett's increasingly restless soul. By early August he had determined to head off to Yosemite, still vivid in his memory from the 1923 trip there with his mother. He arrived on August 4, laid out his campsite on the banks of a tributary of the Merced River, and spent "the most miserable night of my life." By the next morning he could joke about the bivouac in a letter to his family:

> At first it was so hot that my blankets were covered with sweat. But I had to swathe my face in a towel to keep out a few of the millions of mosquitoes. Burrs got stuck to my blankets. After a fitful night's sleep, I woke up in the hot sunshine, and found that thousands of ants were swarming through my pack.

So far, Everett's California travels had been relatively tame, yet the sight of a sixteen-year-old lugging a fifty-pound pack on his solo journey had caught the attention of many a passerby. "On this trip," he wrote his family, "I have been given all kinds of advice, from whether or not one should own a car, and if so, what kind, to whether I should go crooked or straight." It is odd, given Everett's passion for travel, yet somehow characteristic, that he never learned to drive an automobile.

During his days in Yosemite, Everett swam in the Merced, hiked the park's trails, and marveled at the tameness of the wildlife (in broad daylight, a deer entered Everett's camp while he was off hiking, tore loose the wrapper on a loaf of bread, and ate every crumb). Even in 1930, in August Yosemite was thronged with tourists. If Everett sought solitude, he was bound to be disappointed. At Camp 7, "Some people from Oklahoma moved in on one side of me," he wrote home. "Another car is on the other corner, while in back of me, two young men who work for an Insurance Company in Los Angeles, have their tent."

To pose himself a physical challenge, Everett joined a ranger-led group hike from Camp Curry to Glacier Point, a 3,200-foot ascent in only two miles of steep trail. "It took me 3 hours and a quarter to climb up," he boasted. "The usual time is 3 and 1/2. But the record is held by an Indian, who went up in 46 minutes."

In 1930 it was still possible to find prehistoric Indian relics in the park. Guided by an expert amateur who had collected three hundred arrowheads in Yosemite, Everett found his first three points, made of black obsidian, after digging in the ground of an ancient campsite on the valley floor. He pocketed the arrowheads without a second thought.

During the next few days, Everett undertook his first solo hikes. But since there was no escaping the campground crowds, he also embraced the park's makeshift social life. At Camp Curry, his group was treated to "selections on the piano, violin, & banjo in addition to whistling," followed by a "two-reel movie" about Yosemite's bird life. "The Park Naturalist whistled the calls of all the birds."

To his delight, Everett felt that he was getting in shape and tough-ening up as a camper. "As to being lonesome for a good bed," he announced to his family, "I sleep quite well on the ground here and don't mind it at all. . . . I could very happily keep up this life indefi-nitely if I had the money." Instead, he dreaded the onset of September, with its "coming of school time."

Though his parents and his brother were lovers of the outdoors, Everett's backpacking was a self-taught process of trial and error. Mid-way through his Yosemite lark, having exhausted himself on a hike to Merced Lake, he realized that his blankets were unwieldy: he needed a sleeping bag. "You can buy one for $15, that is quite good enough," he hinted to Christopher and Stella. "My blankets weigh far too much, take up too much space, and aren't as warm as a sleeping bag."

In the third week of August, Everett headed for the high country of Tuolomne Meadows. By now he had worn his boot soles "nearly to paper," and had rubbed holes in all his wool socks, so that "I am wearing them with the heels on top." Solo hikes were his preference, but he had not yet concluded that "after all, the lone trail is best." Often Everett joined other hikers on the way to distant lakes. He was curious enough about these chance companions that he could later mail home thumbnail résumés of their lives. Several of these strangers were homesteading in the park, having lost their jobs in the first year of the Great Depression. Others hailed from as far away as Australia.

Yet a certain shyness kept Everett from forming any lasting at-tachments on the trail that summer. On one hike he ran into a party who were in the middle of a nine-day cross-country backpack. Ev-erett envied their ambition; had he known such a long jaunt was possible, he wrote home, he would have signed up for it. The party included "some very nice young women who were from Washington D.C. and Michigan. I hiked with them until I reached Little Yosem-ite, about 8 miles from my camp." But then there is no further men-tion of the women.

On another occasion, Everett struck up a conversation with a woman camping alone at Booth Lake. It turned out that she was from Hollywood, and "She owns a flat four doors from Grandma, whom she knows well. Her name is Mrs. Miller." Everett added, "She wanted me to be her guest at supper, so I had another good meal."

The 1930 letters are not often reflective or deeply personal, and of course no teenager shares all his thoughts and feelings with his parents. Yet, here and there, Everett offers a glimpse of his inner self, foreshadowing the wilderness worshiper he would become in the following years.

> There are many things I do, and which I think out, while on the trail. When I halt for a rest, I watch an ant crawling out of a footprint, or I toss stones, seeing how near I can get them to the edge of the path without making them fall off. As I hike, I count the burro's shoes which have been cast. Or if it is a steep climb, I feel the sweat drip from my face and hair. This morning when I stopped to rest, I found an unfinished arrowhead beneath a tree.

And only rarely in the 1930 letters does Everett attempt to ponder his mission in life: "It seems that my ambitions are always to be allied with the A's—artist, author, archaeologist, and adventurer. Lately, the arrowheads have preceded the art, but I expect to get back to sketching quickly."

Despite selling a few of his watercolors over the summer, Everett was running out of money. On August 12 he wrote to his parents, "I have only a little left as it is, and prices are high in Yosemite." He added, "You might send a dollar or two, but don't send five dollars." The bashful pleas for handouts from home would continue throughout the next four years.

Over the summer, Everett had covered far more miles hitchhiking than he had on foot, even though he calculated that his season's

tramping had added up to two hundred miles. But he finally identified the critical flaw in his first extended campaign of vagabondage:
the fifty-pound pack was too much for him. As early as July 7, from
Carmel, he complained in a letter to Bill Jacobs, "After I hike about
a mile, my both arms begin to go numb from fingertips to shoulders,
because the pack cuts off circulation. After a few more miles, they are
paralyzed, so that I can't tie a knot or even unfasten the pack."

In his last letter home, mailed from Yosemite on August 22, Everett outlined the scheme that would transform his wandering.

> I was becoming extremely weary of being told by everyone
> that I had a load, or, "Say, isn't that heavy," or "what a load
> that boy has," etc. ad nauseum [sic]. So I went to the Camp
> Curry scales and weighed it. What was my surprise to learn
> that, with but a pound of food left, it weighed 48 pounds!
> Evidently I am not as weak as I thought I was.
>
> However, I have thought for some time that I would like
> to have a burro next time I start a hike of this kind. They
> cost $1.50 a day, and you can buy them for $15 or less.

One of the longest letters Everett wrote that summer, covering
four pages in tight pencil scrawl, this missive serves in some ways as
a précis of his apprenticeship in wandering. As always, Everett paid
close attention to the minutest phenomena of the natural world:

> At one of the brooks where I stopped for a drink, I no-
> ticed the curious shadow effect produced by the skaters, or
> water bugs. They have six legs, four large, and two small.
> Each leg, or foot, is placed on a drop of water which some-
> how throws a shadow. As the skaters move, these small
> round dots of shadows skim to and fro on the bottom of
> the pool.

But Everett also had a zest for outdoor play, as he and another hiker climbed the cliff behind camp, seized a log, and pried loose a huge granite boulder to send it plummeting down the precipice. "It finally slid off, and with a great flurry of sparks from the friction, it crashed down," wrote Everett unashamedly. "There was a short silence, and it struck the ground far below, crashing through the brush and over some trees."

During these August days, Everett felt a growing malaise about returning to "normal" life:

> In the morning, I shouldered my pack once more, and started down to the valley. The whole atmosphere was one of anti-climax. I was returning from the mountains and the solitude to the valley, the noisy, uninitiated tourists, and eventually to the city and its sordid buildings and business places.

By the beginning of September, Everett was back in Los Angeles, where he started the last semester of his senior year at Hollywood High School. He could not wait to set out into the wilds again. But he would not immediately return to Big Sur and Yosemite: the goal for the 1931 pilgrimage would be the vast and daunting Southwest, of which Everett's sole experience was his fearful stop at the Grand Canyon in 1923, at the age of nine.

TWO

"I Have Been One Who Loved the Wilderness"

AT THE AGE OF ONLY SIXTEEN, in January 1931, Everett grad-uated from Hollywood High School. His parents hoped that he would soon go to college, but the headstrong youth had a better idea. In early February, he hitchhiked east out of Los Angeles. The rides he got from strangers amounted to a cross-country adventure in its own right: a Buick Eight driven at seventy-five miles an hour by an old man with a dog; a lift in a potato truck; a harrowing lift from "a couple of Long Beach toughs" who drove through the night without headlights and kept running out of gas; and a final jaunt over "a very wild road" from Flagstaff to Kayenta in the car of an Indian mail carrier.

By February 13, Everett was installed in Kayenta, Arizona, smack in the middle of the Navajo reservation. He would crisscross the Southwest continuously throughout the next ten months. But his first item of business was to buy a burro. That transaction marked the start of a complicated and ambivalent relationship that Everett would cul-tivate with Navajo men, women, and children through many weeks in 1931, 1932, and 1934.

There was nothing timid about Everett's initial dealings with the indigenes. Somehow, within days of arriving in Kayenta, he had appropriated a Navajo hogan for his living quarters. (One imagines the sixteen-year-old simply walking up to some family's homestead and knocking on the door, as he had at Edward Weston's house the year before.)

Yet certain cultural criticisms had already crystallized in his mind. Within his first few days in Kayenta, he wrote to his parents:

> I have had a few disillusionments about Indians, here. For one thing the Navajos are scrupulously dishonest. When I leave my hogan for a while, I have to take all my posessions [sic] down to the store. Once I left a few pots and pans behind. When I came back they were outside in the mud.

And to Waldo, he wrote:

> The Indians around here are very poor, having no income except from their sheep and the blankets they sell. A statistician here figured that the per capita income from sheep, including wool and hides, is $13.40 a year. The Navajos live in filth.

In the end, Everett bought a burro for only six dollars. He promptly named the animal Everett, and began signing his letters with the pseudonym Lan Rameau. As others have pointed out, *l'âne* is French for "the donkey." It also has, as a second meaning, "the ass" or "the idiot"—suggesting a self-deprecatory joke on Everett's part. Rameau may have been a nod to the eighteenth-century composer Jean-Philippe Rameau, for since childhood Everett had been passionate about classical music.

This was the first of three occasions on which the vagabond would reject his given name, assuming a temporary alias in its place. The transformation puzzled and apparently disturbed his family and friends. On March 1, Everett wrote to his parents and Waldo: "Please respect my brush name. It is hard to lead a dual existence. . . . How do you say it in French: 'nomme de broushe,' or what? I would like to know. . . . It's not the perfect cognomen but I intend to stick by it."

In taking on a pseudonym, Everett consciously linked his discomfort with his name to a sense of a "dual existence." Here is one of the earliest hints of Everett's melancholy, brooding side, suggestive of a confusion of identity. By calling Lan Rameau a "brush name," the sixteen-year-old made it clear that in the wilderness he felt himself to be an altogether different person from the one who chafed impatiently at home in Los Angeles.

Everett elaborated in a letter to Bill Jacobs:

> As to my pen name, although it is really a brush name, I am still in turmoil, but I think that I will heroically stand firm in the face of all misunderstandings and mispronunciations. I'll simply have to lead a dual existence. . . . The name is LAN RAMEAU, and the friend who helped me select it thought it was quite euphonic and distinctive. Personally, I felt that anything was better than Ruess.

During his first weeks in Arizona, the weather was atrocious. "It has rained, snowed, hailed, or showered every night since I have been here," he wrote his parents in an undated letter. "Now it is blowing an icy gale. Heavy, lead colored clouds are in the offing. On one side, the hills are still covered with snow."

Neither the weather nor the strangeness of reservation life daunted Everett. His first letters home in February and March 1931 brim with zest and eagerness. As he waited for the snow on the mesas to melt, he planned his initial jaunts: they were to be exploratory probes into nearby canyons in search of Anasazi ruins. If Everett's fascination with Indian relics had first been sparked by the arrowheads he found in the forest surrounding Valparaiso, Indiana, now he anticipated far more ambitious quests into Southwestern prehistory. In Kayenta, he traded one of his watercolor paintings to the store clerk for "an ancient Indian bowl"—a decorated Anasazi pot.

In Kayenta, Everett also made the acquaintance of the legendary trader, guide, and self-taught archaeologist John Wetherill, who had found more Anasazi ruins on the Navajo reservation than any other Anglo. "Wetherill is the man who discovered Mesa Verde," Everett wrote Waldo on February 13, "and was in the party which discovered Rainbow Bridge. He is the best guide in the Southwest." Sixty-four years old that February, Wetherill was glad to share his knowledge of the backcountry with the sixteen-year-old greenhorn.

We know that Everett kept a diary in 1931. That book, alas, is lost, just like his diary from his previous journey in California. Once again we have only Everett's letters to family and friends by which to retrace his path during his first ten months in the Southwest.

Almost as soon as he arrived in Kayenta, Everett learned from a letter from his parents that a poster he had entered in a competition had won first prize, with an honorarium of twenty-five dollars. The money could not have come at a better time. On March 1, in a letter to his family, he detailed his purchases:

> I have spent $6 for a burro, $1 for a seamless sack, $2.50 for a Dutch oven, $2.00 for a Navajo woven cinch and some rope, $8 for a tarpaulin to keep out the wind, rain, and snow. I've spent as much again on food, but I have enough to last several weeks now. Bread is not sold in this country, so I have learned to bake squaw bread, corn bread, and biscuits in my Dutch oven. Yesterday the biscuits were perfect.

Despite this boast of self-sufficiency, Everett was not too proud to plead for help from home (as he would throughout the next four years). "I would appreciate it," he wrote, "if you sent some Swedish bread, peanut butter, pop, and Grape Nuts. They are unobtainable luxuries in this country."

Everett failed to keep the letters he received from family and friends while he rambled across the landscape, stopping at one remote post office after another to gather his mail. We have only faint echoes in his own letters by which to judge the tenor of his family's reaction to his headlong flight. Christopher and Stella had always been loving and indulgent, but there is evidence that now they worried about their son's safety. Apparently they planned to make their own trip to the Southwest to check up on Everett's well-being, for on March 21 he deflected their parental anxiety with uneasy humor: "As for hunting for me with Dorinda [the family auto], I don't believe you could get the car here. It would sink in the sand, rattle to pieces on the rocks, get stuck in a river bottom, slide off a cliff, or run out of gas miles from a service station."

Throughout his ten months in the outback in 1931, Everett wrote faithfully to his parents and Waldo, ending each letter with "Love to all" or "Love to everyone" or (while he was still cloaked in his pseudonym) "Love from Lan." And he was still dependent on Christopher and Stella for packages of food and painting equipment. Yet there is no getting around the fact that this first really ambitious journey away from home was in part a flight from the family's intrusive intimacy.

Everett confided to Waldo his need for separation and privacy from their parents. "Of course our letters should be strictly personal," he wrote to his brother. "Surely mother did not read that last letter, worded as it was? Also I wrote that these private letters should not be opened." Because Waldo was still living at home at age twenty-one, this insistence on privacy was awkward. "You ask for a separate letter," Everett wrote in another 1931 missive, "and I presume this is personal, as are your letters to me."

In 1931, of course, the country had not yet begun its painful crawl out of the Depression. Christopher had given up his vocation as a pastor and taken jobs with the Chautauqua Art Desk Company and later as a probation officer in order to support his family and his own ailing parents. Waldo was living at home to save money while he looked for a job. Everett's vagabondage during a time of such widespread poverty, combined with his material dependence on his parents, hints at a streak of self-indulgence fueled by a sense of entitlement.

Apparently he and Waldo quarreled over this matter. Worse, the younger brother had the gall to deride his sibling as a cop-out for adopting a conventional trade. During a brief period, Waldo worked as a secretary for the Fleischmann's Yeast Company. On May 2, 1931, Everett scolded him in a long letter:

> I feel that you are worthy of a better position than the present one. The idea put forward by some, that all necessary work is honorable and beautiful because it must be done, means nothing to me. As far as I am concerned, your work is quite unnecessary, since I can keep very healthy without Fleischmann's yeast. . . .
>
> I myself would sooner walk a whole day behind the burro than spend two hours on the street car.

Waldo, in turn, must have criticized Everett's unwillingness either to go to college or to look for a job, for in the same letter, Everett fires back:

> Somehow, I am very glad not to be home, where civilized life thrusts the thought of money upon one from all sides. With an adequate stock of provisions, I can forget the cursed stuff, or blessed stuff, for days and weeks at a time.
>
> Your censure was quite deserved in regard to providing my needs, but remember that I have asked for no money, and

that most of the equipment I asked for was unprocurable here, and necessary to my life.

"Equipment" such as Grape-Nuts and soda pop may indeed have seemed necessary to Everett's life in Arizona. And before the year was out, he would ask his parents for a sizable sum of money, and receive it with scarcely a murmur on their part.

* * *

From his temporary base in Kayenta, Everett planned his first forays into the canyonlands. It was John Wetherill who turned the young man's attention to Monument Valley and the Tsegi Canyon system. The trader even drew a sketch map for Everett to follow. Everett's thirst for adventure had already focused on the dream of finding Anasazi ruins no other Anglos had ever seen. Forty years earlier, John Wetherill and his four brothers had been able to do that to their hearts' content, but by the 1930s, all but the most minor and remote Anasazi sites had been discovered by government explorers, miners, pot hunters, and archaeologists. Still, Everett wrote Bill Jacobs on March 9:

> I am going to pack up my burro, and take a jaunt thru Monument Valley to a row of cliffs I know of, explore every box canyon, and discover some prehistoric cliff dwellings. Don't laugh. Maybe you thought they were all discovered, but such is not the case.... Most of the country is untouched. Only the Navajos have been there, and they are superstitious. In the event that I find nothing, I shall do some painting and have some interesting camps.

Thanks to an endless stream of classic Western movies, Monument Valley is famous today the world over for its stunning sandstone buttes and pinnacles, but in 1931 it was virtually unknown to tourists. A single rutted two-track dirt road wended its way through dunes and hills to reach the heart of the valley; barely navigable by sedan when dry, the road was impassable after rains. Navajos lived among the monumental geologic formations, as had the Anasazi before them, but the sole permanent Anglo presence was the trading post established by Harry Goulding in 1924. It would not be until John Ford shot the film *Stagecoach* in Monument Valley in 1938 that the place got pasted onto the tourist map. Only in 1958 did it become an official tribal park.

Everett found Monument Valley all that he could handle. In a somewhat dispirited letter to his family, he summarized his visit: "I spent two days, sketching, reading, cooking, and camping. The coyotes howled close at night, and the burro wandered far." Everett's first attempt to probe a box canyon turned into a fiasco. High winds and a snowstorm made traveling miserable; a waterhole he had counted on was dried up; and Everett, the burro, alternately sat down and refused to budge or jostled his load until it shifted so badly that his owner had to stop and lash it back in place. After an overnight in the "gloomy, sunless place," Everett the sixteen-year-old declared himself "very glad to get out of Gloom Canyon." He did find some cliff dwellings, but, to his disappointment, "All the ruins I saw had been investigated before."

The burro that Everett had bought from a Navajo and named after himself was more than a beast of burden; it quickly became a companion. In some of his letters, Everett coyly characterizes the animal's quirks:

> Everett, the burro, has been fattening out and becoming more lively and tractable. The first time I put a real pack on him, he ambled along for a mile and then lay down in the center of a path, but I think he is over that habit. When well treated he is a very droll creature, with his white nose and

stubby ears. Every once in a while he snorts and shakes his
head from side to side, ears flapping. He keeps turning his
ears, individually too.

But learning to train a pack animal by trial and error, with no
lessons from experienced wranglers, was a troublesome business. Everett could not conceal the exasperating failures of that first month
on the trail:

> After sunset I kept going, trying to reach an old Navajo
> hogan of which I knew. Finally I tied the burro to a tree
> and floundered around in the darkness and sandhills until
> I found the hogan. Then I couldn't find the burro. Then I
> couldn't find the hogan, after locating Everett. After two
> more searches for each, I made camp with the burro. A fly-
> ing spark burnt a hole in my packsack. My knife got lost,
> somehow.

If such setbacks discouraged him, or made him wonder whether
he was in over his head on this Southwest pilgrimage, Everett kept
such thoughts to himself. "This country suits me nearly to perfection," he wrote Bill Jacobs on March 9. Anticipating his destiny as a
loner, he added, "The only things I miss are a loyal friend to share my
delights and miseries, and good music."

On March 28, 1931, Everett turned seventeen. That day he opened
a package of food his parents had mailed to Arizona. "What a birthday feast I had!" he exulted in a letter home.

Everett's second backcountry jaunt, into the maze of the Tsegi Canyon system, was a far greater challenge than his tour of Monument
Valley. From eight-thousand-foot-high mesas about ten miles south
of the Utah border, five separate streams run south, carving lordly
canyons in the ruddy sandstone and leaving sheer six-hundred-foot

cliffs riddled with spacious natural alcoves. The streams converge in a single waterway, the Tsegi (Navajo for "canyon"), before emerging from the labyrinth at Marsh Pass, a gentle saddle at 6,750 feet above sea level—now, as in 1931, the highest point on the nearly straight, seventy-mile-long road between Kayenta and Tuba City.

The Tsegi was an Anasazi paradise. Two of the largest and most magnificent cliff dwellings in all of the Southwest, Keet Seel and Betatakin, are hidden away in distant branches of the canyon system. Small squares of land surrounding those ruins define Navajo National Monument today, and visitation at those prehistoric villages is tightly regulated. The rest of the Tsegi is Navajo land, and every branch contains smaller but equally stunning Anasazi cliff dwellings, all of them seldom visited even today. In 1931, the whole of the Tsegi was true wilderness.

The Anglo discovery of Keet Seel came in 1895, by a party including John Wetherill and led by his older brother Richard. The Wetherills spent two seasons digging in the ruins, bringing back an immensely rich trove of artifacts, mummies, and skeletons that ultimately found their way to various museums. Betatakin, tucked away in a short side canyon, was first visited by Anglos only in 1909. The party that discovered it included a prominent archaeologist, Byron Cummings, and was guided by John Wetherill, who learned of the ruin's existence from a Navajo living near the mouth of the Tsegi.

It was natural, then, that John Wetherill would point Everett Ruess to one of the landscapes he most cherished. The Tsegi, moreover, lay only ten miles west of Wetherill's trading post. In early April, Everett led his burro into the canyon system, camping out there for the better part of two weeks. His letters home do not rave about the beauty of the ruins or the scenery, but he was struck by the isolation of the place. "No one was in the valley there," he wrote Bill Jacobs, "not even an Indian, though there was some Navajo stock." At Keet Seel, Everett discovered, kept, and mailed home an artifact that he called "a mother of pearl ornament of value"—most likely a pendant made of shell traded to the Anasazi from the Pacific. More ghoulishly, he also scavenged and sent home "a part of a human jawbone with teeth."

Everett's return to Kayenta triggered one of his dark funks. In an April 16 letter to Bill Jacobs that begins cheerily enough, he reaches a dispirited impasse:

> Somehow I don't feel like writing now, or even talking. Both actions seem superfluous. If you were here, you might understand, but too much is incommunicable. If I were there—but that is unthinkable. You cannot understand what aeons and spaces are between us. I feel very different from the boy who left Hollywood two months ago.

The year before, on his California pilgrimage, even in Big Sur or Yosemite, Everett was seldom alone for as long as a day at a time. It may be that in the Tsegi the loner Everett felt destined to become was born. The April letters to Bill Jacobs reveal a side of his character that he had almost never before let others see. On April 18, Everett wrote again to Jacobs:

> These days away from the city have been the happiest of my life, I believe. It has all been a beautiful dream, sometimes tranquil, sometimes fantastic, and with enough pain and tragedy to make the delights possible by contrast. But the pain too has been unreal.

In this letter, for the first time, Everett articulates the link between solitude and pain, treating both as if they were his inevitable burden as an artist. That tension may have been at the heart of what he called his "dual existence." As he wrote to Jacobs, "A love for everyone and everything has welled up, finding no outlet except in my art."

But tragedy? Surely the nuisances of burro management did not justify such a grandiose term. One wonders whether Everett was simply being melodramatic, dignifying an acute sense of loneliness with a literary conception of irrevocable harm.

It is clear, however, that his journey into the Tsegi had a profound impact on Everett. Never before had he confronted such deep wilderness, much less traveled solo through it for days at a time. The experience changed him for good, as the letters he wrote home demonstrate. The April 18 letter to Bill Jacobs contains the first paragraph that stands by itself as a conscious performance, almost a prose poem. And that paragraph marks the first time that Everett lapsed into his strange usage of the perfect tense, as if he were looking back on a life that lay behind him:

> Music has been in my heart all the time, and poetry in my thoughts. Alone on the open desert, I have made up and sung songs of wild, poignant rejoicing and transcendent melancholy. The world has seemed more beautiful to me than ever before. I have loved the red rocks, the twisted trees, the red sand blowing in the wind, the low, sunny clouds crossing the sky, the shafts of moonlight on my bed at night. . . . I have been happy in my work, and I have exulted in my play. I have really lived.

Yet in Everett's heart, joy was inextricably tied up with a sense of doom. On May 2, he wrote to Waldo:

> I must pack my short life full of interesting events and creative activity. Philosophy and aesthetic contemplation are not enough. I intend to do everything possible to broaden my experiences and allow myself to reach the fullest development. Then, and before physical deterioration obtrudes,

I shall go on some last wilderness trip, to a place I have
known and loved. I shall not return.

As if to certify his transformation, Everett now dropped the pseudonym he had adopted for the last three months and invented a new
one. In the same letter to Waldo, he explained:

> Once again, I have changed my name, this time to Evert
> Rulan. It is not as euphonious or unusual as Lan Rameau,
> but to those who knew me formerly the name seemed an
> affectation. Evert Rulan can be spelled, pronounced, and
> remembered, and is fairly distinctive. I changed the donkey's
> name to Pegasus.

"Rulan" looks like an amalgam of "Ruess" and "Lan," and of
course "Evert" is much closer to "Everett" than "Lan Rameau" had
been. The new pseudonym seems to signify a shift in Everett's mind
as he edged back toward acceptance of his given name and his true
identity. By the middle of September 1931, he was once again signing
his letters "Everett." It would be more than three years before he assumed his third and last alter ego, giving himself an alias stranger and
more ominous than either Lan Rameau or Evert Rulan.

By May, Everett was ready to push on from his Kayenta base
camp. In a letter to Waldo, he outlined a planned itinerary that was
so ambitious, it has the stamp of fantasy about it:

> After the Grand Canyon, Kaibab and Zion, I shall go South
> for the winter, perhaps pausing in Mesa [Arizona], where
> a friend has relations. After working in the cactus country
> of southern Arizona, I may go northward thru New Mex-
> ico, Rocky Mt. Park, and Yellowstone to Glacier. . . . At all

events I intend to spend a year or two in the open, working
hard with my art. Then I shall wish for city life again, and
to see my old friends if they still exist.

Such a journey would have covered, at a very minimum, 1,700
miles. Everett did not specify to Waldo whether he planned to cross
such expanses on foot with his burro, or give up tramping for the hitchhiking that had propelled him through California the previous year.

This long May 2 letter really amounts to a blueprint for the life
Everett imagined himself leading:

After having lived intensely in the city for a while (It may
not be in Hollywood), I feel that I must go to some foreign
country. Europe makes no appeal to me as it is too civilized.
Possibly some unfrequented place in the South Seas. Australia holds little allure for me now. Alaska is too cold and
Mexico is largely barren, as is most of S. America. Ecua-
dor is an interesting place with its snow capped volcanoes,
jungles, and varied topography. As to ways and means, that
problem will be solved somehow.

This worldly-wise appraisal of foreign lands by a teenager who
had never been outside the United States may be tongue-in-cheek. But
about his goal as an artist, Everett was dead serious.

It is my intention to accomplish something very definite in
Art. When I have a large collection of pictures, done as well
as I can do them, then I am going to make a damn vicious
stab at getting them exhibited and sold. If this fails, I'll give
them away to friends and those who might appreciate them.

What is so striking about Everett's life-plan is that he saw his
wandering not as a distraction from the business of becoming an

artist, but as a crucial prerequisite for it. Other artists and writers (one thinks of Gauguin in Tahiti, Sir Richard Burton in Africa and the Near East) shared the same kind of vision, linking travel to exotic lands with creativity itself, but to find that conviction so firmly fixed in a seventeen-year-old is rare indeed.

Meanwhile, Everett had gained a new companion. Somewhere near Kayenta in April, he had adopted a "rez dog"—a mongrel, probably abused and abandoned, of the sort that hung around trading posts scrounging for scraps of food from strangers. "I found him last night, lost and squealing for help," Everett wrote to Waldo on April 19.

All the longing for friendship that had gnawed away at Everett during his solitary canyon jaunts was now directed toward the dog. As he wrote to his brother:

> He is a little roly poly puppy with fluffy white fur, and blue brown patches on his head and near his tail. His eyes are blue, and his nose is short. . . .
>
> I haven't yet decided about his name, but may call him Curly, because of his tail. When he is large enough, I am going to train him to go behind the burro, occasionally nipping the donkey's heels, so that we shall be able to go faster.

Curly would be Everett's constant companion through the next thirteen months. Rather than nipping at the burro's heels, the pup learned to ride on its back, comfortably seated between the saddlebags. After Everett finished his 1931 ramble through the Southwest, he would take Curly home to Los Angeles with him, then back to Arizona in March 1932.

As he left Kayenta in early May, Everett set off to the southeast toward Canyon de Chelly. The great twin-forked sandstone labyrinth at the head of Chinle Wash, as John Wetherill no doubt told Everett, was full of Anasazi ruins, some of them, including Antelope House, White House, and Mummy Cave, as spectacular as any in Arizona. Canyon de Chelly was also one of the most sacred places in the Navajo universe.

Only a month before Everett set out, on April 1, 1931, President Herbert Hoover had declared Canyon de Chelly a national monument—in celebration of the Anasazi ruins, not of the Navajo presence. (The people who lived in the canyon were never consulted about the governmental decree.) If Everett was aware that the place had just been made a national monument, he did not mention the fact in his letters. Eighty years after Hoover's fiat, Canyon de Chelly remains unique in the National Park System, the only park or monument devoted to prehistoric ruins but inhabited solely by Native Americans who endure the uneasy compromise of leading their private lives while tourists tramp and truck-ride through their backyards.

It took Everett four days to cover the seventy miles from Kayenta to the ramshackle town of Chinle, at the mouth of the canyon system. His first several days there served to sour his feelings about Navajos. The poverty of the town struck him forcefully, as he tried unsuccessfully to snag even the most menial temporary job to boost his meager funds. But the prejudices of his privileged upbringing trumped his compassion. On May 10, he wrote to Bill Jacobs:

> The Indians are not very lovable here. This morning, when I looked for my burro, I found that his bell and tie rope had been stolen (from his neck). Peg[asus] had evidently been mistreated, as his legs were skinned. . . . Experienced Indian traders say that a Navajo is your friend only as long as you give to him. Certainly none of them would go to church if the missionaries did not give them food and clothes.

Once launched in this vein, Everett vented his pent-up disdain:

> The Navajos do not help one another. If one Indian is try-
> ing to corrall a herd of horses, and they start to escape past
> another Indian, the latter will stir neither hand nor foot,
> but will only laugh. When a Navajo begins to be helpless
> and decrepit, the others cease to have anything to do with
> him. The government used to give such Indians a few ra-
> tions once a week, but now times are hard and they only get
> grub once a month. In consequence they go to all the white
> people and beg.

Since its first publication by Bud Rusho in *A Vagabond for Beauty*
in 1983, this May 10 letter has triggered an endless stream of speculation, for Everett signed it

> Love and kisses,
> Desperately yours,
>   Evert.

Amateur psychologists have seized upon this scrap of verbiage to
buttress their arguments that Everett was gay, or at least bisexual. But
it seems far more likely that the sign-off was mere badinage between
long-time buddies, as Everett parodied the style of teenage love letters.

Everett spent nine days in Canyon del Muerto, the system's northern branch, and three in Canyon de Chelly proper. Exploring Anasazi
ruins was his chief objective, painting with watercolors his main diversion. Upon his return to Chinle, he bragged in a letter to Bill Jacobs, "Saw a goodly portion of the 1200 cliff dwellings, & made half
a dozen paintings." (There are actually even more than 1,200 Anasazi
sites in Canyon de Chelly, but in a mere twelve days no mortal could

have seen more than a small fraction of them.) "Many of the ruins are well nigh inaccessible," Everett added, detailing the kinds of risks he was willing to take to get into a remote prehistoric site: "I made a foolhardy ascent to one safely situated dwelling. Part of the time I had to snake my way along a horizontal cleft with half my body hanging out over the sheer precipice."

To his disappointment, Everett saw that the ruin "had already been rifled" by previous pot hunters (or archaeologists). Even so, it was here that he made the finest discovery yet of his short career as a wilderness sleuth:

> One room, however, was rocked shut, & on opening it, I thot for a moment I saw a cliff dweller in his last resting place. But the blankets, tho mouldering with age, were factory made, & a Navajo baby was buried therein. Odd, because the Navajos are superstitious about the Moquis [Anasazi]. However, in sifting dirt in a corner, I found a cliff dweller's necklace, a thousand or so yrs. old. About 250 beads, 8 bone pendants, 2 turquoise beads, & one pendant of green turquoise.

Odd indeed. As Everett had learned, Navajos generally steer well clear of prehistoric ruins, for they believe that places of the dead are full of physical and spiritual danger. Although not unheard-of, a Navajo burial in an Anasazi ruin was a rare phenomenon, bespeaking some shamanistic ritual that an Anglo latecomer could only guess at.

Everett kept the necklace and later mailed it home. It was, as he had written in the poem he had composed at age thirteen, "a very precious treasure find," one he remained proud of throughout the rest of his short life.

In another Anasazi ruin nearby, Everett found a baby's cradleboard. This relic he left in place. Some fourteen months later he would return to the site, under very strange circumstances.

The twelve-day journey into the sandstone labyrinth was not without its tribulations. Three times Pegasus got stuck in quicksand. Another debacle was caused by a burro that was a resident of the canyon. Everett solved it with the shotgun he had carried throughout his 1931 journey so far, but which he had almost mailed home as unnecessary. The only use he had made of it before entering Canyon de Chelly was to kill a chipmunk that turned out to be "too small to eat."

In the May 23 letter to Bill Jacobs, Everett recounted the drama with the local burro as quixotic comedy:

> Au printemps [in the spring], a young burro's fancy seriously swings to thots of homosexual love. My burro is old & virtuous, but was handicapped by the pack, which he swung under him, then dented both canteens, & dragged about till it came off. Then the white ass pursued him about the country while Pegasus kicked constantly & ineffectively, only drawing blood once. I wanted to continue my way, but tho I pelted the ass with stones, he didn't seem to mind. Then I peiced [sic] the old Stevens together, loaded it with 7 1/2, & almost shot off the animals [sic] anus. But the next day, when I repassed, he came for more trouble, & I gave it to him in the legs.

Back in Chinle, Everett managed to sell one of his paintings for a dollar. In the letter to Jacobs, Everett narrates the transaction in the arch, worldly-wise tone that seems to have been the default mode of communication between the teenage friends. But the scene reverberates with an ambivalence about relationships that had already become part of Everett's makeup.

> Pretty soon I can start in as a columnist giving advice about how to be happy in love. Pretending interest in my pictures, the doctor's wife enticed me to her home & spent almost 4

solid hours this aft. telling me about her troubles. Her husband, 43, is going with a young nurse, & she's disconsolate. All about her little boy that died & how she's getting estranged from her husband. She couldn't decide whether to go away or stick it out. . . . Another of the tragedies of life.

Was the doctor's wife flirting with Everett? If so, was he interested? This encounter may have been another of those half-glimpsed possibilities with women, like the lakeside invitation to dinner by a woman friend of his family camping alone in Yosemite the previous summer.

On the same day that he wrote to Jacobs, Everett mailed a far less personal letter to his parents and Waldo. The jaunty note amounts to a plea for financial support. Ever solicitous, Christopher and Stella had mailed their son a package containing groceries and cash, which he opened upon his return to Chinle. Everett expressed surprise at such parental generosity, especially when, as he wrote back, "the financial situation is so pitiful at home." One item in the package delighted him: "Secretly, I had wished for puppy biscuits, but never dreamed you'd be thoughtful enough to send them."

Yet Everett was still strapped for funds to continue his journey. He had long since spent the twenty-five dollars in prize money he had won in the poster competition. He had tried to wangle odd jobs, but "All attempts to find work have failed. Hard times prevail [in Chinle] as elsewhere." As if embarrassed by having to beg for an allowance, Everett sketched out a mock-serious budget of his living expenses. Opposite such items as "rent," "electricity," and "telephone," he proudly entered "nothing." Likewise for "burro insurance" and "doctor bills." Totaling up the column, he wrote "usually under $20."

There is no question that Everett was practicing an extremely frugal existence. But the odd one-dollar sale of a painting was not going to tide him through the months of further ramblings he still craved. In the May 23 letter to his parents, he announced his next destination: "the Hopi country and Grand Canyon—about 200 miles distant." As the crow flies, the three Hopi mesas lay only about sixty-five miles west of Canyon de Chelly. But the nearest rim of the Grand Canyon was another seventy-five miles farther west. Two hundred miles was a reasonable guess as to how far Everett would have to travel on foot. And the country between Canyon de Chelly and the Grand Canyon was some of the starkest in all the Southwest.

Everett did not write home again until June 8, a little more than two weeks later. In the interim, he made his way to the Hopi mesas, which on this first visit disappointed him (he would later change his mind about those ancient villages). "The pueblo of Walpi was rather a disillusionment," he reported to his family. "There is an element of incongruity in the juxtaposition of old stonework and fences made of bedsteads." Oraibi, which vies with Walpi for the claim of being the oldest continuously inhabited town in the United States, was also a letdown. Everett's only comment: "The dust and heat were extreme."

The truth of the matter was that on this trudge across the Arizona badlands during the scorching days of early June, Everett got into serious trouble. On June 7, somewhere near the outpost of Cameron, a pair of teenage boys driving a pickup south toward Flagstaff encountered the loner with his burro and his dog. One of them, Pat Jenks, nineteeen at the time, never forgot this chance meeting. In 2009, at the age of ninety-seven, he recounted it to a Tucson newspaper reporter. Jenks and his friend Tad Nichols were surprised to see "a boy hunched over without a cap to protect him. He looked forlorn and he looked very sad.

"We stopped the car," Jenks went on, "got out and talked to him. He told us who he was. He was discouraged because he hadn't been able to sell his woodblocks.

"We asked him, 'You want a drink of water?' He misunderstood. Handed us *his* canteen—it was almost used up.

"I said to Tad, 'We're not leaving him out in the desert this way. We can't do that.' " The boys tied Everett's gear to the roof, unloaded the back of the pickup, and managed to coax Pegasus onto the flatbed. They drove on to Jenks's family's Deerwater Ranch, west of Flagstaff. "I guess he stayed about a month," Jenks recalled in 2009. (The actual stay, according to Everett's letters, was less than two weeks, but ranch life among the cool pines and aspens at eight thousand feet on the slopes of the San Francisco Peaks served to rejuvenate a badly depleted youth.)

In his June 8 letters to his family and to Bill Jacobs, Everett completely played down his semi-rescue by the boys with the pickup. To Jacobs he wrote,

> [W]hen I was at the Little Colorado river yesterday, about to turn westward [toward the Grand Canyon], two boys in a light Ford truck stopped to talk. They were very much interested in what I was doing. One of them wanted to buy my picture of a cliff dwelling, but he didn't have the money, of course. Suddenly he decided to take me, my burro, and Curly to a ranch of his in the Coconino forest in the San Francisco peaks. I didn't think it feasible, but the three of us lengthily shunted the donkey on, after much maneuvering.

In Everett's telling, this change in his plans was simply an unplanned lark, a chance to make new friends and to explore yet another corner of the country. But in the same letter, he admitted that his burro was in bad shape: "Peg is old and broken down, and his broken leg scrapes the other and bleeds. Tho I gave him a couple of days rest, his back is sore. He is really only half a burro." How the animal broke its leg, Everett never explained—much less why he had tried to push on with a crippled beast of burden.

More vaguely, Everett admitted to Jacobs, "A host of misadventures have occurred, and while they were very unpleasant at the time of happening, I don't regret one of them now." In the letter he wrote the same day to his family, Everett did not even hint at such "misadventures," nor did he mention the maimed and worn-out condition of his burro.

At the Deerwater Ranch, Everett chipped in with the chores of cutting down aspen trees and building fences. He also hiked up some of the peaks that towered to the east. Six months later, back home in Los Angeles, Everett wrote a thank-you note to Pat Jenks, as he conjured up the delights of his recuperative stay at the ranch. He spent hours, he remembered, "lying in the long, cool grass or on a flat-topped rock, looking up at the exquisitely curved, cleanly smooth aspen limbs, watching the slow clouds go by."

Before he left, Everett gave Jenks one of his paintings, a canyon landscape. The two young men corresponded for the next three years, and after Everett's disappearance, Jenks stayed in contact with his family. In 2009, the old man still had Everett's watercolor painting hung on his wall.

Still bent on exploring the Grand Canyon, Everett headed north from the Deerwater Ranch around June 20. En route, he stopped for six days at a sheep camp, where he earned a bit of cash by chopping wood and watering and branding lambs. The camp was full of "interesting characters," as well as an abundance of burros. Eventually Everett traded his shotgun for a fresh burro, which he named Pericles, or Perry for short. To Bill Jacobs he wrote, "The new burro, though older than Pegasus (about 25), has four sound legs, a strong back, and is far handsomer. . . . Pegasus was left behind, free to kick his heels as he listed."

By June 30, Everett was camped on the South Rim of the Grand Canyon. From Chinle he had walked, by his own reckoning, three hundred miles to get there. The whole of his 1930 ramble up the California coast to Yosemite had lasted two months. Now Everett was almost five months into his far more ambitious peregrination across the Southwest. Despite his trials and setbacks, and his poverty—"My total

monetary wealth is 4 cents," he wrote Jacobs, only half-facetiously—
Everett had not the slightest urge to head for home. He would stay on
the trail, in fact, for another five and a half months.

*   *   *

The adventure Everett had been living since early February had
changed and shaped his character. In June 1931 he was still only
seventeen years old. The surviving letters that he periodically mailed
from wayside post offices give us the only window into Everett's personal development during that year, but they are full of potent hints.

By the end of June, the wanderer was still signing himself Evert
Rulan. The notion of a "dual existence" was all tied up with Everett's
quest to understand himself. In his mind, that duality had much to do
with the difficulty of intimacy with others.

By 1931, apparently, Bill Jacobs was Everett's best friend, replac-
ing Waldo as his closest confidant. The letters to Jacobs are deeper,
more private, and more confessional than the missives he headed
"Dear Father, Mother, and Waldo" or simply "Dear Family." The
bond between the two adolescents was a strong friendship bordering
on a kind of love. But to express that affection, Everett took refuge in
the mannerisms of boys feigning learned pomposities with fancy vo-
cabularies. Lapsing into this mannered style, Everett produced some
truly clunky sentences. From the June 30 letter to Jacobs: "Not having enjoyed a college course in psychology, I surmise from your writings that you feel rather belabored by circumstance, and, unable to
strike back, have striven, in a small way, to bolster up your ego by
laying bare to me my frailties." It is not hard to read between the
lines, however, to see the teasing fondness beneath the put-down. In
a sense, the banter between Everett and Bill was not unlike that of
athletes trading locker-room insults.

In the June 30 letter, Everett admits that he is writing regularly to
other friends.

You inquire . . . about my other correspondants [*sic*]. . . .
Aside from my parents, three "fortunates" are blessed by
my letters. One is five years your senior, the other four years
younger than you. Of the three, you are by far the most
prompt in replying. By all means hold your place.

It seems weird that Everett did not identify the other two correspondents by name. Today we have no idea who they were. But the
tenor of Everett's coy admission is akin to that of a man taunting his
lover with the threat of unspecified rivals.

Something to do with intimacy scared Everett, even while he
fiercely craved it, and that tension lay at the core of the insatiable
wandering loner he was fast becoming. It is tempting to trace the
tension to the intrusive closeness Christopher and Stella had forced
upon both their sons. Yet in his letters to his parents, from childhood
through age twenty, Everett never once lashed back, never shouted
"Leave me alone!" Nor did he ever cut off communication with them.

In the same letter to Jacobs, Everett commented, "My grandmother
wrote one solicitous letter. 'When are you coming home?' she asked."
It was a question not worth answering. To Jacobs, as to his family,
Everett reveled instead in the open-air freedom and self-sufficiency of
his new life, even while he seemed a bit surprised that he was capable
of pulling it off:

I throw my camps in all manner of places. I have slept under
cedars, aspens, oaks, cottonwoods, pinyons, poplars, pines,
maples (not the typical maple), and under the sky, clouded
or starry. Right now I am under cedars [junipers], with pines
all around. Cedar bark is excellent tinder.

Desert rats have told me few camping secrets, but here
and there I've gleaned some. I can take care of myself rather
well now. Before I had the pack saddle, I used the squaw

hitch, but now I throw a double diamond hitch. It wasn't
hard to learn.

Everett spent the next five weeks in the Grand Canyon—two weeks
on the South Rim, two weeks in the canyon depths, and a last week
on the North Rim. The majesty of the landscape clearly held him in
thrall, for he would return in future years to make further probes into
the colossal chasm. Yet the letters home are strangely lacking in evocations of the beauty of the place. One such effort appears in a July
16 letter to Everett's father:

> I followed obscure trails and revelled in the rugged gran-
> deur of the crags, and in the mad, plunging glory of the
> Colorado river. Then one sunset I threw the pack on the
> burro again and took the long, steep uptrail. I traveled for
> several hours by starlight. A warm wind rushed down the
> side cañon, singing in the pinyons. Above—the blue night
> sky, powdered with stars. Beside—the rocks, breathing back
> to the air the stored up heat of the day. Below—the black
> void. Ahead—the burro, cautiously picking his way over the
> barely discernible trail. Behind—a moving white blotch that
> was Curly.

The heat in the inner gorge in mid-July was debilitating. Everett
claimed that the thermometer rose above 140 degrees Fahrenheit—an
exaggeration, for the all-time record at Phantom Ranch, at the foot of
the Bright Angel Trail, is 120 degrees. The average daily maximum on
the river in July, however, is a searing 106.

Everett cooled off by swimming in the turbulent Colorado, unin-
tentionally "drinking gallons of the muddy water" as he did so. Then
he lay on the sand in the shade of the suspension bridge across the river
and watched damselflies flitting through the air. To get Pericles to cross
the bridge, however, proved a strenuous challenge. The burro balked

time and again, until, as Everett wrote to Jacobs, "I finally banged him across with an old shovel." This initial difficulty in getting a pack animal to cross a major river, even on the secure span of a bridge, would be repeated on future outings. And it would eventually furnish a critical clue in the mystery of Everett's disappearance in 1934.

The reticence of Everett's letters during his five weeks in the Grand Canyon (he writes more about Pericles and Curly than about his own doings) is curious. Only a single cryptic sentence in an August 1 letter to Bill Jacobs hints at an adventure of consequence: "Recently I had the most terrific physical experiences of my life, but recovery was rapid." Recovery from what? An accident? A bad scare? Simple exhaustion?

It would be understandable for Everett to minimize close calls and hardships in his letters to his family, but for Bill Jacobs's ears, such ordeals ought to have made for juicy telling. By July, Christopher and Stella were getting even more worried about their wayward son. Once again they proposed an auto trip out to Arizona to meet him, apparently with the idea of bringing him back to Los Angeles, even if it meant bringing Pericles and Curly to California as well. And once again, in a letter to his father, Everett fended off their solicitude:

> You must be definite in any plans you make for me, as I am crossing to Utah before much longer. It would cost money to have the burro fed and cared for, and the city is no place for a dog. Again, could you spare the time for the trip—two days each way? Eight days altogether. Then too, you would probably have trouble with the car. Personally, I feel no craving for city life, unless it is for the more expensive aspects of it. But use your own judgment in the matter.

Christopher and Stella took the hint and stayed at home.

From the North Rim, Everett headed toward Zion National Park. It took him nine days to cover 130 trail miles—slow going for Everett, because each day he hunkered down in the shade through the hottest afternoon hours. "Zion Canyon is all I had hoped it would be," he wrote to his family on August 18. But except for a single passage in a letter to Bill Jacobs a month later, Everett sent home no account of what he saw or did in the park. One paragraph in a letter written to Jacobs while he was still in Zion hints at a certain burnout: "I write by firelight. The crest of the sandstone cliffs is bathed in moonlight. I know it is beautiful, but I can't feel the beauty."

But this blasé mood may have had a mundane cause. In Zion, Everett contracted a bad case of poison ivy. To Jacobs, he vividly described the rash's torments:

> For six days I've been suffering from the semi annual poison ivy case—my sufferings are far from over. For two days, I couldn't tell whether I was dead or alive. I writhed and twisted in the heat, with swarms of ants and flies crawling over me, while the poison oozed and crusted on my face and arms and back. I ate nothing—there was nothing to do but suffer philosophically.

As he had the year before in California, Everett seems to have regarded poison ivy as a congenital predisposition to which he had the bad luck to be prone, not as an infection that could easily be avoided. He complained to Jacobs,

> You may remember that last year I took antitoxin injections and bounced happily off on my vacation—within a few days I was suffering it again with dull resignation. One chap says to use saltwater, another gasoline, another claims tomato juice is a sure cure. Nothing I used in times past alleviated the raging perceptibly.

The only inkling of Everett's awareness of the cause and effect of poison ivy emerges in a defiant line in the same letter: "I get it every time, but I refuse to be driven out of the woods."

The low mood brought on by the poison ivy nudged Everett toward some unusually deep reflections upon his own nature. In the August 27–28 letter to Jacobs appears one of the paragraphs most often quoted by latter-day analysts of Everett Ruess:

> My friends have been few because I'm a freakish person and few share my interests. My solitary tramps have been made alone because I couldn't find anyone congenial—you know it's better to go alone than with a person one wearies of soon. I've done things alone chiefly because I never found people who cared about the things I've cared for enough to suffer the attendant hardships. But a true companion halves the misery and doubles the joys.

To those who want to see Everett as homosexual, the phrase "a freakish person" rings as a veiled admission of that orientation. Yet even if it implies nothing more than that Everett felt too different from others to kindle lasting friendships, one wonders just how hard he tried to find a "true companion." In California the year before, he had made instant pals of Edward Weston's teenage sons, and in Yosemite he had had no trouble finding hikers to share a trail with. But in Arizona and Utah in 1931, there is no indication that Everett invited anyone to set off into the backcountry with him.

In any event, this letter marks the first unambiguous expression of the longing for a soul mate that would plague Everett throughout his short life. He never acknowledged the kind of terrible loneliness that the extraordinary solo journeys he was undertaking would have inflicted on a normal seventeen-year-old. But he would return now and again to the lament that he could not find that "true companion"—whether or not he meant lover, mentor, or partner in the wilderness.

There is more, however, to this manifesto of a solitary aesthetic than meets the eye—or less, depending on how one parses it. In *Vagabond,* Rusho published only part of the letter to Bill Jacobs. The full text gives a personal context to Everett's oft-quoted statement about being "a freakish person."

The paragraph that in Rusho's book begins with "My friends have been few . . ." actually starts with a preceding sentence: "What's all this poppycock about half formulated plans and half hearted invitations?" Then, after penning his manifesto for the solitary life, Everett complains,

> Then too I never could make anyone do anything for me; I'd feel like someone if you actually kept your promise; it was one, you know.
>
> How I looked forward to that Christmas trip with you—it fell thru. Always then you told me you'd certainly be with me this summer; you waived my doubts. Yet we both feel the undeniable lure of far places.
>
> But I know there are many drawbacks to my way of living & traveling—things you wouldn't want to do. Don't come unless you want to.
>
> Your letter was good; I couldn't complain—but letters are poor substitutes for speech and companionship.

It seems clear, then, that Jacobs had backed out of a promise to share the 1931 ramble through the Southwest—or at least the summer portion of it—with Everett. And a planned Christmas trip before that had failed to materialize, presumably because of Jacobs's change of heart. "Don't come unless you want to" may imply that Everett had renewed the invitation in mid-journey, asking Bill to join him somewhere near Zion.

Worse, Jacobs had gone off on other trips with other friends. "Why do you say no news," Everett went on, "tho you tell me nothing of your trips except that you took them; what sort of companions did you have? what were the ups and downs?"

The August 27–28 letter thus serves in part as the wounded outcry of a jilted friend. The pain and jealousy Everett cannot hide imply nothing about overt homosexuality, but Bill Jacobs was the true companion with whom Everett had hoped to share his wandering quest. Yet the letter modulates away from anger, as Everett tries to repair the friendship with news of his own adventures. Toward the close, he quotes the first four lines of a poem he had been working on, written in a loose blank verse:

> *I have been one who loved the wilderness—*
> *Swaggered and softly crept between the mountain peaks*
> *I listened long to the sea's brave music;*
> *I sang my songs above the shriek of desert winds.*

Everett would continue to work on this poem—arguably the best he ever wrote—for another two years. It was published posthumously in 1935, under the title "Wilderness Song," in the *Los Angeles Daily News*. Its penultimate stanza (quoted in the prologue to this book) has served ever since as a kind of autobiographical epitaph for Everett:

> *Say that I starved; that I was lost and weary;*
> *That I was burned and blinded by the desert sun;*
> *Footsore, thirsty, sick with strange diseases;*
> *Lonely and wet and cold . . . but that I kept my dream!*

The remarkable August 27–28 letter to Jacobs, signed simply "Evert," contains another important declaration: "I expect to resume my old name soon."

*   *   *

Seven months into his 1931 expedition, recovering from the bout of poison ivy, worn out by the desert heat, and perhaps beginning to tire of the natural beauty he so ardently sought, Everett might have been expected to pack it in and head for home. But nothing could have been further from his thoughts. On August 28 he wrote his family, "I expect to continue my wanderings for a year more at least—my itinerary is planned, & I have work to do." This letter, which Christopher and Stella must have read with dismay, also elaborates on Everett's intention to revert to his given name: "Uncle Alfred was mistaken or trying to be ironic when he said I went back to the old name. However I expect to do so anyway very soon. I tire of the experimentation & entanglements, and after all there's not much in a name." He closed the letter, "Love from Evert." Only on September 18, for the first time all year, did he write "Everett" at the bottom of a page of correspondence.

From Zion, Everett planned to return to the Grand Canyon, then, as the days grew chillier, push on farther south. "As to what I'll do when it's cold," he wrote his family on September 9, "I expect to spend the winter in the cactus country of southern Arizona. I've never seen that country, and it's warmer there." Everett's resumption of his given name was tied up in some psychic way with the geography of his journey. "I think it would be better to use [Evert] Rulan until I am out of the Grand Canyon country," he explained.

The young man's haughty assertions of independence were undercut by his need for regular shipments of food and money from his parents. On September 18, for instance, he wrote, "If you want to send food don't send Eusey's jell a teen—it tastes like glue. It is a long time since I've had cookies. The peanut butter, raisins, & prunes you sent were good." The day before, "I cashed the welcome 5 dollar m.o. [money order]. Money doesn't seem to go very far, tho. Soon I must buy new shirts, socks, and shoes." Everett was aware that his parents' own budget was stretched to the breaking point. On September 17 he sympathized, "I don't understand how you scrape along now that Mrs. Ryall's rent is gone."

The unabated affection in Everett's letters to his parents does not ring of cynical manipulation, as if he were posing as a dutiful son in order to keep up the flow of his allowance. The love sounds genuine. One must chalk up Everett's fending off his parents' attempts to control his life at the same time as he pleaded for supplies and cash to the sense of entitlement in which he had basked since childhood. At his most selfish, he treated his parents almost as though they were patrons committed to supporting a budding artist through thick and thin. Thus: "If you wish to send things, you might send a bottle of India ink. The bottles it is sold in are not much good, for the corks always come out easily." Or: "Some time in October you will receive some negatives of pictures of Curly, Pericles, & me. A hiker from New York took them. I wish you would make four prints of each, sending three of each to me."

Yet Everett did not even feign politeness as he rejected his parents' attempts to bend his life's path. Christopher and Stella were deeply disturbed that Everett showed no interest in going to college. Sometime that summer, they sent him a brochure for a junior college. On September 17, Everett wrote back,

> I studied the Junior College pamphlet, and I don't feel enthusiastic. The place must be like a jail, with all the rules and regulations. What an anticlimax it would be after the free life. There was nothing in the art course that seemed worthwhile.

At some point, Christopher and Stella also asked Everett if he would send home his diary so that they could read it. The sharing of diaries had been a mandatory family ritual since both Everett and Waldo were old enough to write. But now Everett responded, "Regarding the diary, I must dash your hopes. I've finished writing it, true, but I'm not done with it. It is too personal to be read by anyone but the author, in its present state." (It is this 1931 diary that has long since gone missing, probably for good.)

It took Everett eight days to reach the North Rim of the Grand Canyon, as he traced a different return path from the one he had followed heading out toward Zion in August. On September 30, writing to Bill Jacobs again, he announced his plan to "start down the hole," cross the Colorado River, and make the five-thousand-foot ascent to the South Rim. On the North Rim, at an altitude of eight thousand feet, Everett sensed the changing of the season:

> Winter is close at hand; the maples are crimson, and flurries of yellow aspen leaves swirl about with each breeze. On many hillsides the yellow leaves have blackened, and the trees stand bare and silent. Soon the snows will be here, but I won't.

Such lyrical evocations of the countryside are increasingly rare in the letters Everett sent home from September on. It may be that he poured all his poetic energy into his diary. A single letter to Waldo quotes eight paragraphs from the diary—the only passages from his 1931 journal that have survived. And those sentences brim with the rhapsodic:

> Sunset made all the misery worth enduring. Far to the north and east stretched the purple mesas, with cloudbanks everywhere above them. Some were golden brown and vermillion [sic] where sunshafts pierced the low clouds. A rainbow glowed for a moment in the south. That was a promise.

Clouds of all kinds and shapes arched overhead, stretching
in long lines to the horizons. Some were like swirls of smoke.
Then twilight—a rim of orange on the treeless western hills.
The full moon appeared, rolling through the clouds.

On the strength of paragraphs such as these, we can safely judge
that, eight months into his 1931 expedition, Everett had not even
begun to burn out on natural beauty.

By the second week in October he was camped on the South Rim.
Not since May 2 had he written a letter to Waldo: all the epistles
home bore the salutation "Dear Father, Mother, and Waldo," or simply "Dear Family." On October 9, however, Everett sent two long letters to his brother. Along with the letters to Bill Jacobs, these are the
most personal and heartfelt that Everett penned in 1931. The first one
begins, "I was delighted to hear from you yesterday. I'd almost given
you up—thought you were tired of me." Apparently the fact that for
months Waldo had not bothered to send a letter separate from the
ones their parents had mailed had led Everett to fear an estrangement.
Now he half-confides a secret in the first paragraph: "I would have
replied yesterday, but I was expecting an important change which has
not occurred. The season is changing—cold winds shriek ominously,
and then there is meaningful silence. I expect change in my life too."

The allusion remains cryptic, for Everett never made clear what
the change in his life would have been. But the tone of both the October 9 letters is almost conspiratorial against the parents. In the first
(as quoted above), Everett writes, "Of course our letters should be
strictly personal. Surely mother did not read that last letter, worded
as it was?"

A few paragraphs later, Everett makes another cryptic remark:
"My only choice between getting out on my own and going home is
the first alternative. I couldn't go back—not defeated, at least." One
wonders what sort of defeat Everett contemplated. He had already

performed a momentous solo journey full of intense experiences and discoveries. The defeat may have been attached to his financial dependence on his parents, for Everett goes on, "In that last letter I told you to tell father to send no money; I wish you had made that clear to him. It might have saved me more trouble than the money saved."

Money in fact preoccupied Everett's worries, and a defensive mixture of pride and shame pierced his sense of entitlement. To Waldo, he reported that in eight months their parents had sent him "only 52 dollars." He felt that he had to give his brother a full accounting of his finances on the trail.

> I started with 50 dollars, parents sent 52, 35 came from prizes, I procured 15 from various sources.
>
> I have spent 136 dollars altogether. Considerably more than a third went for equipment—all the rest for food. Needless to say, I have earned dozens and dozens of meals.

But this reckoning stirred Everett to a sudden fit of anger. "Not for God's sake," he wrote, "or yet for Hell's sake can I sell any of my paintings. The world does not want Art—only the artists do."

Everett was not so self-centered as to be oblivious of the Depression in which the country still floundered; his letters mention the poverty of every town he visited, the scarcity of work. Waldo was living at home at the age of twenty-one, taking what stopgap jobs he could find to support himself, while Everett was cruising across the Southwest, trying to "become" an artist. Yet "It is unfair to you to be chained at home," he wrote to his brother.

In the second October 9 letter to Waldo, Everett mentioned that he was mailing home "a small pink arrowhead" and the beautiful Anasazi necklace he had dug out of the cliff dwelling in Canyon de Chelly. He also dropped a comment that for Everett's devotees today still reverberates as a bombshell:

Whatever I have suffered in the months past has been nothing compared with the beauty in which I have steeped my
soul, so to speak. It has been a priceless experience—and I
am glad it is not over. What I would have missed if I had
ended everything last summer!

After Everett's disappearance in 1934, some observers speculated
that he might have committed suicide. Seventy-seven years later, there
are still theorists who argue that suicide is the most likely explanation
of the wanderer's fate. The paragraph quoted above forms those theorists' prime piece of evidence. It remains the only extant statement in
Everett's hand that he ever seriously thought about killing himself.

Most of the summer of 1930, Everett had spent hiking and hitchhiking in California. There is no hint of the suicidal in any of the
surviving letters he wrote from Carmel, Big Sur, or Yosemite. Yet the
implication of the October 9 passage is not only that Everett had contemplated suicide, but that Waldo knew about it.

*   *   *

Camped on the South Rim, Everett had reached an impasse. In the first
of the October 9 letters to Waldo, he complained, "For the present I
am stranded here, with no means of moving my equipment. My clothes
are fairly well worn out. As soon as I can procure two good burros,
which is my greatest concern at present, I'll be traveling south."

What must have stranded Everett was the condition of Pericles.
None of the letters mention the old burro breaking down, but after
traveling hundreds of miles, including two traverses of the immense
gorge of the Grand Canyon, Pericles may have been too worn out to
continue. Evidently, Everett abandoned or sold the faithful burro on
the South Rim.

The answer to his logistical woes was to double the number of
his pack animals. (Was this the "important change" in his life that

he hinted at to Waldo?) The problem was that he couldn't afford to buy two burros. Swallowing his pride, Everett sent a telegram home begging for money. Loyal as ever, Christopher and Stella sent cash to their prodigal son, but the transaction sparked some hard feelings. On October 23, Everett wrote defensively to his mother, "I could not buy two burros with my ten dollars, so I wired you to send some money. It came this noon, and I felt much better. This is the first time on this trip that I've asked you outright for money, and I needed it."

Before acquiring his new burros, however, Everett made his way to Mesa, Arizona, probably by hitching a ride with Grand Canyon tourists. Today a suburb of Phoenix, Mesa even in 1931 was far from wilderness. After the solitary remoteness of the Tsegi, Canyon de Chelly, the Grand Canyon, and backcountry Zion, southern Arizona must have seemed bland and civilized to the vagabond.

From Mesa, Everett made his way east along U.S. Highway 60 to the largely Hispanic mining town of Superior. As Everett wrote his mother, "The Mexicans use burros to haul wood, and there are dozens of them here." With his new allowance from home, Everett purchased two fresh pack animals, which he named Cynthia and Percival. The bickering with his parents continued. "It hurts me to think you consider me selfish for wanting another burro," Everett wrote to his mother. And, "Neither Pegasus nor Perry were good burros—they were too old, and suffered under their loads. I had to travel light and carry part of the pack myself."

One can hardly blame Christopher and Stella for their resentment. Pinching pennies themselves, they were effectively subsidizing their son to stay away from home as long as he pleased. More than a month after the burro purchase, Everett was still arguing about it with his parents. "[Y]our idea of a burro's load is hardly correct," he wrote them on November 28. "The blankets and the canteens alone weigh more than 60 pounds. There is usually a hundred pounds on each burro. When I only had one, he occasionally had a burden of 150 pounds."

Through the rest of October and all of November, Everett made minor excursions around the parched hills and scrubby desert east of Phoenix. He visited the Tonto Cliff Dwellings (today, Tonto National Monument) on the Salt River, ruins of villages built not by the Anasazi, but by their contemporary neighbors to the south, the little-known Salado. He fell in with some tourists from New York who were determined to visit an "amethyst mine" in the Four Peaks area just north of the Salt. Everett talked these greenhorns into hiring him to burro-pack their gear for the three-day excursion. Later he used the burros to gather firewood that he sold to other tourists. Money was Everett's constant concern. On November 13 he wrote Bill Jacobs, "The outlook was quite dismal for a time, but now I am assured of enough to keep me going for a month or so."

Those weeks spent in the comparative warmth of the lowland desert lacked the adventurous spark of Everett's bold wilderness forays during the preceding months. Instead of solitude, he found himself constantly in the company of strangers, some of them interesting. To Jacobs he wrote,

> I have been meeting all types of people—artists, writers, hoboes, cooks, cowmen, miners, bootleggers. . . . The bootlegger said that as soon as he sold his stock on hand he could offer me a job guarding his still in the mountains and packing barrels to the retreat.

Nothing came, however, of that odd job offer.

For a while, Everett pursued an ambitious scheme to make decent money. A shopkeeper named Mr. Dupre encouraged him to transform a drawing Everett had made of the Tonto Cliff Dwellings into mass-produced Christmas cards that the two of them would sell. To do so, however, Everett had to send home the drawing, beseech his mother to make a linoleum block based on it, and then ask her to print a thousand copies. In several letters to Stella, Everett made peremptory demands: "We want this card to be stiff paper, cream color perhaps, and larger than a post card. There must be a thousand envelopes too." Poor Stella dutifully made and sent the blockprint, only to have Everett complain, "The printing is terrible. . . . There is no use printing the thing unless larger type is used." In the end, the Christmas cards got made and sent to Arizona, but it seems doubtful that Everett ever sold more than a handful (at the then exorbitant price of forty cents apiece).

After nearly ten months in the Southwest, Everett still did not want to go home. He had set his heart on wandering indefinitely as he slowly built up a practice as a landscape artist. He shared his dream with Bill Jacobs:

> I am confident that I can make something of my work—the problem is how to keep alive until I have succeeded in a larger measure. My plan is to ramble about the Southwest with donkeys for a couple of years more, gathering plenty of material and mastering water color technique—then to get some windfall so I can work with oils and do things on a larger scale, perfect my field studies, and then do something with what I have.

Instead, Everett had painted himself into a corner. The only windfall was the dribs and drabs of allowance his indulgent parents kept mailing to him. Everett's blind idealism kept him from recognizing just how naïve it was for a seventeen-year-old in the middle of the Depression to hope to build a career as an itinerant painter carrying all his belongings on a pair of burros.

Sending home treasures like the Anasazi arrowhead and necklace was a way of trying to placate his parents. Yet even in this respect, Everett misjudged their tolerance. In October he wrote his mother:

I now have another trophy to put on the wall of my imaginary studio. It is the skin of a Gila monster which I caught.
It took me all morning to separate the skin from the monster, and then it wrinkled when I stretched it. In a few days I
will have it dried, and I can send it to you. It should be sewn
with fine thread on a piece of felt.

Throughout his several years of traveling in the Southwest, Everett would gleefully kill every rattlesnake he could find—even though
he knew that his mother (an environmentalist before her time) was
appalled by that practice. Stella may have been an artist, but it is hard
to imagine her making a wall hanging out of a Gila monster skin.

By the end of November, Everett was reconciled to returning
home. "I want to be in the city for a couple of months this winter,"
he wrote his parents on November 28, "but I'm not sure just how I'll
get there. I would like to spend hours in a library, and to put some
of my sketches in oils." Not once in his letters home did Everett let
down his guard enough to offer his parents or Waldo even a perfunctory gesture of affection, such as "I miss you" or "It'll be good to see
you again."

On Thanksgiving Day, feeling a bit sorry for himself, Everett wrote
Bill Jacobs, "I suppose you are sitting around a groaning table now
while I am all alone in a tent with my feet frozen." He had a proposi-
tion to make. He would give Bill one of his best paintings if he would
drive out to Arizona and pick him up. "The proper time for you to
arrive here would be December 6th, 8th, 10th, or 12th," he wrote. "If
you drive rapidly, you could be under parental wings again within five
or six days." The edge of annoyance toward the friend who had stood
him up in the summer tainted this letter. "Here is how you can earn my
everlasting gratitude and respect," he threatened, "or fail to do so."

Jacobs evidently declined. On December 6, Everett wrote a petu-
lant letter to his mother. "I had no intention of paying Bill anything,"

he griped. "I told him it was an opportunity for him to earn the picture he has been clamoring for me to give him." This letter reveals Everett at his most spoiled and selfish. "I wish you would please send me more Christmas cards soon," he demanded of his mother. "I think I had some unused pieces of linoleum in my droor [sic]. Please send them—large and small, and any others you can spare. If you have an extra carving knife, I'd like to have it."

Then, in the next paragraph, "I am not coming home. . . . I'd never have thought of coming home if you hadn't spoken of it two or three times."

But Everett had nowhere else to go. Toward the end of December, he hitchhiked to Los Angeles. He left his burros, Cynthia and Percival, in Roosevelt, Arizona, entrusting them to a local Apache to keep through the winter. With him on the road, however, Everett brought Curly, the "roly poly puppy with fluffy white fur" he had adopted on the Navajo reservation in April.

By all indications, Everett returned to Los Angeles in a sullen mood, weighed down by a crushing sense of failure. Yet he had behind him an exploratory adventure the likes of which few Americans so young had ever accomplished. In ten months he had traveled perhaps a thousand miles on foot, most of it solo, and seen more obscure and beautiful corners of the wilderness than other devotees of the canyon country do in a lifetime.

Of Everett's next three months at home with his family, we know almost nothing, except that he could not wait to get back to the Southwest. By the end of March 1932, he had arrived in Roosevelt once more, ready to reclaim his burros and hit the trail. Ahead of Everett lay another aimless but purposeful pilgrimage.

THREE

"The Crazy Man Is in Solitude Again"

IN THE CHRONICLES OF AMERICAN HISTORY, a quest such as the one Everett Ruess had launched in the Southwest in 1931 was virtually unique. Few vagabonds before him had attempted anything comparable.

Most of the great explorations of the terrain that would become the fifty United States had been undertaken by well-organized teams. On the traverse of the continent led by Lewis and Clark between 1804 and 1806, thirty-three men served in various capacities, and the team was famously aided by the Shoshone woman Sacajawea. On the five expeditions led by John C. Frémont between 1842 and 1853, the man later known as the Pathfinder and hailed by his foremost biographer as "The West's Greatest Adventurer" never set out into the field with fewer than fifteen accomplices.

Among Ruess's predecessors, it was the mountain men hunting beaver across the West between 1806 and 1840 who were closest in spirit to the wanderer from California. We know very little about those bold explorers because most of them were illiterate, and nearly all of them thought their deeds were not worth recording. It was not unusual, however, for a trapper to set off into the wilds by himself, and some of the mountain men began their careers at relatively tender ages.

The template for solo discovery among those fearless wanderers was set by John Colter between 1806 and 1808. An ace hunter on the Lewis and Clark expedition, Colter was so little fazed by the hardships of that monumental voyage that on the way home, in what is now North Dakota, he asked to be discharged early so that he could turn around and guide a pair of trappers who had showed up in the government camp back into the regions mapped by Lewis and Clark. During the winter of 1807–8, traveling alone, Colter became the first Anglo-American to discover the thermal wonders of Yellowstone. His reports of geysers, hot springs, and lava pools were almost universally discounted as nonsense, and for a while the unknown region was nicknamed Colter's Hell.

Even before Colter, a visionary Dartmouth College student named John Ledyard dropped out of school in 1773, at the age of twenty-one, and rode a canoe he had fashioned out of a fallen log down the Connecticut River to his grandfather's farm. His appetite whetted by this minor voyage, three years later Ledyard joined Captain James Cook's third expedition into the Pacific Ocean. During his four years before the mast, Ledyard participated in the European discovery of Hawaii, where his commander was killed by natives.

In Paris in 1786, encouraged by the American ambassador, Thomas Jefferson, Ledyard concocted a wild plan to travel from London across Europe, traversing Russia, crossing the Bering Strait, traipsing south through Alaska and Canada, and resurfacing in Jefferson's Virginia. Ledyard made it as far as Siberia before he was arrested and deported by Catherine the Great.

Two years later, Ledyard proposed a traverse of Africa from the Red Sea to the Atlantic Ocean. He got only as far as Cairo, however, before he came down with a mysterious illness, of which he died at the untimely age of thirty-seven. The unmarked grave in which he was buried on the banks of the Nile is lost to posterity.

Explorers, surveyors, mountain men, and miners were the first Anglo-Americans to penetrate most of the remote regions of the American wilderness. But nearly all these men had utilitarian motives—to claim land for the United States, to scout a railroad route, to find gold, or to bring back beaver pelts to be converted into stylish top hats. An explorer venturing out for purely aesthetic reasons was a much rarer creature.

In this respect, the two renowned American lovers of the outdoors who most closely prefigure Everett Ruess are Henry David Thoreau and John Muir. For Thoreau, walking through the woods or along the seashore (much of his rambling performed alone) was a direct conduit to the metaphysical insights that stitch together his quirky and inimitable books. Like Ruess, Thoreau had a keen eye for nature on its most intimate scale: just as Everett in Yosemite could attentively study the flitting of water bugs on the surface of a stream pool, so Thoreau, strolling the shore of Walden Pond, could observe how "the bullfrogs trump to usher in the night, and the note from the whip-poor-will is borne on the rippling wind from over the water. Sympathy with the fluttering alder and poplar leaves almost takes away my breath."

But Thoreau did not really launch his celebrated wanderings until he was in his late twenties. The Walden experiment began in the summer of 1845, when Thoreau was twenty-eight, and his most daring excursion, an early ascent of Mount Katahdin in Maine, came the following year. Nor did any of Thoreau's expeditions quite compare in ambition or sheer distances covered to the ten-month voyage Everett had made at age seventeen.

John Muir, whose journeys equaled and even exceeded Everett's in boldness, did not get started as a wanderer before the age of twenty-six, when he made an extended plant-collecting journey along the shores of Lake Huron. Muir's personal discovery of Yosemite, the landscape with which he is most often associated in the public mind, came at age thirty.

One of Muir's most famous exploits, climbing a hundred-foot-tall Douglas fir to ride out a Sierra thunderstorm in the treetop, is the kind of *jeu d'esprit* Everett might have indulged in himself. With the good fortune to live till the age of seventy-six, Muir matured and developed as he became a pioneering environmentalist, co-founder of the Sierra Club, and probably America's greatest nature writer. (It would seem inevitable that Everett must have read Muir, especially given their overlapping fascination with Yosemite, but the explorer-naturalist's books are not among the scores that Everett mentions reading in his diaries and his letters. In a June 10, 1933, diary entry, however, in the high Sierra Nevada, Everett writes, "I thought of John Muir and his solitary strolls here, long ago.")

None of Everett's predecessors or potential role models, however, launched their wandering careers at anything like the early age of sixteen. And we are left to speculate whether, had he lived as long as Muir, Everett Ruess might be acclaimed today as the artist and writer who, more than any other American, championed the quest for beauty for its own sake as he pursued an insatiable solo vagabondage through the landscapes of his heart's content.

*   *   *

On March 22, 1932, Everett arrived once more in Roosevelt, Arizona, having hitchhiked from Los Angeles with his dog, Curly. At the Tonto Cliff Dwellings just south of Roosevelt, Everett rendezvoused with a friend named Clark, who had preceded him to Arizona. We know so little about Clark that even his last name has escaped the record. The young man seems to have been a crony of both Everett and Bill Jacobs, perhaps a former high school classmate. Everett's plan was evidently to share another ambitious sojourn throughout the Southwest with a good companion. In his first letter home, Everett wrote,

"Everyone here is favourably impressed with Clark." Yet from the start, it was obvious that Clark was a relative novice in the outdoors. He would have to play acolyte to Everett's wilderness priest.

The excursion got off to a dismal start. The Apache to whom Everett had entrusted his burros over the winter had let Percival get stolen (or so he told Everett), while Cynthia was now pregnant. In the end, Everett sold Cynthia to a couple in Roosevelt, who fancied the burro as a pet for their young son.

The feckless behavior of the Apache triggered an outburst against Indians in general. "I have learned that all Indians are children," Everett wrote to Waldo, "unable to attain to anything like the white man's intelligence, and what this [Apache] could not understand, he counted as nothing."

On March 28, Everett turned eighteen. Unlike the previous year, he made no mention of this milestone in his letters home, preoccupied as he was with getting his vexed expedition under way.

From Arizona, Everett wrote to Bill Jacobs about the travels in the vicinity of Roosevelt that he and Clark took as warm-up hikes. Sometimes the letters record boyish fun: "I am enclosing for you the rattle of a snake I killed. Clark skinned him and I ate him." But early on, Clark disappointed Everett. In a long letter to Waldo, Everett wrote, "Clark is a childlike slave to tobacco, his grammar is faulty, he has little understanding of art, and he himself has admitted that he is very selfish."

One curiosity is that in these first 1932 letters to Jacobs, Everett reverts to signing himself "Evert." At the same time, he is "Everett" in his letters to his family. The "dual existence," perhaps, had kept its grip on the young man through his winter months at home.

The delay in setting out from Roosevelt was caused by the unavailability of the burros, and by the fact that even at the start of the journey, both Everett and Clark were almost out of cash. As early as March 30, in his first letter to his parents, Everett complained,

It is very peaceful here now—too peaceful. Clark and I are
both sick of waiting, and we want to hit the trail as soon as
possible. . . .

I spent thirteen dollars on food and utensils, and have
four dollars left. Clark is broke. . . .

If you are going to send any money in April, right now is
the time to send it.

At the end of his 1931 journey, Everett had seemed embarrassed
by his financial dependence on his parents. Now, just a few months
later, his tone is almost arrogant, as he not only prods Christopher
and Stella to send money, but orders from them a minor lending library of books. The works that Everett demands his parents mail
to him are Mann's *The Magic Mountain,* Dostoevsky's *The Brothers Karamazov,* Voltaire's *Candide,* Petronius's *Satyricon,* Virginia
Woolf's *Mrs. Dalloway,* Zola's *Nana,* and Rabelais's *Gargantua and
Pantagruel.* Of the Mann and the Dostoevsky, Everett writes, "Get
them in the modern library series, otherwise they will be too bulky.
These two will not cost more than two or three dollars."

The literary heft of this reading list sounds ostentatious, as if Everett were trying to prove to his parents that he didn't need college
to provide him with a good education. Christopher and Stella dutifully shipped their son the books, although they substituted works
by Balzac and Lord Dunsany for the Mann. By April 20, less than
three weeks after placing his order, Everett had read all the books
his parents sent him except *The Brothers Karamazov.* Still moored in
Roosevelt, he mailed the other books home.

The new tone in these letters to his parents smacks of the entitlement
that Everett was always in danger of slipping into half-aware. "Other
things you might send," he adds in the March 30 letter, "are, a sheaf of
this paper, the dog biscuits, and a pair of thick white socks which I think
are in one of my droors." As if to soften the peremptoriness, near the

end of the letter he teases, "If you send all the things I have mentioned you will be doing very well indeed."

Hanging around Roosevelt as they tried to organize the logistics of a major journey drove both Clark and Everett to frustration, and they started to get on each other's nerves. When Clark finally received money from his own parents, as Everett complained in a letter to Waldo, instead of contributing it to the purchase of supplies, he spent it on "his hotel bill." That glancing remark reveals that rather than camping out, the boys were squandering their diminishing funds on lodging and hotel meals.

By early May, Clark and Everett were still stuck in Roosevelt. And by now they had agreed to part ways. We lack, of course, Clark's version of the story of the falling-out, but Everett later explained his side of it to Waldo.

> I bought grub, candy and cigarettes for Clark and myself for five weeks, then I told him I did not intend to wait any longer. I invited Clark to leave with me, but he refused to consider it unless he could have a horse and saddle. As I did not have one myself I certainly couldn't offer him one.

At this point, sometime in early May, Bill Jacobs arrived in Roosevelt. To Waldo, Everett wrote,

> Earlier in the day Bill had come and persuaded Clark to join him. Bill invited me to go with him, but I had no faith in him and wanted to carry out my plans. I didn't really believe I'd like them as traveling companions anyway. I had grown tired of Clark already.

After parting from Bill and Clark and setting out alone, Everett had no regrets, though the rancor among the three friends still perturbed him. On May 22 he wrote in his diary, "[Two words illegible] put distance between me and Clark. As companions they don't fit the bill. Neither has anything to teach me, tho they seem to think so. If they had, why wouldn't I respect them instead of pitying them?"

In 1998, Bud Rusho published Everett's 1932 and 1933 diaries, under the title *Wilderness Journals of Everett Ruess*. Except for a pastiche of extracts printed in the 1940 volume *On Desert Trails with Everett Ruess*, the only published versions of Everett's letters and diaries until now are those that appear in Rusho's *A Vagabond for Beauty* and *Wilderness Journals*. But Rusho omits some letters entirely, and cuts passages from others without indicating his excisions. He also silently removes passages from the 1932 and 1933 diaries, even though he purports to present verbatim everything Everett wrote.

Rusho's omissions in both books smack of deliberate expurgation. Sometimes the cuts may be dictated by a sense that certain passages may be simply boring or unimportant—long discussions by Everett in letters to his mother, for instance, about the specific materials he needs to make his paintings and blockprints. But other excisions seem aimed at camouflaging unpleasant episodes in Everett's life. Just as Stella was appalled by her son's penchant for killing rattlesnakes, so Rusho seems discomfited by some of Everett's behavior—his thoughtless looting of Anasazi ruins, for instance, and his mailing home the treasures he had unearthed. Rusho likewise edited out Everett's criticisms of others, or even passages that detail conflict. It is almost as though Rusho were at pains to protect Everett from himself, or from the occasionally childish or churlish sides of himself, and at pains as well to protect those others (Clark, Bill, Waldo, his parents, even the Apache he entrusted with his burros) who, were they living today, might be hurt by what Everett had to say about them.

The cumulative effect, sadly, is to bowdlerize Everett, if ever so slightly. Rusho's portrait of the vagabond who has by now become such a cult figure needs to be restored to its unretouched state. There is no danger that a fuller picture of Everett Ruess, warts and all, will damage his legacy. He was far too interesting and complex a person for that. Everett survives his faults and foibles.

*   *   *

Just before saying goodbye to Clark and Bill, Everett paid a local rancher ten dollars for a horse, named Pacer by his owner. At the beginning of his 1932 outing, Everett had decided to use a horse rather than burros to carry his gear. And he intended to ride the horse as much as he could, rather than use it only as a pack animal. It was a trade-off that would vex him throughout his season in the Southwest.

Leaving Roosevelt, Everett forded the Salt River and climbed high into the Sierra Ancha mountains to camp. On his second day out, a disaster of sorts occurred. In a telegraphic shorthand bespeaking Everett's exhaustion, his diary captures the dark feelings of that panic-stricken night. In the middle of preparing his dinner, Everett realized Pacer was missing.

Dashed frantically in all directions for half an hour, then found his trail back up the road. Half a mile along was the rope, broken again. Soon sighted Pacer and he galloped off ahead. Prayed to God and cussed him. Dark, but half moon. Shouted to car but he went around it. Another car stopped and the driver had Pacer by the neck but I didn't have the rope ready, and Pacer got off over the hill. Driver must have thot me stupid. Ran and ran. Pacer kept slowing and looking back. . . . Finally got a loop over his head. Both drenched with sweat. Tied both ends of the rawhide on his neck and rode him back. . . . Curly had eaten all my supper. I called him and beat him severely. Fried spuds and wrote. Thot of fluent, blistering swearing.

The diary reveals Everett's ever-present doubt, despite his marathon journey of the year before, concerning his competence to perform such basic trail tasks as keeping track of a hobbled horse. And it makes clear the source of Everett's fury at his once-beloved dog. A few days before leaving Roosevelt, while Everett was off on an errand, Curly had broken into the henhouse of a resident named Wilson and killed three chickens, for which Everett had to reimburse the owner.

The morning after the moonlight chase, Everett wrote,

> Slept late. Curly was not in camp. Called and called as I left. Thot I heard barking, but he didn't come and I didn't search. I thot he would trail me but he didn't. . . . No signs of Curly. Probably when he finds I'm gone he'll go back to Wilson's, kill more chickens, and J.C. will write to my parents. I wish he were shot. His distemper is still bad. He doesn't know enough to get out of the road. He kills chickens and steals food. I can't afford to feed him. I can't trust Clark at all. Curly might drown in the river, but its unlikely.

Poor Curly! Killing chickens and gobbling down what must have looked like leftover supper amounted to normal canine behavior. But the former rez dog may have remembered beatings from before Everett had adopted him, and to slink away for good was a matter of sheer survival.

Both the 1932 and 1933 diaries, in general, are utterly different in tone from Everett's letters. In this sense, they emphasize how increasingly Everett turned to his letters to craft memorable and rhapsodic passages evoking the beauty and power of the wilderness. They are conscious performances in a way the diary entries are not. Moreover, the diaries reveal the funks, the depressions, even the despair into which Everett periodically lapsed, a side of his personality he tried to keep out of the letters. What a fuller understanding of this enigmatic adventurer we would have if the 1930, 1931, and 1934 diaries were not irretrievably lost!

The diaries also present another conundrum. Everett wrote in pencil, and in the pages of the surviving bound ledger books that he used as journals, many passages have been erased. Rusho indicates these blanks in *Wilderness Diaries* by inserting brackets, as follows: "[9 lines erased]."

After Everett's disappearance, one of his parents, probably Christopher, typed up passages that seemed particularly eloquent. In so doing, that parent regularly made minor revisions to Everett's prose. From this known fact, Rusho leaps to the conclusion that in the diaries themselves "the Ruess family . . . actually erased sentences that might prove embarrassing to them or to other people."

There is strong internal evidence, however, that the person who erased the passages was Everett himself.

What is maddening is that the erasures often come just as Everett is probing most deeply into his psyche. For example, on May 19, four days after Curly ran away, Everett reaches a truly low point. The diary: "I'm in a bad position. No dog. An old broken down horse. [2 lines erased.] I may not be able to trade Pacer for a burro. I will die if he gives out on me."

If it was Everett who erased the passages, his motive may have been simply to guard his privacy, just as, responding to his parents' wish to read his 1931 diary at the end of the summer, he had refused, citing it as "too personal to be read by anyone but the author, in its present state." The evidence that it was Everett who later erased the passages emerges in another lacuna at the end of his despondent May 19 entry. As Rusho publishes the text, it reads,

Killed a scorpion in the gunny sack pack. Gnats and mosquitoes. Alone again. The crazy man is in solitude again. . . . Pacer munched foxtails. The full moon, round and yellow,

in the chalky blue sky over distant mesas. No Curly to pet.
No [word missing] to hold [8 lines erased].

In the diary itself, however, the eight-line erasure is more accurately rendered as follows:

[1 line erased]
stupid
[2 lines erased]
I'd
[2 lines erased]
be done.

Whoever erased the passage left four words intact—"stupid," "I'd," and "be done"—each at the left margin of the page. This practice, repeated often in both the 1932 and 1933 diaries, would have been a very odd thing for a parent determined to expunge embarrassing entries to do. If Everett left those few floating words unerased, they must have served some arcane purpose. To remind himself, perhaps, in later years what the self-censored passage had been about—or perhaps to tantalize a future reader with a kind of cryptogram hinting at secrets too dark to share.

The 1932 journey seemed jinxed from the start. The diary entries through the end of May record almost no joy, and precious little pleasure. For one thing, the country north of Roosevelt, through which Everett now traveled, was not true wilderness, but cattle country. Everett kept running into ranchers, and now and again he performed odd jobs for them to earn a bit of cash.

He seemed, however, to be physically worn out much of the time. On May 18 he wrote, "I felt too weary to climb to the cliff dwellings, so followed the old man about working in the gardens and making fence. I was so weak I could hardly listen to what he said."

In a July 12 letter to Waldo, Everett confessed his frailty, even while it shamed him:

> Physically, I am not very tough. I haven't the constitution of a day laborer. I soon wear out at a job like road building, or digging & lifting. This seems to be my physical make up, because tho I have tried many times, I find I can't do a man's work in physical labor.

This weakness, in Everett's mind, was tied up with his loneliness: "I don't have much trouble getting along with people, but I have the greatest difficulty in finding the sort of companionship I want."

Later commentators, notably Gary James Bergera, have specu-lated that Everett may have suffered all his life from either pernicious or folic anemia. The former is caused by a deficiency of vitamin B12, the latter from an absence in one's diet of green leafy vegetables. In a revealing July 21 diary entry, Everett wrote, "Physically I feel very weak. I would not be surprised to learn that pernicious anaemia has set in again. A slight bruise has taken three weeks to heal." This pas-sage is immediately followed by five erased lines. But once again, not all the words are erased. The cryptic remaining text reads:

Clark   I
  [2 lines erased]
                                         happy
  H   as. _If_ not by   happy.

In the letters from 1931, there is virtually no mention of exhaus-tion or weakness, much less of anemia. Instead, Everett brags about his fitness and his energy. It is hard to disentangle the 1932 diary's confessions of fatigue and weariness from Everett's depression and his lingering upset over the rupture with Clark and Bill. Every few days in his diary, he drops a disparaging remark about his former pals, as if to convince himself all over again that he was right to leave them behind in Roosevelt and strike off on his own.

Everett's immediate goal, as he wandered north and east, was to find more prehistoric ruins. But even these disappointed him. In Pueblo Canyon, where a local had told him he could find a seventy-room cliff dwelling, Everett found far fewer structures, and they were "all crumbled." "I was unwilling to push thru more brush," he wrote in his diary. "I was scratched sufficiently as it was. I took one photograph. There was nothing to paint."

It is striking how seldom Everett mentions painting or drawing in either his diary or his letters from 1932. In the comprehensive July 12 letter to Waldo, Everett admits, "I have not been able to paint for some time, but I am going to try some more before I admit defeat."

A fog of depression, then, hung over Everett's first four months in the Southwest in 1932. The traveling seemed to be reduced to a process of going through the motions. And every now and then, the leaden reportage of his daily doings in the diary was interrupted by a wail of existential anguish, as on May 22: "I often wish people meant something to one another, and one could find people to one's taste."

On May 23, near the small settlement of Young, Arizona, Everett made a deal with a local rancher to trade Pacer for two burros. He named his new charges Peggy and Wendy, though he later claimed that neither name really fit. Now Everett concocted a modus operandi he had not previously tried: he would ride Wendy, pack his belongings on Peggy, and connect the two animals with a leash. But his progress was thwarted by one snafu after another. The horse saddle, modified to fit a burro, was too big for Wendy and kept slipping off. Peggy stubbornly tugged on her leash, trying to head off in a different direction, thereby stopping Wendy in her tracks. And both burros balked at every stream crossing.

During the last weeks of May and into early June, Everett climbed north through pine forests toward the high escarpment of the Mogollon Rim, which he then followed east before dropping down to the town of Holbrook. His itinerary matched the routes of today's state highways 288, 260, and 377. Even in 1932, an auto road covered this ground. "Half a dozen cars passed," Everett noted on May 30, "and one tourist stopped and took my picture for me."

How far from the true wilderness forays of the previous year was this dispirited trudge with recalcitrant burros! Everett was not even sure where he was headed, or why. During his down moments, the whole journey started to seem pointless. "Felt that the trip was foredoomed to failure," he noted on May 31, "that I'd be overcome with melancholy if I visited the places I've seen before. Afraid to go home because that would be an admission of failure & I'd be ashamed to face Bill and Clark. [2 lines erased.]" The blank in the diary immediately preceded another cryptic complaint:

> If only Sam would write to me about New York. I can't yet believe that he has left me in the lurch. I felt distinctly different from other people, knew that I was a freak, in spite of Jean's angry denial of it. Already I've drifted too far away from other people. I want to be different anyhow, I can't help being different, but I get no joy from it, and all common joys are forbidden me.

At this remove, we have no idea who Sam or Jean was, or what they meant to Everett.

However obliquely or privately, in passages such as this Everett was slowly coming to terms with the destiny he felt forced upon him, which was to be a lifelong loner. A little more than a month later he would announce his fate in a triumphant postscript to Waldo, but now there was more gloom than gratification in the realization. To be

a loner meant to be condemned to loneliness. On May 29, Everett's
diary recorded another anguished outburst:

> I wish I had a companion or someone who was interested in
> me. Bill and Clark, however, would be worse than none. I
> would like to be influenced, taken in hand by someone, but I
> don't think there is anyone in the world who knows enough
> to be able to advise me. I can't find any ideal anywhere. So I
> am rather afraid of myself. Obscurantism.

During his slow burro march toward Holbrook, Everett was going
through a dark night of the soul. But that ordeal would ultimately
have a curative power. After Holbrook, Everett's wandering regained
purpose and even a modicum of joy, although the transports of 1932
would never match those of the previous year.

Since he was seldom alone for very long on the road to Holbrook,
Everett began to strike up casual friendships among the local ranchers.
Most of them were Mormons, who with characteristic hospitality offered the young man a place to stay and free meals. During the month
of June, in fact, Everett spent more time sleeping in ranch houses and
barns than he did camping out.

Frustrated by the tribulations of managing Peggy and Wendy, Everett changed his mind about burros and decided he wanted to buy
or trade for a pair of horses before continuing his journey. From June
6 to 27, he lingered in and around Holbrook. At several different
ranches he helped men break wild horses, castrate cattle, brand cows,
build a shack, and other chores. Everett was thus getting an excellent
apprenticeship as a cowboy, but he knew that was not his ultimate
goal. The hard work seemed to justify the free room and board his
new acquaintances offered the vagabond, but if one reads between the
lines of the diary, it seems that Everett was essentially mooching off
the generosity of the locals.

All this interplay with Arizona families, however, distracted the young man from his solitary woes. The diary abounds in pithy appraisals of these new friends. Of a drifter nicknamed Hot Cakes, Everett wrote, "[He] has an inferiority complex, I think, and he talks big in order to hide it." Of another ranch hand, "Oscar is a small man, all muscle, with a turned up red nose. I like him the best of the bunch."

Everett hung around Holbrook long enough to attend the town's June 25 parade and rodeo, which culminated in a drunken brawl (a wide-eyed bystander, he recounted every blow and insult in his diary). He argued with a Mormon host about whether the Earth was only six thousand years old and had been created in six days. To humor the man, Everett attended church, where he rose and read out loud a favorite passage from the Book of Ruth ("Whither thou goest, I will go; and where thou lodgest, I will lodge: thy people shall be my people, and thy God my God"). "On the whole, it was quite interesting," Everett recorded in his diary, "and Mr. Crosby must have thot I behaved quite well for an unbeliever."

Yet true companionship still eluded him. "I haven't met anyone to talk to since Bill and Clark," he lamented on June 22. "Yesterday I wrote them a good long letter, with any irrepressible superiority complex showing thru. Clark says I antagonize everyone and whoever learns to know me finally becomes disgusted. There may be some truth in that. I don't try to please people I don't respect."

In keeping up a correspondence with the friends he had left behind in Roosevelt, Everett evidently was not willing to burn all the bridges between himself and Clark and Bill. Bill and Everett would in fact stay friends and trade letters through the rest of Everett's life. Yet in Holbrook, he was still contemptuous of his unambitious pals. In that town he received several letters from his parents, who also sent money and a whole new package of books, including Mann's *The Magic Mountain*. From Stella, he got news about Bill. "Mother wrote that Bill's mother drove out to take him home," he noted in his diary.

"What a fuss about him. I suppose Bill and Clark went, because they certainly couldn't do anything in this country."

After much haggling in and around Holbrook, Everett secured two horses. There he abandoned Wendy and Peggy, without bothering to mention in his diary what happened to the burros, just as he had traded away Pacer near the town of Young without apparent regret. The first of the two horses, purchased from a rancher for six dollars, was "skinny as a rail, and twelve years old." A local man colorfully disparaged this nag by telling Everett that "he wouldn't give two hoots for the powder to blow my horse to hell." It would be a prescient appraisal.

For the next several weeks, Everett called his horses Bay and Whitie, before renaming them Jonathan and Nuflo, respectively. By the end of June, he was restless to hit the trail. All the socializing and the indoor comfort had worn thin. On June 23 he wrote in his diary,

> I will be glad when I am alone again. It is too much work
> for me to get along with other people. Yesterday I lay on the
> bed looking at the ceiling papered with ragged yellow news-
> papers, and thot of other ceilings I had looked at dismally.
> Trees and skies don't give the same futile feeling.

Even before Holbrook, Everett's spirits had started to take a turn upward. Camped near Zeniff, a straggling Mormon community below the Mogollon Rim (a ghost town today, Zeniff is reduced to three crumbling adobe buildings), Everett recorded a gleam of hope on June 3:

> Again I am in the desert—the desert that I know, red sand,
> cedars, great spaces, distant mesas, and behind, the blue of
> the Mogollons.
>   The fire flamed straight up, and for awhile, I was almost
> able to be happy in the present, rather than in anticipation.

*   *   *

On June 27, Everett made his getaway from Holbrook, heading north-east. Despite his fear that he would be "overcome with melancholy if I visited the places I've seen before," he had decided to return to Canyon de Chelly, where he had had some of his most transcendent experiences in 1931.

Twenty miles north of Holbrook, Everett crossed the boundary of the Navajo reservation. Now the strangers whose paths he crossed were not Mormon ranchers, but Indians. As he had started to do the year before, Everett made an effort to befriend Navajos and to learn about their culture. Sharing their campfires, he unsqueamishly ate native food—coffee, mutton broiled over the fire, and *naneskadi*, or Navajo bread. One man agreed to teach Everett Navajo phrases. He dutifully recorded his lessons in his diary: "Chynn ya go—I want to eat. . . . Ado beg zduh ut si seh ut-t-ih ha day sha to—Don't be afraid, little girl, I'm going," and the like. The next day, Everett learned that the man had been pulling his leg, uttering nonsense syllables and proffering bogus translations, while his friends listened in silent amusement.

The xenophobia of some of the Navajos, Everett handled in stride. "They talk about me in Navajo," he noted on July 7, "and I retaliate by speaking French." On the reservation, Everett regularly sought out empty hogans in which to sleep—a practice that would have offended the natives, had they known about it. (Even though he carried a tent, he pitched it and slept in it only rarely.) On July 2, Everett unabashedly recorded in his diary how he had broken the lock on one hogan and forced his way inside. A week later he took apart a half-ruined hogan and burned its logs in his campfire. Such deeds shock the modern reader, but they were not uncommon in the 1930s. Everett's thoughtless appropriation of Navajo dwellings can also be seen as stemming from his sense of entitlement, the same cockiness that allowed him to knock on Edward Weston's door and introduce himself (as he would with other famous artists in 1933 and 1934).

Along the trail, after killing every rattlesnake he could find, Everett kept the rattles as souvenirs. Once that summer he horrified some Navajos by flaunting a newly killed rattlesnake. (In Diné mythology, the Great Snake is a supernatural being woven into the very geology of the landscape.) In his diary, after he showed the dead snake to some young men, he recorded their reaction: "They said I would die, and looked at the snake. They ran like little girls when I waved it at them."

Everett's ambivalence about Native Americans emerged in another set piece, as he sermonized in his diary about the limitations of Navajo culture:

> I have been observing more and more fully that the Navajo owes everything he has to the white man. His food is mutton, bread, and coffee. All these were brought by the white man. [Sheep, to be precise, had been introduced to the Diné not by Anglos but by the Spanish.] His clothes are borrowed. All he has left is his language, ceremonies, and a few customs. In spite of all the things he did not have before, he seems a pitiful creature to me. Yet he is always ready to laugh and sing.

Yet tempering such pronouncements was Everett's openness to individual Navajos. In Ganado, near the famous trading post established by John Lorenzo Hubbell in 1883 (the first Anglo trading post on the rez), Everett was invited to stay in the hogan of a Navajo who lived nearby. "His oldest daughter, Alice," Everett wrote, "is the most beautiful Navajo girl I have ever seen." During the next few days, Everett paid inordinate but shyly mute attention to Alice's comings and goings.

Such an observation could be cited to argue that Everett's orientation was firmly heterosexual. Yet only two days after meeting Alice, a strange episode involving a young Navajo named Lefty (Everett calls him "a boy") with whom he had shared some ranch chores occurred.

> At night he wanted to sleep with me, outside. He crawled under and snored irritatingly. Late at night the sky darkened, wind whistled, and a light shower moistened the air. We moved inside.
>
> [The next morning] I managed to awaken but fell asleep again while Lefty was preparing breakfast. I had an ugly dream about him.

Even as his spirits gradually improved, Everett continued to suffer from the exhaustion that had debilitated him since setting out from Roosevelt two months before. His stupor was intensified by the desert heat of summer. And he had developed a new problem with his eyesight. On June 28 he wrote, "My eyes are wretched. They have been paining me severely. I couldn't recognize my horses until I was upon them." Two days later, "For hours I lay half dead on the sand under the pinion, feeling too weak to rise. My eyes burned when I read, and nothing seemed to give joy. Mentally I wrote my last letter."

Despite the pain in his eyes, Everett voraciously read the books his parents had mailed him. In June and July his diary records the consumption of Mann's *The Magic Mountain* (which alternately bored and enthralled him); the *Arabian Nights;* Shakespeare's plays; Ibsen's *Ghosts;* Emerson's essays; a collection of letters from famous men (Everett singles out Mendelssohn, Wagner, Liszt, Jules Breton, and the sculptor-poet W. W. Story); an anthology called *The Fifty Best Poems of America;* a travel narrative about the Pacific by Frederick O'Brien; William Morris's medieval novel *A Dream of John Ball;* Irving's "Rip Van Winkle" and "The Legend of Sleepy Hollow"; George Bernard

Shaw's *Socialism for Millionaires;* a government report of a survey among Navajos; religious tracts the zealous Mormon Mr. Crosby had given him; and assorted newspapers and magazines he found in stores and homes along the way.

In terms of his own Southwest odyssey, the most interesting book Everett read that summer is one whose title and author he does not name. On July 12 his diary reports that he

> read a book about the Navajo country & a boy who started in New Mexico, had money, good horses & equipment but was the grossest sort of tenderfoot, stayed on the highways for several months, met a friend in Santa Fe, then together they went up thru Frijoles to Mesa Verde & to the reservation. They were here several years ago when things were much wilder. There was hardly any trail to rainbow bridge—they picked their way very adventurously. They were always changing horses—trading one & paying 8 to 15 dollars to boot. They got to see the Indian dances & sand paintings, met all kinds of interesting people.

The book was Clyde Kluckhohn's *To the Foot of the Rainbow,* today regarded as a Southwest classic. Despite Everett's put-down of the "greenhorn" who was a rich kid and who overpaid for horses, Kluckhohn and Everett were kindred souls. (It is a pity they never met.) The book recounts a 2,500-mile ramble across the Southwest undertaken in 1925 by Kluckhohn, twenty years old at the time, and two buddies of the same age. Kluckhohn had the same appreciation for scenic beauty and the same curiosity about Indian cultures and prehistoric ruins that Everett did. He would go on to become a Harvard professor and the leading Navajo ethnographer of his era.

Despite his suffering and his loneliness, on the reservation Everett was reawakening to the magnificence of the landscape. On July 1, in the midst of a storm, Everett wrote in his diary, "The rain beat down steadily. I made a sketch and photographed a butte. The beauty of the wet desert was overpowering. I was not happy for there was no one with whom I could share it, but I thought how much better than to be in a school room with rain on the windows."

On July 11, Everett reached Chinle. Renewing his friendship with some of the residents gave his morale another boost. There, at the gateway to Canyon de Chelly, he made a new resolve, writing in his diary, "I think I'll extend my leave another year. I'll get a couple of good horses and a good saddle." At last, it seems, Everett had not only come to terms with his destiny as a loner, but had embraced it with passionate conviction. On July 12 in Chinle, he wrote five densely crowded pages to Waldo, summing up the first four months of his 1932 adventure. It is one of the longest and richest letters Everett ever sent to anyone. The epistle is penned in ink, but at the bottom of the last page he added a postscript in pencil:

> I have been thinking more and more that I shall always be a lone wanderer of the wildernesses. God, how the trail lures me. You cannot comprehend its resistless fascination for me. After all the lone trail is best. I hope I'll be able to buy good horses and a better saddle. I'll never stop wandering. And when the time comes to die, I'll find the wildest, loneliest, most desolate spot there is.

This manifesto has become the most oft-quoted statement that Everett ever wrote. And in light of his subsequent disappearance, the sibylline final sentence has stood as a kind of epitaph for the vagabond for the last seventy-seven years.

*   *   *

Now, instead of wandering somewhat aimlessly, Everett had mapped out his destinations for the next few weeks. He would ride up both

Canyon de Chelly and Canyon del Muerto, emerging at the headwaters of the latter branch, then cross the Lukachukai Mountains
to arrive at Shiprock, New Mexico. Resupplying in that town in the
northeast corner of the reservation, he would head farther north to
expore Mesa Verde. In 1931 his looping forays had never taken him
so far east. Except for the trip by train across the country at the age
of nine, Everett had never before entered New Mexico or Colorado.

Riding up Canyon de Chelly, Everett was assailed by nostalgic
memories of his 1931 jaunt.

> I passed the sandspit where I shot the burro last year, and
> came to the fork of Monument Canyon and Upper Canyon
> de Chelly recognizing the spot where Pegasus had stuck in
> the quicksand. I saw my old campsite and remembered how
> I raised my cocoa to my lips and drank "to the long, long
> dead whose bones are there above me" (in the dwellings). I
> remembered how I fondled Curly, then a small puppy, and
> sang to the moon and the rising night wind.

At last Everett started painting again, and he spent hours copying
Anasazi pictographs and petroglyphs. Every day he greeted Navajos
living in the canyon, yet once more he unhesitatingly spent nights in
disused hogans. And at least once, he again burned the logs of an old
hogan in his campfire, for he records that an elderly Navajo woman
"taunted" him for doing so. (The taunting was more likely a stern be-
rating. Navajos will usually abandon a hogan after someone has died
in it, and sometimes they will break down a wall "to let the spirit out"
or even burn the structure. But for an Anglo to take apart a hogan just
to feed his campfire would amount to a serious profanation.)

Once more, Everett sought out "untouched" prehistoric ruins—
ones that he hoped no one had visited since the Anasazi abandoned
them in the thirteenth century. He made a daring climb toward a high

cliff dwelling, but backed off fifty feet below it. "For a long time I looked at the dwelling and shuddered," he wrote that evening in his diary. "Once I made as if to climb up, but the rock crumbled. . . . I might have climbed up the narrow crack of soft sandstone, but I knew I would be terrified at descending, with no place to put my feet and the rock crumbling in my hands."

In Canyon de Chelly, Everett seemed rejuvenated. At night, he "chanted" poetry out loud as he perused his anthology by flashlight. Reading Emerson's essay "Self-Reliance" provoked a meditation on his own belief system:

> [Emerson] like many others I have read is horrified at the atheist, or rather, he pities him. Personally I seem to be an agnosticist. I don't see how an intelligent person can believe anything, even determinism. . . . I can't believe in a God just because other people do. . . . Prayer is foreign to my nature. I could not seriously attend church and worship.

Although he did not need to say so in his diary, this declaration was an implicit rejection of his father's faith, for Christopher had not only graduated from the Harvard Divinity School, but had served for years as a Unitarian minister.

Digging in Anasazi ruins, Everett found arrowheads that he undoubtedly kept. Scraping away the floor of a subterranean kiva, he unearthed a yucca sandal. But on July 19 he recorded another onset of the pain afflicting his eyes: "I felt drunken. I reeled and swayed in the saddle and felt decidedly out of my usual nature. For some time I could hardly see."

Somewhere near Spider Rock, the striking 810-foot-tall, free-standing pinnacle, Everett turned around and headed back down Canyon de Chelly to its junction with its northern branch, Canyon del Muerto. Whether or not the pain in his eyes darkened his spirits,

Everett plunged abruptly into the doldrums. All at once, the manifesto he had sent as a postscript to his July 12 letter to Waldo seemed
hollow. After spending a whole afternoon sitting in a hogan reading
Emerson and Ibsen, Everett wrote in his diary,

> I felt futile. It seems after all that a solitary life is not good.
> I wish I could experience a great love. I find that I cannot
> consider working, even in art. To be a real artist one must
> work incessantly, and I have not the vitality. . . . More and
> more I feel that I don't belong in the world. I am losing con-
> tact with life. It seems useless to paint, when Nature is here,
> and I can't paint anyway.

Three days later his mood had not changed. "I think I have seen
too much and known too much—" he wrote, "so much that it has put
me in a dream from which I cannot waken and be like other people. I
love beauty but have no longer the desire to recreate it." In his funk,
Everett once more pondered death, as he misquoted from memory
two lines from Edwin Arlington Robinson: " 'Who goes too far to
find his grave, / Mostly alone he goes.' "

Such passages reveal how invaluable the surviving diaries are
for anyone who wishes to comprehend the mind and soul of Everett
Ruess. Nearly all the "famous" Ruess quotes—the ones reprinted as
mottos on calendars and posters—come from the letters. The 1932
and 1933 diaries are far less deliberately poetic than the letters he sent
home from the trail, but they are truer to his real experience. If we
had only Everett's 1932 letters by which to judge his second Southwest expedition, we would have almost no awareness of the doubt
and despondency that plagued him throughout the journey.

Several students of Ruess, combing the texts of both the diaries and
the letters, have advanced the theory that he was bipolar—or, to use
the term current in the 1930s, manic-depressive. Certainly the evidence

is there of extreme and sudden mood swings. But to lay a psychiatric diagnosis on a person one has never met (*pace* Freud on Leonardo) is all too facile a guessing game. In the effort to understand Everett's sexuality, it is more important to attend to all the nuances of his attraction to various friends and strangers than to label him as gay or bisexual. In the same way, the mood swings speak for themselves, and to deduce that Everett had a bipolar disorder does little or nothing to aid our understanding of this complicated and articulate young adventurer.

Despite his gloom, Everett pushed on up Canyon del Muerto. On July 21 he finally renamed his horses. Bay became Jonathan "because he is so sweet tempered, meek and gentle," wrote Everett; Whitie became Nuflo "after the mischievous old guardian of Rima in [W. H. Hudson's] *Green Mansions*." By a twist of fate, the renaming would have the effect of a malediction.

Fifteen months earlier, after his April 1931 foray into the Tsegi, Everett had written to Bill Jacobs about suffering "enough pain and tragedy to make the delights possible by contrast," but he never made clear what that pain and tragedy were. Now a real tragedy occurred.

On July 22, at the head of del Muerto, Everett started his horses up the steep trail leading out of the canyon. That evening he vividly recorded what happened:

> It was so steep that I led Nuflo, and Jonathan had to be urged. Finally he fell or lay down at a rough spot about half way up. I thwacked him but he would not rise, so I unpacked him there. . . . When I pulled out the pack saddle, Jon slid off the trail, turned over three times on the downslope, and tottered to his feet. I led him up, put Nuflo's saddle on him, packed Nuflo, and slowly descended.

Instead of continuing his ascent out of the canyon, Everett wisely returned to his previous night's camp. But then:

I unloaded and led the horses on the bank where the grass was very sparse. I didn't hobble Jonathan. He went around in circles and didn't eat. I washed a cut on his leg and he stood for a while, then staggered sidewise and fell into a clump of cactus where he lay awhile. Then he got groggily to his feet, tottered again and collapsed. Then I prepared myself for the worst and began looking at my maps to see how near a railroad was. In a little while, I looked at Jonathan again, and he was dead—eyes glassy green, teeth showing, flies in his mouth.

"So for me," Everett sermonized that evening, "Canyon del Muerto is indeed the canyon of death—the end of the trail for gentle old Jonathan."

On the spot, Everett devised an unusual funerary rite. Carrying Jonathan's saddle, he climbed up to the ruin where the year before he had discovered the Anasazi cradleboard. There he deposited the saddle. In his diary he wrote,

I don't think anyone will find the saddle. The baby board was where I left it last May, except that the hoops had fallen into the bin. My printing on the board—Evert Rulan etc., was almost obscured. The rain washed away my tracks. The saddle is well cached. The ghosts of the cliff dwellers will guard it.

This is the only surviving admission that Everett ever made about carving or writing his name as a graffito in a prehistoric ruin. It was not the last time he would do so, however. (If, in subsequent years, some Navajo or pot hunter or archaeologist revisited the ruin and found the strange assemblage, with Everett's 1931 alias inscribed on the cradleboard, he or she left no record of the discovery.)

Jonathan's body, of course, Everett had to leave in the grass where the horse had collapsed. "I suppose the Navajos will steal his shoes," he noted in his diary.

The remark about pulling out his maps to look for the nearest railroad seems to indicate that at the moment of Jonathan's death, Everett realized the rest of his journey was doomed. But later in the same diary entry, he mused, "I don't think I'll buy another horse. I haven't the money and one will do. Having only Nuflo, I'll care for him more solicitously."

Gamely, Everett coaxed the heavily laden horse up the steep trail out of Canyon del Muerto. At a trading post near the Navajo settlement of Tsaile, he bought supplies—not only cookies, peanut butter, and cereal, but cigarettes. The 1932 diary first reveals the fact that Everett regularly smoked on the trail. One entry a few days after his resupply makes no bones about the pleasures of tobacco. Ensconced in yet another hogan, "I smoked half a dozen cigarettes, watching the beautiful spirals of blue smoke, blowing rings, and looking at the fungus on the rafters." Everett's mother had voiced her concern about her son's habit, for in his next letter to Stella, he minimized his usage: "No, I haven't smoked regularly, just once in a few weeks."

Even as he struggled on, crossing the Lukachukai range, walking beside Nuflo more often than riding, Everett felt his weariness spread through his whole body. On July 23 he confessed, "[T]here was such a stiffness and soreness in my limbs as I had never known before. My shoulders seemed bruised and my thighs ached piercingly when we climbed."

On July 26, Everett crossed the state border into New Mexico. The town of Shiprock, the largest he would pass through since having left Holbrook, lay a mere twenty miles ahead. The day before, he had jotted down a cryptic testimony about his private feelings:

> I went swimming, made pop corn, and wrote a good letter
> to Bill. While there is life, there is hope. I still think at times

that the future may hold happiness. I shall wait and see. I
have waited three years already, and not in vain.

Despite his falling-out with Bill and Clark in May, Everett was
determined to preserve his friendship, at least with Bill. The "good
letter" devoted several pages to recounting Everett's adventures of the
previous months, including a long passage (much of it copied verbatim from his diary) detailing Jonathan's death and Everett's caching of
his saddle in the cliff dwelling. Yet toward the end, Everett complains
about his old friend's failure to keep up his end of the communication:
"Now I expect some kind of reply from you—if it isn't a better letter
than the last one, I really won't answer."

Yet Everett was unwilling to end on a sour note. Instead, he
mooted the question of some later voyage with his pal. Everett closed,

> I might be back there [in Los Angeles] in a few months, tho
> I don't know how I would get back. If I did, would we have
> a chance to hit the trail together into the Sierra wilds? Give
> me some advice, tell me my faults, my virtues, if any, open
> up your heart, and write lengthily if you love me.

The tone here is quite different from the "Love and kisses, / Desperately yours" sign-off of Everett's May 1931 letter to Jacobs. In
some sense, Everett genuinely loved Bill, and the feeling may have
been mutual. This says little or nothing, however, about any overtly
homosexual relationship between the young men.

From Chinle, Everett had announced in his letters home that his
next post office would be Shiprock. But when he arrived in that flat-
land town on the banks of the San Juan River, he was disappointed
to pick up only a single letter, from his mother. He wrote her back,
offering a short account of Jonathan's death. "I'm going on to Mesa

Verde," he vowed, "about 70 miles by highway and trail. There I expect to rest awhile, and if I can find a tourist who will take me to Los Angeles, with my luggage, I'll go with him."

Jonathan's death and Everett's physical ailments had taken their toll. On July 27 he wrote, "My legs are weaker than ever. I'm filled with a violent desire to go home." Yet he would stick it out in the Southwest for another month, and castigate himself for not staying longer and attempting more. On July 29 he wrote in his diary,

> I could not sleep for thinking of the future. I was sure I wanted to go on thru the Carrizos to Kayenta and Monument Valley, Betatakin, Keet Seel, Inscription House, Rainbow bridge, and Grand Canyon. I felt I'd never forgive myself if I went away without seeing more of the West.

Such an itinerary would have effectively doubled the mileage of Everett's 1932 wandering, as he would have looped back westward to revisit the places that had meant the most to him the year before, throwing in some new destinations (Rainbow Bridge, Inscription House) to boot.

Instead, from Shiprock Everett headed north toward Mesa Verde. For almost twenty miles, he followed a highway, the old Route 666 (today's U. S. Highway 491). At one point he hitched a ride in a truck driven by a Navajo. Nuflo was tied to the back of the vehicle. "It irked him," Everett noted, "to be obliged to step along at a proper pace." Other autos passed by as Everett walked or rode his horse.

> There were two comely girls who slowed their car to look at me. One, in a red and black shirt, looked quite nice. Then there was a Louisiana car, with a haughty young fellow with black mustache and sombrero and a longhaired black beauty beside him.

On July 29, Everett crossed another state border and entered Colorado, at the same moment also leaving the Navajo reservation. At a trading post on the Mancos River, he left Highway 666, planning to head east up Mancos Canyon. The trader, however, professed to know nothing about this southern approach to Mesa Verde.

Everett bought new supplies, including half a watermelon, and set off, following a faint trail that paralleled the river. He had gone only a quarter of a mile when the second disaster of his 1932 campaign occurred. Once again, his diary vividly recounts the fiasco.

> [T]he trail led along the edge of a bank in a quite narrow pass with the high bank above & below. I supposed it was passable, because it was there. Nuflo went ahead, scraped safely by, but around the turn, the ledge was narrower. There was nothing to do but go on, and Nuflo was within a few yards of safety when at a particularly narrow spot, his kyak [pack sack] pushed him out and he began to slip off. He lunged up again, but once more, the pack pushed him off. He clawed the ledge frantically, then fell down into the current of the muddy Mancos. It was deep near the bank, and he floundered about and wet his pack. When the kyaks were full of water, he could not lift them, and he floundered miserably and floated downstream several yards. He could not stand up.

Petrified, Everett stood on the bank and yelled, "Oh, for God's sake, for GOD's sake." Then he sprang into action, leaping into the river up to his waist. As he tried to pull the horse back onto the bank, a neck strap broke and the saddle and pack sacks fell off. Everett got Nuflo onto shore, tied him to a cottonwood, then went back into the river after the sodden gear. A precious blanket floated away. At last, hauling his equipment in pieces, Everett got the rest of it onto dry land. "I . . . heaved at the bedroll," he later wrote. "It weighed like lead. I had to try a dozen times before I could get it on the bank."

Everything he owned was soaked through. His camera and flash-light were ruined. With a sense of desperation, Everett hung every-thing on a nearby fence, hoping to dry out his gear. To his further dismay, his precious sketch case was also soaked. He spread out the papers on which he had made his paintings and drawings, but, as he recorded, "Most of them are spoiled." His food had turned to mush. Even the diary was soaked. (Later, in Los Angeles, after Ever-ett disappeared, his mother wrote on the cover of the bound record book: "1932 diary. This fell into the River with all of Jonathan's pack, in Canyon del Muerto." Stella had confused the two horse catastrophes, but her pride at saving the diary in legible form was self-evident.)

As he had started up Mancos canyon, Everett entered the Ute Mountain Ute Reservation. He was no longer in Navajo country. While he struggled with his gear, he wrote later, "Two women came by—smiled, but did not offer to help."

To his further dismay, it started to rain. Everett flung a tarp over the "wreckage," left Nuflo tied to the tree, and hiked back to the trad-ing post. There he bought cigarettes and candy and borrowed clothes, a rug, and a canvas to sleep in before returning to the debris of his camp. At the end of the long day, Everett wrote, "Tho I had not let it show, I really felt overwhelmed by what had happened."

During the next few days, Everett struggled slowly up Mancos Canyon, searching for any of several tributary gorges that would lead up onto the high tabletop of Mesa Verde. His mood was dismal. Sev-eral times he got lost, but Utes more helpful than the two women who had smiled at his river predicament put him back on the right trails. "Nuflo was exasperating," Everett wrote on July 31. "If I tried to lead him he pulled back like a burro, and if I drove him, he was constantly turning around and leaving the trail."

The next day, Everett recorded, "I am in no great rush to reach the park. It will mark the termination of my wanderings—my independence.

I can't even see the [cliff] dwellings independently. All tourists go in an auto caravan with a ranger."

On August 2, Everett entered the national park, visited the head-quarters, and then adjourned to the group campground. He was dis-appointed to find not a single letter awaiting his arrival. The next day he wrote to his family, putting up a brave front:

> In spite of all the reverses, hardships, and difficulties, I find the wilderness trail very fascinating. . . . I think it would be cowardly to turn back at this stage of the game. . . . You have no idea how flabby and pale the city is, compared with the reality, the meaningful beauty, of the wilderness.

But Mesa Verde, thronged with tourists, was not wilderness. And Everett was played out. During the next few days, as he joined those auto caravans to visit the famous ruins, he looked hard for a tourist from California who would be willing to drive him home.

*   *   *

After August 2, Everett stopped writing in his diary. The reason was not that he had lost interest in keeping a record, but simply that he had run out of pages. In the last six pages of his bound journal, Ev-erett had transcribed quotations from famous poets. These passages had been entered earlier, perhaps even before he left Los Angeles.

The quotations form a small anthology of some of the verses that meant much to Everett. The poets cited range from Stephen Vincent Benét to John Masefield, from Keats to Yeats, from Euripides to Baudelaire. Everett may have been quoting from memory, for in his transcription of parts of Swinburne's "The Garden of Proserpine," he inadvertently dropped the sixth line of the famous penultimate stanza:

From too much love of living,
  From hope and fear set free,
We thank with brief thanksgiving
  Whatever gods may be
That no life lives for ever;
That dead men rise up never;
That even the weariest river
  Winds somewhere safe to sea.

The diary situation is further clarified by a line in Everett's August 3 letter to his family, asking them to mail not only books by Baudelaire and Blake but "a diary book (mine is full)." When the new diary did not arrive in time, Everett scrounged some loose pages on which he made highly telegraphic entries from August 3 to August 17 (those pages are folded and tucked inside the bound, river-soaked original journal, now housed in the Marriott Library at the University of Utah).

However brief, those entries record a series of visits to Anasazi ruins. What Everett did with Nuflo during his two weeks in Mesa Verde is unclear, but he got to the ruins by riding with tourists in their automobiles, and he put up with the regimen of ranger-guided tours. By now Everett had given up camping as well, as he spent his nights in a ranger cabin.

The entries read like a laundry list of ruins knocked off: "On to Kodak House." "Jug House ruin." "Over to No. 11. Couldn't get in." Occasionally, Everett elaborates: "Went to No. 16. Upper terrace well preserved—Fine doors. Skeleton ex. preserved. Fondled skull." On August 11, Everett wrote, "JW 1890." In some ruin, he had found the inscription of the Kayenta trader and self-taught archaeologist John Wetherill, engraved in the rock forty-one years before Wetherill would meet Everett and set him on his Anasazi path toward the Tsegi Canyon system.

Despite the blasé tone of these entries, constrained as they are by a shortage of paper, Mesa Verde made a lasting impression on Everett. One of his best blockprints is a deft rendering of the four-story ruin called Square Tower House, as seen from the rim above.

In Mesa Verde, Everett managed to get poison ivy again. He met a few strangers interesting enough to consider as friends, but backed away: "Herb very travelled—music, studied at Chi. Art In. [the Art Institute of Chicago]. Yet we don't seem to strike a note."

What Everett did not find was a tourist willing to drive him to Los Angeles. After making a four-day excursion to some of the more remote western arms of the national park, Everett wrote a last letter home on August 25. Then he started hitchhiking. What happened to Nuflo, he did not bother to record.

From Mesa Verde, Everett got a ride not all the way to Los Angeles, but only to Gallup, New Mexico. From there, as he wrote a friend seven months later, "I persuaded an unwilling chauffeur to take me as far as Williams [Arizona]. Then he wanted to drop me again, but helped by my magnetic personality I persuaded him that he was foolish not to take me to the [Grand] Canyon, which he finally did."

The great chasm briefly reawakened Everett's wanderlust. He lingered long enough to make two round trips down five-thousand-foot trails to the Colorado River and back up to the South Rim. Both times he carried his own gear in a knapsack, rather than rent a burro from the Park Service. Somewhere in the canyon depths he killed his eighth rattlesnake of the summer—"a rare species found only in the Grand Canyon," he bragged unabashedly.

At last Everett got a ride to Kingman, Arizona, just thirty miles east of the Nevada border. From Kingman he mailed home most of his gear. But during the next few days he managed only to patch together short rides westward. "Stranded" (his word) in the blazing heat of Needles, California, Everett sent a telegram home pleading for rescue, "but the wire was never received," he later wrote, "and I got a ride straight through, arriving in dense fog in a strange part of the city."

It was a fitting end to Everett's star-crossed 1932 expedition. Looking back on that journey, Everett could not have failed to be disappointed by how far short his accomplishment had fallen from the standards he had set during his 1931 excursion. He had spent five months in the Southwest, not ten, and during some ten weeks of his time, he had effectively been marooned, first in Roosevelt, then in Holbrook. His 1932 journey had covered less than half the distance of his previous year's pilgrimage, and relatively little of his traveling had taken him through true wilderness. Much of the time on the trail in 1932, Everett was plagued by exhaustion, by aching throughout his body, and by some kind of painful eye affliction. He never sorted out the logistical problems posed by a series of inadequate pack animals. And he had suffered four calamities—the schism with Bill and Clark, the beating and disappearance of his dog Curly, the death of Jonathan, and Nuflo's plunge into the Mancos River.

Back home, Everett was not at all sure what he wanted to do with his life. His parents had plans for their younger son, however, and they had nothing to do with further vagabondage in the outdoors.

FOUR

"I Go to Make My Destiny"

IT WOULD BE ALMOST NINE MONTHS before Everett hit the trail again—the longest hiatus in his five years of wandering. Soon after arriving home in September 1932, he enrolled as a freshman at UCLA, almost certainly in response to pressure from his parents. Although he had done well in high school, Everett insisted in a letter to a California friend that "I got in [to college] by rather a fluke."

Since he did not keep a diary during the time he was anchored at home, and there was no reason to write letters to his family or to local friends such as Bill Jacobs, this nine-month span remains the haziest period in Everett's life after the age of sixteen. A few scraps of his college essays survive. They suggest that academe brought out a stiff, dutiful formality in his prose, so different from the rhapsodic flights of his letters from the trail. One specimen: a single-page essay on the English Reformation, which earned Everett a D in History 5A. "There is nothing permanent in the world except change, which is inevitable and omnipresent," Everett wrote, veering dangerously astray, before he closed the essay with a lame pronouncement: "If we believe in evolution, then we must believe that the English reformation was fated, and that Henry was only the tool, if a good tool, to bring it about."

Even when he chose a subject dear to his heart, as in another one-pager that he titled "Navajo Hardships," the woodenness prevailed: "The Navajo seems to thrive on his meager diet, which consists of three staples, coffee, mutton, and *naneskadi* or squaw bread."

A single piece from his UCLA semester transcends the humdrum plod. It is titled "I Go to Make My Destiny," and it closes with the kind of proud yet tragic manifesto that was becoming the stamp of Everett's vision:

> Bitter pain is in store for me, but I shall bear it. Beauty beyond all power to convey shall be mine; I will search diligently for it. Death may await me; with vitality, impetuosity and confidence I will combat it. . . .
>
> My heart beats high, but my eyelids droop; tomorrow I will go. Adventure is for the adventurous. Life is a dream. I am young, and a fool; forgive me, and read on.

In 1983, Bud Rusho transcribed parts or all of five letters written by Everett between September 1932 and March 1933. The originals of all five have since disappeared. Passages in these letters, however, sketchily document the young man's moods and intentions during his nine months at home. In January, having completed only one semester, Everett dropped out of UCLA, putting college behind him for good. To one friend, he dismissed the experience in the mock-pompous style he and Bill Jacobs had started to affect in 1931: "How little you know me to think that I could still be in the University! How could a lofty, unconquerable soul like mine remain imprisoned in that academic backwater, wherein all but the most docile wallow in a hopeless slough?" Less ironically, Everett added, "Even after climbing out of the maelstrom of college, I find that life is still awhirl, though no

longer a swirl. I have, however, been on several Bacchic revels and
musical orgies."

What those revels and orgies really amounted to, we have little
idea today, but they may have consisted of nothing more than listening to records and attending the occasional concert. "Music means
more to me than any other art, I think," Everett wrote to one friend.
Another letter opens, "I have just been listening to Cesar Franck's
Symphony in D Minor. I turned out all the lights and danced to
it—then to Saint-Saens' bacchanal in 'Samson and Delilah,' until everything whirred."

Over Christmas vacation, Everett visited Carmel and Monterey, renewing acquaintances he had forged in 1930, including his friendship
with Edward Weston. On the seacoast, he tried to sketch, but the winter cold defeated his efforts: "[M]y fingers shiver and I have paper after
paper covered with wavy, erratic lines which are hard to decipher."

One of the few memorable experiences Everett had had at UCLA
was hearing T. S. Eliot give a poetry reading. And sometime in February, probably in Los Angeles, Everett attended a concert recital
by Sergei Rachmaninoff, the great Russian composer and pianist,
fifty-nine years old at the time but still at the peak of his performing
powers. The event so moved Everett that he wrote a short essay (for
himself, not UCLA) trying to render Rachmaninoff's pianistic leger-
demain in prose:

> His long tapering hands dart over the ivory like shadows
> shifting and interweaving under a tree as the wind blows
> through the leaves above. He hunches forward farther. One
> hand shifts to a single point and pounces on a key like a cat
> on a pixie. It is a large Persian cat, and having missed, it
> recoils and withdraws its paw in a flash, but not the slightest
> discomfiture is reflected in its face.
>
> The other hand is the pixie.

On February 13, Everett wrote Rachmaninoff a letter. After fulsomely praising the Russian's performance, he offered him his essay:

I myself am a young artist. . . . I thought that you might
be interested in the phantasy which you in your turn have
inspired, so I am sending you what I wrote Monday night
after your concert.
  With no tinge of hypocrisy,
    Everett Ruess.

Rachmaninoff was a cooler genius than Edward Weston. If he in fact received Everett's brash homage, he never bothered to respond to it.

With college out of the question, still feeling no pressing need to land a real job, Everett turned his thoughts back to wandering. By the spring of 1933 he had decided not to return to Arizona and the canyons, but to make a second jaunt into the high country of California. "In a month or so when it is hot," he wrote a friend on March 23, "I am going to shoulder my pack and go up into the Sierras, with some rice and oatmeal, a few books, paper, and paints. It will be good for me to be on the trail again."

Why California, when the true Southwest had proved so much more powerful for Everett? In a September 1932 letter, he elaborated, "After months in the desert, I long for the seacaves, the crashing breakers in the tunnels, the still, multi-colored lagoons, the jagged cliffs and ancient warrior cypresses." Yet it would not be the coast of Big Sur to which Everett headed in late May 1933, but Sequoia National Forest.

Above all, the restless young man needed to get away from home. About to turn nineteen, he was eager to cut loose from the family bonds that confined him to the house on North Kingsley Drive in Los Angeles. In his March 23 letter, Everett projected beyond the summer:

"After the Sierras, I may stay in San Francisco and have the experience of another city."

But already he was concocting a campaign for 1934, an expedition on a grander scale than anything he had yet attempted: "Next year I expect to spend the whole year in the red wastes of the Navajo country, painting industriously."

*   *   *

Waldo, having turned twenty-three, was still living with his parents. He had taken yet another stopgap job as a temporary stenographer in a Los Angeles office. That summer he would land a steadier post with a water company in San Bernardino, some fifty miles east of L.A., which required him to move out of the family house and rent a place of his own. On learning this news, Everett wrote in his diary, "It must have been a wrench for him to pull up stakes."

Some might chalk up the oddity of two ambitious brothers still living at home at the ages of nineteen and twenty-three to the familial closeness that Christopher and Stella had imposed on their sons since they were infants. More likely, however, it was simply a by-product of the Depression, for during all the years of Everett's vagabondage, Christopher was struggling to make ends meet for the whole family.

Certainly Waldo had demonstrated plenty of footloose independence long before the age of twenty-three. During the two summers when he was twelve and fourteen, he had worked on a ranch in Montana, far from the family's residence at that time on the East Coast. (Waldo's ranch idylls filled the much younger Everett with envy.) At only sixteen, Waldo had gone off to Antioch for college, though he failed to graduate. One reason may have been that his restless itch to see the world led him to interrupt his schooling as he cadged a job as a deckhand on the transatlantic liner *Leviathan*. To get hired, he had to fudge his age by four years, claiming a birth date of 1905, not his actual 1909.

Only eighteen months after Everett set off for the Sierra Nevada, moreover, Waldo would take a job that uprooted him from California and transplanted him to China, where he would linger contentedly for years, even while Christopher and Stella pleaded with him to come home.

There is no evidence that Everett ever tried to land a steady job. In a UCLA essay, he sneered like a Nietzschean *Übermensch,*

> Work is a malevolent goddess, made impossibly conceited by unlimited and untempered flattery. . . .
>
> When I am bowled over and trampled upon by the contemptible fools who rush madly to cast themselves upon her pyre, my face flushes to the roots of my hair, but I do not look back to see the evil leer in the eyes of the thwarted goddess as I pick myself up, flick decorously at my smirched clothes, and thread my way past the pitiable throngs swarming to her sacrificial altar.

A sense of entitlement unmistakably runs through such grandiose pronouncements. Yet at the same time, on the trail Everett strove to be as frugal as possible, and to earn enough money by selling his paintings and hiring on for short-term jobs (chopping wood, rounding up cattle, packing for tourists with his burros, and the like) to get out from under the burden of accepting handouts from his parents.

Sometime shortly after his 1931 expedition, Everett wrote down two columns accounting for his profit and loss during the ten-month ramble. "Earned income" began with the twenty-five-dollar poster prize he had won, and included such minutiae as "Posing Pericles . . . $.20" and "Burro's load of wood; Roosevelt . . . $1.00." The column totaled $76.50. On a separate page, headed "Expenditures, other than for food," Everett confessed not only to such necessities as buying his burros, but also "Shoe repair . . . $2.00," "Haircut . . . $.50," and "Telegram . . . $.65." Significantly, Everett failed to add up this column. Had he done so, he would have arrived at a total expenditure of $62.50. He might then have prided himself on coming out fourteen bucks in the black for his ten-month odyssey, except that he knew that the cost of food had plunged him deep into the red. And on a third page, in a spidery hand so cramped it breathes embarrassment, he noted:

        Unearned Income
        Dee's gift   2.00
        Bill's   1.00
        Parents   53.
                           5
                          <u>10</u>
                          71
                          15

There was no getting around the truth. Everett's campaign to become a self-sufficient itinerant artist had to be bankrolled by Christopher and Stella.

The letters home from Sequoia and the Sierras during the summer of 1933 not only dutifully thank his parents for a steady stream of "stipends," but make many a request for goods and books to be mailed as soon as possible. Thus on June 16, only three weeks into his journey:

> I received the note from father and one from mother, also a letter from Waldo and the 5 dollar order from father. . . . I find that my shoes are wearing out, and I am forced to ask you to send me my boots. . . . In the same package I wish you would send my can of Viscol, which was on the back porch, a bottle of India ink, a few pencils for writing . . . an old pair of sunglasses for the snow (gray or blue), if you

have an extra pair, and "Casuals of the Sea," a Modern Library book on my shelf in the closet. After you've sent them, you might send what is left of my allowance, because if I leave [Sequoia National Forest] before July, I shall need it to outfit myself.

From Everett's four-and-a-half-month exploration of the Sierra Nevada in 1933, only a handful of letters to family and friends survive. It would be hard to trace the journey of his body and soul that summer and early autumn, but for the fact that his 1933 diary is intact. That journal is so different from the one he kept in 1932 that it seems as though the author has been magically transformed. Everett made an entry every day between May 27 and October 12, and most of those entries are substantial. Although he records down moods and self-doubts, the general tone of the diary is hearty and exuberant. There is scarcely a vestige of the exhaustion and despair that haunted him through his 1932 traverse of the Southwest.

That his parents had worried about his psychological state during his nine months at home is revealed in the closing lines of one letter home: "No, I am in no danger of a nervous breakdown at present. How about you?"

Everett launched his 1933 journey by getting Waldo to drive him from Los Angeles to the southern portal of Sequoia National Forest. And Waldo brought along his girlfriend. "Betty and Waldo necked at fifty per," Everett noted in his diary, but added, "Betty seems a good sport, no matter what she does."

The very first diary entry on May 27 records a turn of events that might well have set Everett off on the wrong foot. As he packed his belongings in Los Angeles, he wrote, "Bill Jacobs did not call, so I called, and his mother said he was asleep, having decided to go some other time. She sounded heartbroken, but I was relieved."

Everett's best friend had stood him up in 1931, after promising

to share his Southwest excursion with him. Before that, he had re-
neged on some Christmas trip together. In 1932, Jacobs had belatedly
showed up in Roosevelt, where he pried Clark away from Everett's
sojourn to go off on a far less ambitious project—from which his
mother had driven him home to Los Angeles. Now, it seems, Bill had
once more backed out of a journey with his chum, deciding at the last
minute to sleep in rather than bother to telephone Everett with news
of his change of heart.

Such feckless behavior might well have exhausted the tolerance of
the most magnanimous of companions. It may be evidence of Everett's lingering annoyance at Bill that none of the surviving 1933 letters is addressed to him. Yet Everett forgave once more, and in 1934
wrote some of the deepest and most intimate letters of his short life to
his stay-at-home pal.

On his second day in Sequoia, Everett bought two burros from a
local wrangler. For a week or so in his diary, he referred to them simply as "the black burro" (or "Blackie") and "the gray." By June 3 he
had named his animals, not with classical allusions such as Pericles or
Pegasus but with the homely tags of Betsy (the black) and Grandma
(the gray).

It was Everett's intention to climb through the Sequoia National
Forest to reach the high Sierra, but upon his arrival he learned that
there was far too much snow in the backcountry to set out for alpine
regions in early June. Instead, for a full month he made jaunt after
looping jaunt out of an essentially stationary base camp, effectively
going nowhere.

The diary during these weeks is uncharacteristically impersonal.
Granted, Everett was not recording his doings in hopes of impressing
any future reader, but there is a sameness—even a tedious attention to
detail—about the entries, as Everett records every single thing he did
each day. A sample:

I tried to write in the studio, then in the lodge. I talked to John, who clerks there and is studying medicine at Stanford. Then Mickey McGuire, the information girl, came in for a while. I couldn't write there, so I went back to the Post Office to wait for the mail. The Postmaster and his wife looked at my pictures.

In 1932, despite his setbacks and fatigue, Everett's journey had an overriding design, as he followed his northeast vector 260 miles as the crow flies from Roosevelt to Mesa Verde. But the tramps of his first month in Sequoia in 1933—many of them day hikes without his burros—seem aimless and arbitrary. He spent almost as much time swimming in streams and fishing as he did hiking. He was seldom far from a road, and he often hitched rides from passing cars to get where he wanted to go for a day or two.

And during that month, he ran into a constant stream of strangers, many of whom he stopped and talked to at length, while with others he set out on hikes and fishing trips. The year before, Everett had declared as his abiding principle, "After all the lone trail is best." But there weren't many lone trails in the Sequoia forest in June 1933, and, oddly enough, Everett did not seem to mind that fact. To be sure, on June 23 he complained to his diary, "Thus far, I've had only two days of uninterrupted solitude." But a more characteristic entry was the one he wrote on June 12: "It was delightful to sit in the shade of the redwoods, watch the flag flutter and the men digging in the sun, everyone happy and smiling, working, conversing or watching. The whole atmosphere was of spaciousness, peace, and contentment."

In 1933 there were many sectors of the Sierra Nevada in which Everett could have wandered through true wilderness without running into other people. The north fork of the Palisades, for instance, where the ruggedest mountains in California thrust into the sky, was seldom visited. Later in the summer Everett would climb Mount Whitney, at 14,505 feet the highest summit in the forty-eight United States, but even in 1933 that hike was a popular tourist outing along a gentle and monotonous trail.

Besides the deep snow in the backcountry, another excuse for Everett's ensconcement in the lower part of the Sequoia National Forest (which adjoins Sequoia National Park) was the effort to find buyers for his paintings to help finance his trip. Yet by heading straight for a popular national forest and park, Everett guaranteed that he would not find much solitude. His diary through June records encounters with park rangers, Civilian Conservation Corps workers, roadbuilders, telephone-line workmen, post office personnel, policemen, and of course tourists. On July 5, after a short probe into more-remote regions, Everett groused in a letter to his family, "When I came down from the back country, I found the park overrun with tourists."

What did he expect? The diary makes it clear that what kept Everett rubbing elbows with strangers was his eternal longing for true, deep friendship. As unintrospective as most of the entries are, a few veer into the murky depths of that longing. On May 28, his second day in Sequoia, he fell in with a stranger named Wes Leverin, with whom he took a moonlight hike. "I like Wes," he wrote. "He had delicate, handsome features." The hike, he added, "was a glorious experience for me."

Then, just as the diary becomes reflective, three lines have been erased—but not entirely. The cryptogram left on the page reads,

Bill   old when all
                  Im glad   I   without
                              by can.

Just two sentences after the partially expunged passage, Everett wrote, "It was good to be called by name and made one of them." Who the "them" refers to is unclear.

On June 20, Everett recorded another glancing encounter with attractive strangers, as he hiked along Colony Creek.

> Three willowy young school teachers with glasses on passed on the other side of the stream. Apparently they did not trust me, for they would not reply to my greeting. I am again mistrusting myself in relation to other people.

This provocative remark is immediately followed by an eighteen-line erasure, one of the longest in either of the two surviving diaries.

Whatever Everett wrote in those missing lines must have been provoked by the glum insight about "mistrusting myself in relation to other people," for when the text resurfaces, he is still miffed by the schoolteachers' snub:

> The girls came back, and I crossed to meet them, speaking to them as I crossed the brook. They went right on in silence. Not to be outdone even in ill breeding and insolence, I went straight up the hill as if that had been my intention.

Despite these occasional fits of melancholy, Everett's diary records day after day of enthusiasm and joy. He was reading voraciously again—Apuleius's *The Golden Ass* ("I was rather disappointed in it"); the rest of *Gargantua and Pantagruel*, which he had begun in 1932, and which delighted him; H. M. Tomlinson's *The Sea and the Jungle*, which grew on him after a shaky start; and Norman Douglas's witty novel of decadence on Capri, *South Wind*. The last book prompted a curious diary entry: "Finally I finished 'South Wind,' enjoying the final Bacchic scene. It is truly amusing to me what people say before they pass out. Everyone should have the experience, I think."

We know that Everett smoked an occasional cigarette. Whether he regularly drank alcohol is uncertain. In all his surviving writings, there are only a few glancing mentions of beer or wine. When others got drunk, as at the Holbrook parade and rodeo, Everett seemed to play the role of the sober bystander. Yet there are those odd allusions to "Bacchic revels."

Of course, Prohibition had been in effect since 1920, and would not be repealed until December 1933. Because drinking was illegal, Everett would not readily have confessed in print (even in the privacy of his diary) to any personal indulgence in alcohol. Moreover, we know that Stella was a lifelong teetotaler. It may be that if Everett drank, or ever got truly drunk, he would have had an additional reason to keep it to himself, for fear of offending his mother.

As he hiked in the forest, Everett often sang out loud. Sea chanties and cowboy ballads, he mentions in one entry, but more often he hummed his favorite classical music. "I drank at a stream," he wrote on June 12, "and strode gallantly up, singing some Dvorak melodies, putting all the volume I had into them. The forest boomed with my rollicking song. Then the transmuted melodies of Beethoven, Brahms, and the Bolero rang thru the silent forest."

That day or the next, Everett mailed a curious letter. It has no salutation, but after Everett's disappearance, one of his parents added an annotation after Everett's signature, "To friends from the high Sierra in 1933." The letter opens with a proclamation of happiness the pitch of which Everett would seldom again match:

> During the last few weeks, I have been having the time of my life. Much of the time I feel so exuberant that I can hardly contain myself. The colors are so glorious, the forests so magnificent, the mountains so splendid, and the streams so utterly, wildly, tumultuously, effervescently joyful that to me at least, the world is a riot of intense sensual delight. In addition to [which] all the people are genial and generous and happy, & everyone seems to be at his best.

Yet two paragraphs later in this atypical letter, Everett slips into his odd usage of the perfect tense, as if the joys of the summer—of life itself—were already over: "Oh, I have lived intensely, drinking deep!"

Everett's extreme high spirits in 1933 after a 1932 campaign so riddled with gloom and despair form one paradox. His comfort surrounded by strangers in the Sequoia after glorying in solitude in Arizona forms another. And yet a third lies in the two landscapes, as different from each other as can be found in the United States. In the canyons and deserts of the Southwest, one treasures openness, distant horizons, and azure skies, even barrenness itself. In the Sequoia National Forest there is little openness and only the odd glimpse of the sky: instead, one is surrounded by towering trees—not only the famous ancient redwoods, but cedars, firs, and lodgepole pines. That Everett could equally love both landscapes may testify to the omnivorousness of his passion for nature. Or it may simply reflect that to be outdoors, on his own, on the move, with no end to the journey in sight, amounted to him to the most important thing in life.

* * *

On June 26, Everett claimed in his diary, "I plotted my course for the next two months to my entire satisfaction." If so, the vagaries of his rambling through July and August make it hard to discern the shape of that course. In general terms, his plans involved traveling north into the high Sierra, climbing Mount Whitney, and eventually making his way to Yosemite National Park, which he had last visited in 1930. But the actual route of his wandering veered far from a steady trek along that northern and northwestern compass bearing.

By the end of June, the deep snow in the high country had started to melt. On June 29, with a friend met along the trail, Everett climbed Alta Peak, a modest summit 11,204 feet above sea level. Reaching the top in late afternoon, he gazed to the north and for the first time saw Mount Whitney.

In the beginning of July, launched on the High Sierra Trail, Everett escaped the shadowy woods and began to traverse alpine meadows and glades. He left the national forest behind and entered Sequoia National Park, which encloses Mount Whitney. By now, Everett was riding Betsy and using Grandma as his pack animal. The streams were running high everywhere, and the greatest obstacle to his progress was coaxing his balky burros to ford even the shallowest brooks.

In the high country, Everett still ran into strangers virtually every day—backpackers, mule- and horse-packers, trail-building crews, and rangers. By the 1930s, the High Sierra Trail had become a standard objective for outdoorsmen and women who were hardier than the casual tourists who flocked to Sequoia to drive up and park next to such prodigies as the General Sherman Tree. Although it traversed mountain passes and rocky boulderfields, the trail was excellently maintained. Everett's daily task was not to blaze his own route through the wilderness, as he had for long stretches in Arizona in 1931 and 1932, but to sort out the signposts along the trail that would guide him from one valley to the next. Nor was this alpine terrain deep wilderness, for Everett records regular visits to ranger stations, old cabins, and working ranches.

In early July, the mosquitoes "tormented me fiercely," he complained, making it hard to paint or even to write in his diary. Yet his spirits stayed high. Fishing had become a serious diversion. For bait, he usually stuck grasshoppers and other bugs on the barb of his hook, but strangers he met along the trail traded or gave him dry flies (the Royal Coachman was his favorite). What kind of fishing rod he had, Everett does not mention. His technique was crude but effective: once he had snagged a trout, rather than play it toward shore, he would jerk it out of the water, then retrieve it as it thrashed in the weeds. More than once, he catapulted a fish to shore, snapping it loose from the hook, but then couldn't find his catch in the underbrush.

Everett's diary lavishes many paragraphs on the wiles and pleasures of trout fishing. On July 30,

> After patient casting in a deep pool, I felt a tug on my line,
> and, thrilled to the core, swung the pole, and the biggest fish
> I ever caught thudded up on the bank. I hunted five minutes
> before I found him in the deep brake, but he was still flop-
> ping. I could hardly close my fist on him. He was a foot long
> and weighed at least a pound. How I shouted.

On his best day, Everett caught forty fish. For breakfast on July 27,
he ate eighteen trout, fried in cornmeal and bacon grease.

One of the highlights of Everett's July adventure was an epic
battle with a rattlesnake. He spotted the serpent coiled and rattling
beside the trail, threw rocks at it to no avail, then tried to prod it
with a stick. He succeeded in stabbing the snake, then forcing its
head into the dirt, but his prey slithered away into underbrush and
rocks. Without the slightest sense of shame, Everett described what
happened next:

> The brush was almost impenetrable. Taking my life in
> my hands, I reached down and caught his tail, loosed the
> makeshift spear, and whipped him out on the rocks. He was
> very much alive, but after a few tries, I mashed his flat head
> and cut it off. . . . Only six rattles, and he is not long, but
> what a fight we had. It was true sport.
>
> Hunting rattler's as I do comes nearer to real sport than
> almost anything I know. It has the necessary element of
> danger, for it is not sport unless opponents are somewhat
> evenly matched, and the quarry can turn the tables on the
> pursuer. By comparison, fishing is a diversion for senescent
> bachelors.

Despite this gloating credo, Everett would continue to fish avidly throughout the rest of his time in the Sierras.

During this part of the summer, Everett was reading two works "with the greatest of pleasure": Richard Burton's unexpurgated translation of the *Arabian Nights* and Edward FitzGerald's brilliant and idiosyncratic rendering of Omar Khayyam's *Rubaiyat*. At regular intervals, he transcribed stanzas of the latter into his diary, as well as summaries of the tales in the *Arabian Nights*. Everett's enthusiasm for these Victorian versions of Near Eastern classics is significant, for both works are paeans to the hedonistic life. Yet both are full of *carpe diem* reminders of mortality.

On July 22, after transcribing FitzGerald's lines, "Drink! for you know not whence you came, nor why; / Drink, for you know not why you go, nor where," Everett wrote, "I was completely swayed by Omar's thoughts, and I decided I'd certainly get some wine from Lee if I could." This comment is the closest Everett would come in either of the extant journals to admitting to a craving for alcohol.

On July 14, at the Kern River Hot Springs, Everett bumped into two teenagers named Ned and Charley, who happened to be students at Hollywood High School, from which Everett had graduated in 1931. Both also turned out to be Bible-reading Christians, and on the spot Ned tried to convert Everett to his fundamentalist beliefs. In his diary, Everett assessed the pair: "Ned has some intelligence, but Charley is rather callow." Nonetheless, he paired up with the youngsters to climb Mount Whitney. Six days later they reached the summit—the highest point of land Everett would reach in his short life. On top,

> Charley counted the names in the registry book and I took pictures. In the book we entered our names and a legend from the tale of Abu Hasan [from the *Arabian Nights*] which nearly made us die of laughter. No doubt coming visitors will be affected by it too.

The next day, Everett parted ways with the young lads.

From Whitney, Everett might well have headed northwest along the John Muir Trail, which runs 211 miles from the summit of that peak to Yosemite, as it links up a series of mountain valleys and high passes. (Construction of the trail began in 1915. By 1933 it was complete except for one section at the headwaters of the Kings River.) Instead, Everett wandered up and down the Kern River, lingering in Sequoia National Park and eventually turning back south to the lower national forest where he had begun his journey in late May. For the first time, a certain disappointment undercut his exuberance. "I have found Kern Canyon rather monotonous and depressing," he wrote on July 28. "There is no variety. The rocks are a dull gray, and the forest is an impenetrable tangle that cuts off all outlook."

Then a series of minor mishaps interfered with his plans. The first was his discovery that Grandma was pregnant. "Poor ignorant creature," Everett wrote, "she had no knowledge of contraceptives!" A passerby experienced with livestock examined the burro and told Everett that Grandma would give birth in about a month. The second setback came when Everett developed an infection on the palm of his right hand that festered and spread. "I hardly slept, the pain in my hand was so great," he wrote on August 2.

As the infection worsened, Everett pushed his way south and down toward the outskirts of civilization. In early August, in order to see doctors, he retreated all the way to the towns of Visalia and Tulare, out on the flat farmlands of the Central Valley, which was scorching hot at the height of summer. One physician soaked Everett's hand in Lysol and hot water. The next day, he wrote, "[T]he nurse laid me out on the operating table, and after my hand had soaked, the doctor injected Novocain and slashed and probed in four places." Four days later, another doctor diagnosed blood poisoning.

Despite the seriousness of his injury, Everett kept hitching rides back into the near edges of the forest, where he retrieved his burros and tried to resume his vagabondage. "I am not a good left handed camper, but I did my best," he recorded on August 4. He wrote a letter home using his left hand, the script slanted backward, the scrawl like a child's. This was, however, a somewhat theatrical gesture, for at the same time, Everett kept up his diary entries with his right hand.

Contact with the outer world plunged Everett into a new depression. In a ranger cabin, he listened to a radio broadcast. "I heard the San Francisco news by radio," he wrote, "and was disgusted at the advertising and the vulgar quality of the news & sports." But in Visalia, he caught a broadcast of classical music on another radio. "The concert was glorious," he wrote. "I was drunk with the beauty of it." To the strains of Mussorgsky's "Night on Bald Mountain," Everett "whirled and wove a dexterous pattern with my feet, reaching and maintaining a frenziedly fantastic mood until I was exhausted."

At last Everett's hand healed, and he resumed his journey. Something was troubling him beyond the infection and Grandma's pregnancy, however. The 1933 diary had become such an unintrospective habit that, reading between the lines, one guesses that in some half-conscious way, Everett was censoring his own darkest ruminations. Thus he ended an August 21 entry, full of the trivial happenings of the day, with a single, unelaborated line, "I had a huge fire, and some hot stew, then thought long long thoughts."

On August 28 he let down his guard ever so slightly: "I thought strange thoughts, and looked forward to San Francisco. My longing for the desert has increased." Already anticipating a 1934 return to Arizona, he started chanting not melodies from Dvořák or Beethoven, but Navajo songs and words. That same day he made a confession of which there is no hint in the previous three months of diary entries: "I find sleep very unpleasant. I cannot bear to yield consciousness without a struggle, especially as I sleep so poorly. I call sleep temporary death."

Despite these inklings that the exuberance of summer in the Sierras had faded, Everett determined to complete his journey by reaching Yosemite. At the beginning of September, somewhere in the high country, he at last intersected the John Muir Trail. Even here, traveling most of each day above timberline, he was seldom alone for more than a few hours at a time. On October 2 he met a solitary rider, who told him he had come from Yosemite in only eleven days, but in Everett's judgment, the man had "completely ridden down" his horse by pushing the traverse so fast. In the end, it would take Everett twenty-seven more days to reach Yosemite.

The diary hints at periodic spasms of gloom. "Supper and thoughts," Everett wrote on September 11. The next five lines are erased, with not a single word left standing. Another entry begins, "After a woeful, restless night full of evil dreams . . ." Everett's dread of sleep may have sprung from those recurrent evil dreams, as his unconscious took over, mocking the joys that filled his waking days. But the content of those dreams, he was unwilling to confide even to his diary. On September 6, however, he announced, "I set less and less value on human life, as I learn more about it. I admit the reality of pain in the moment, but its opposite is not strong."

On September 8 a minor accident threatened to abort the whole journey. The detailed account of it in Everett's diary reads like a surreal nightmare. Thrashing through "a tangle of prickly brush" on Goddard Creek, Everett stirred up a bees' nest. He was stung at least a dozen times.

> I struggled frenziedly down to the water, tearing my shirt. I had to leap down onto some wet rocks, then I climbed up on some more, pulled out the stings and the bees in my hair, threw off my clothes, and plunged into the water. Then I seemed to burn all over, and looking down, I discovered that my body was a mass of poison oak blisters. The shock nearly broke me, and I felt sick all over. When I was trying to put on my shirt, I fell into the water, and could not find the strength to get out until I was half drowned.

It took Everett hours to get back on the trail, as he vomited up his breakfast. "I could see nothing but blackness," he reported, "and fell back, exhausted, dizzy, and faint." Struggling to bash his way out of the undergrowth, he fell down repeatedly.

It seems probable that the reeling, staggering fit that Everett suffered had nothing to do with poison oak, but was instead caused by anaphylactic shock brought on by the bee stings. Depending upon the victim's allergic susceptibility, the reaction to a dozen or more bee stings can range from annoying to fatal. Back in camp that evening, Everett searched for old lemon peels to rub on his skin, for one trail acquaintance had told him that was a good remedy for poison oak. Two days later, Everett still had swollen lips and eyelids. But by September 13 he admitted to his diary that the poison oak rash had disappeared entirely. "Either it was something else," he wrote, "or some powerful counter agent stopped it."

Anaphylactic shock was first diagnosed in 1902, but by 1933 it was little understood or recognized, and its relationship to insect bites and stings was not fully clarified until the latter half of the twentieth century. In all likelihood, Everett had a close call with death in the tangle of underbrush on Goddard Creek.

Beginning on September 18, when Everett stumbled upon "a camp of disappointed hunters," he embarked upon a nine-day detour in his jaunt toward Yosemite. The six hunters hired the nineteen-year-old to burro-pack their supplies into the upper reaches of Fish and Silver creeks in the high Sierra, and to cook and wash dishes for them. The diary account of this junket reads like a chapter out of *Don Quixote*, as the incompetent hunters miss one shot after another, but finally kill a deer too young to be legal game. They also shoot a doe (another violation) just to enrich their dinners with venison. Much of the men's camp time is taken up with drinking, cursing one another, and worrying about game wardens. One of the hunters regularly gets lost on his daily prowls in search of four-point bucks.

Everett seems to have tolerated this nonsense with good humor, gotten along fine with the drunken bumblers, and kept his appraisal of their follies to the privacy of his journal. On parting, the men gave Everett ten dollars, a pack of cigarettes, and some of their poached venison.

Throughout the last leg of his 1933 journey, thoughts of the desert Southwest increasingly swam through Everett's head. Near Mono Creek on September 15, he stared at an escarpment called Vermilion Cliffs, then wrote, "They are a very pale pink, and make me wish for the real Vermilion cliffs of Utah and Arizona."

At last, on September 29, Everett reached Yosemite. To his surprise, Grandma had lasted the whole trip without yet giving birth. By now, most of the tourists were gone. "The deer hunters are discouraged or sated," he wrote, "the school boys have gone back to their studies, and vacation time is over for the populace. But this is not vacation time for me. This is my life."

Despite this boast, Everett spent only two weeks in Yosemite. He climbed Half Dome by the cable route and made several forays along trails he had not explored in 1930. But his diary captures few expressions of the glories of the landscape, and the fulfillment of his goal to return to Yosemite sounds like an anticlimax. Everett spent as much time in the park headquarters, museum, library, and store as he did in the outdoors. The mail from home that he gathered was "disappointing," although he was pleased to cash the latest of the unfailing string of money orders from his parents that he had received throughout the last four months. Buying groceries, he splurged on such luxuries as caviar and foie gras. Washing up in the Ahwanee Lodge, Everett saw himself in the mirror, perhaps for the first time in months. "My self confidence dropped to zero at once," he wrote tellingly. "I looked like a ghoul or an ogre." At once he tried to improve his appearance by going to a barber, who not only gave him a haircut but shaved off his beard and whiskers.

Everett's plan was not to head back to Los Angeles, but to proceed directly to San Francisco and launch the life of a bohemian artist. On October 3, he recorded his fantasy:

> I planned how I would rent a little garret on some city hill-top, and have a place all my own. From it I would sally forth to make color studies of tropical fish in the park, to concerts, to library expeditions, and devil may care wanderings in the city and on the sea front.

The unspoken assumption behind this pipe dream was that Christopher and Stella would continue to subsidize their son as he crafted his artistic career.

Despite the optimism of that vision, Everett's mood was glum. The same day he wrote, "My thoughts were bleak. At dark I made a fire to cheer myself." On October 8 he recorded matter-of-factly that he had spent the last seventy straight hours without sleep.

From the park library, he borrowed a novel by Charles Morgan called *The Fountain*. A best-seller when it was published in 1932, but virtually unread today, it revolves around the saga of a British soldier interned in Holland during World War I, who gets entangled in a passionate affair with a German officer's wife.

From its opening pages on, the book made a strong impact on Everett. "[M]y heart leaped when I learned the subject," he wrote, "the contemplative life, the inner stillness which I too am striving to attain, tho I am not done with the wild songs of youth." He devoured the novel in a day and a half. Midway through the book, stirred by the forbidden love affair around which it pivots, Everett paused to record the deepest statement that he had made that year in 194 pages of tightly scrawled diary entries: "I suppose a great and soul filling love is perhaps the greatest experience a man may have, but it is such a rarity as to be almost negligible."

In some sense, that sentence, with its mingled hope and despair, could stand as an epigraph to Everett's life.

Everett finished his diary on October 12, as he prepared to sell his burros, leave Yosemite, and make his way to San Francisco. But at the bottom of a last, otherwise blank page, he wrote a final line: "What a strange dream about Waldo!"

*   *   *

Judging from the letters and the diary, it is hard to know what the 1933 expedition meant to Everett. From it emerged no deep reflections about his purpose in life, no manifestos comparable to the one embodied in the postscript to the letter to Waldo mailed from Chinle, Arizona, in July 1932. Except for the admirable push in September along the John Muir Trail to Yosemite, Everett's wandering seemed rather aimless. There was little true exploration about it, for throughout his four and a half months in national forests and parks, Everett almost never strayed from a well-maintained trail.

If the purpose of the journey was to find inspiring landscapes to capture on paper, there is surprisingly scanty mention in the diary of hours spent sketching with pen and pencil or painting with watercolors. Far more paragraphs (and more zestful ones) narrate Everett's toil as a fisherman. But the stalking, landing, and devouring of trout sound like the play of a boy at summer camp, not the quest of an artist.

Nor did Everett find much of his treasured solitude in 1933. If his goal instead was to discover a lasting companion, a soul mate of the sort he had given up hoping Bill Jacobs could ever be, he came up empty. Not only did the Sierras fail to give Everett even a glimpse of a "great and soul filling love," but he did not forge a single serious friendship there that survived the journey. The dozens of strangers who briefly shared a camp or trail with Everett flit in and out of his diary like shadows. As early as June 8, in his first letter to Waldo, Everett had written, "What I miss most here is intellectual companionship, but that is always difficult to find." Difficult indeed, for none of the Neds or Charleys or park rangers or willowy young schoolteachers whose lives briefly crossed Everett's seemed to promise intellectual friendship.

The hunger for the desert Southwest, for real wilderness, that assailed Everett during the last weeks of his trek through the Sierras would point his life in a truer direction—the direction around which the cult of Everett Ruess that has grown ever since his disappearance is based. But before he could return to Arizona, Everett had high hopes for San Francisco.

In his last letter from Yosemite to his parents, on October 4, Everett pleaded, "I'd also like to have another 200-page diary book if you can find one reasonably." But if he kept a diary during his months in San Francisco, it has disappeared. Once again we have only Everett's letters to speak for his experiment in living as a starving artist in the city.

In El Portal, near the western gateway to Yosemite, Everett managed to sell Betsy and Grandma to an acquaintance from Visalia whom he had met in Sequoia. It was a good bargain, for Everett unloaded the animals for the same price he had paid for them in late May. The buyer drove Everett to the town of Merced. From there he hopped a freight to Sacramento—the first time, so far as we know, that Everett dabbled in the hoboes' preferred means of transportation. It was all fun and games, as more-seasoned vagabonds taught him the ropes. "When we pulled out," Everett wrote home on October 17, "one of the fellows found a reefer [a refrigerator car], and while the cars were gathering speed, we ran the length of the train on top, leaping from one car to another, till we reached it." Inside the "reefer," Everett lounged on a pile of fresh cantaloupes as he "swapped yarns" with his fellow railroad bums.

After a couple of other freight-train rides, Everett "dismounted in Oakland." From the railroad yard he proceeded to the house of friends of his family, who put him up while he searched for an apartment across the bay in San Francisco.

It took him a week to find and rent a small place on Polk Street—today a chic gay district, but in 1933 a less lively and slightly rundown neighborhood. After he was established there, he wrote home a droll description of his garret. Three of his own blockprints hung on the wall, along with one by Hiroshige for which he had traded, and the battered sombrero he had worn in the Sierras. His saddlebags and Navajo blanket lay on the floor. A simple table served as his desk, from which he could look out onto the street. At night, a neon light outside bathed the curtains with "a rosy glow." "There are no cooking possibilities," Everett explained. "I have eaten three cooked meals in the last two weeks. I get along famously on fruit, sandwiches, and milk."

Shortly after arriving in this city of artists and intellectuals, Everett started pounding the pavement in search of dealers who might show some interest in his work. His mother had sent him linoleum blocks, so he was able to carve, ink, and process new prints; Stella also mailed him prints he had made in previous years. On November 24, Everett reported a gratifying breakthrough. Paul Elder, who ran an influential bookstore-cum-gallery, took the whole batch of prints Everett showed him on consignment. But later, Everett reported, "I went to Paul Elder's today, and they haven't even got around to putting my stuff up, so naturally they haven't sold any." In January he passed on gloomier news: "A while ago I was reliably informed that Paul Elder's are and have been on the verge of bankruptcy for a long time, and that I should take my stuff out as soon as possible, as they would not pay me anything even if they sold all my stuff."

Everett was able to sell prints here and there to new acquaintances, or trade them for such luxuries as concert tickets. He threw himself into the cultural life of San Francisco. During his first two months there, he went to lectures by the muckraking journalist Lincoln Steffens and the artist Rockwell Kent (himself a bold adventurer who captured such remote landscapes as Greenland and Alaska in masterly woodcuts and paintings); a concert by the Russian violinist Mischa Elman; a chamber music recital featuring Italian music; and operatic performances of Rimsky-Korsakov's *Le Coq d'Or* and Wagner's *Tristan und Isolde*. He also signed up for life classes in drawing (at fifty cents a session). No sketches of nude women, however, seem to have survived in Everett's portfolio.

The would-be artist could not fool himself with the presumption that he was making money or even breaking even. When Waldo sent him an unexpected check as a Christmas gift, Everett responded with embarrassment: "[M]y first feeling was that I did not want it. I know too that you could ill afford to spare it." But he went on to confess, "I sold a couple of pictures today, and spent the money already. Half the time I am broke or without money for carfare and telephone."

The truth was that at nineteen, Everett was still completely dependent on the "allowance" that his parents regularly mailed him. And there are signs that he was now taking their generosity for granted. On October 29 he wrote to his parents, "In regard to the remittance, I suggest that you put $10 of the October money (if you haven't already sent it) in the bank for me against the desert trip, and send the other 15 odd as soon as you can."

As he had with Edward Weston in Carmel in 1930, now in San Francisco Everett had no compunctions about presenting himself on the doorsteps of famous artists. He had long admired the paintings of Maynard Dixon, who as a young man, two decades earlier, had himself crisscrossed the Southwest and captured its landscapes in oils and watercolors. Only a little more than a week after landing in San Francisco, Everett sought out Dixon's studio and introduced himself. Like Weston, Dixon was charmed rather than put off by this pushy young stranger.

The linkage with Dixon would prove one of the most fortuitous of Everett's brief career. One day the master gave him what Everett called "perhaps the best art lesson I ever had." It was, he wrote his mother, "a lesson in simplicity."

The main thing Maynard did was to make me see what is meaningless in a picture, and have the strength to eliminate it; and see what was significant, and how to stress it. This he showed me with little scraps of black and white paper, placed over my drawings.

It was not Dixon who had the crucial impact on Everett's development so much as his wife, the photographer Dorothea Lange. Not yet famous for her portraits of Dust Bowl refugees and victims of the Great Depression, Lange at the time was far less well known than her husband, whom she would divorce two years later. She took Everett under her wing, introducing him to other artists (including Rockwell Kent and the composer Ernst Bacon), and attended concerts with him. Lange was evidently taken with Everett's looks, for, as he wrote home on October 31, "On Thursday I have a sitting with Dorothea Lange, who wants to make some photographic studies."

The series of portraits of Everett that Lange took, posing him against a black backdrop, are by far the finest photographs ever made of the young vagabond. Lange captured, as Everett's own snapshots failed to do, the beguiling mixture of innocence and sensuality in his countenance. Seventy-six years after she made the portraits, they would play a pivotal role in an ongoing controversy about Everett's ultimate fate. At the time, however, Lange seemed dissatisfied with her work, for Everett wrote home on January 2, "I would have sent you one of Mrs. Dixon's photographs, but she did not think they were good enough, and wants to make some others."

With his blithe self-confidence, in October Everett knocked on the door of Ansel Adams's studio and introduced himself. He wrote his family, "Ansel Adams waxed very enthusiastic about my black and white work. He could not exhibit it in his gallery, but he gave me a number of suggestions which I am following out. He is going to trade me one of his photographs for one of my prints." The composition that Everett chose was a picture of "a mysterious lake" at Kaweah Gap, a pass in the Sierras that he had traversed in July.

Even Everett's staunchest devotees have wondered whether his claim about trading pictures with the great black-and-white photographer was a fictitious boast. But at a conference in southern Utah in 2009, Gibbs Smith, founder of Peregrine Smith Books and the publisher of Rusho's *A Vagabond for Beauty*, related an intriguing story. Many decades after Everett had met Adams, Smith studied with the master. "One time I asked him," Smith recalled, " 'Did you ever meet Everett Ruess?' He said, 'No.' But then his wife, Virginia, asked him to come into the bedroom. There on the wall was Everett's woodcut."

By the end of the year, Everett was getting restless. "I am tired of the place where I am staying," he wrote to Waldo just before Christmas. And to his parents, even before that: "As to the duration of my stay [in San Francisco], I am not yet certain. . . . I would like to spend a whole year in the desert, but I might not go until March or April."

With the restlessness came a renewed curiosity about basic matters of morality and purpose. On December 4, in a letter addressed solely to his father, Everett opened, "I have been asking myself some questions latterly, and I wrote some of them down, thinking you might be interested." The document that Everett's questions provoked is one of the most extraordinary in the chronicle of his life. It is, in fact, the only letter from Christopher to Everett after the age of fifteen that has survived. In it, Christopher copies Everett's eighteen philosophical questions and answers them at length and with passionate earnestness.

It is characteristic of his ambivalence about intimacy that Everett turned to his father for answers to what seem like veiled but intimate questions. Among them: "Must pain spring from pleasure?" "Is bodily love empty or to be forgotten?" and "Can one be happy while others are miserable?" In Christopher's answers, the Unitarian pastor comes to the fore. To Everett's inquiry "Is it possible to be truly unselfish?" Christopher answered, "No, because even Jesus fed his ego: a man who dies for a cause does express himself, achieve his goal, perhaps. God does not ask unselfishness in an absurd sense." As to whether bodily love was "empty," Christopher asserted, "No, it is a part of life. It is not all of life. I do not see that it should ever be outgrown, but it changes form; it begins animal and always remains healthily animal, but it is refined and sublimated."

There is something excruciatingly awkward about this extended colloquy. Everett seems in effect to be asking his father about his parents' sex life. He may even have been seeking permission to have a sex life of his own. Christopher himself was a bit nonplussed by Everett's far-ranging but impersonally phrased probes into the meaning of life. "Now you tell me," he closed the long letter, "where did you get all these mind-twisters anyway?"

Everett wrote back like a dutiful schoolboy—or perhaps schoolmaster: "I was very pleased with your carefully considered replies to my questions, and I think you have answered them well."

By December, in fact, Everett's life had taken what may have been a momentous turn. On the thirteenth of that month, in a letter to Waldo, he alluded to it in a guarded fashion: "I have met some fine, sincere men, and several fine women, and one girl with whom I am intimate."

In 1983, after transcribing this letter in *Vagabond,* Bud Rusho wrote, "This girl was undoubtedly Frances. Who she was or how Everett met her, remains unknown. But for a brief period, at least, romance had entered Everett's life."

Rusho copied five of Everett's letters to Frances, three written in December 1933, two in May 1934. They are unmistakably love letters. On December 14:

> I have just acquired the most heart-rending symphony you
> ever heard. You must come out to my mean hovel Saturday
> night to hear it, for I have to share it with you. In addition,

there are two things I want to read to you, and a new picture I want you to see. Don't refuse, for I must see you, and I have laid in a store of Roquefort cheese as a special inducement. . . . I saw two girls on the streets this morning who reminded me of you.

A second letter, only one line long, is dated simply "Monday Afternoon":

Frances dear,
    Teresine dances tomorrow night at 8:20, so sleep sweetly tonight.
Everett.

And another one-liner on December 19:

To Frances,
    I wish the most blithe and serene Christmas that anyone could wish.
Everett.

From these fragments alone, one must conclude that Everett had fallen in love. Whether he had a brief affair with Frances (if so, probably the only affair of his life), or merely nursed a crush on her, it is impossible to say. Something did not work out, for on May 5, 1934, from an outpost in Arizona, Everett wrote a long letter to Frances in which he voiced a lament:

I was sorry, though, that our intimacy, like many things that are and will be, had to die with a dying fall. I do not greatly mind endings, for my life is made up of them, but sometimes they come too soon or too late, and sometimes they leave a feeling of regret as of an old mistake or an indirect futility.

The whole Frances business is one of the knottiest and most baffling riddles in Everett's life. Sometime since 1983, the five letters to
Frances, like so many other primary documents, have gone missing.
The obvious puzzle, which Rusho did not address in 1983, is why the
texts had survived for half a century in the keeping of the Ruess family, and yet no one knew who Frances was. The letters to Bill Jacobs
survive because Jacobs gave them to the family after Everett's disappearance, as did several other family friends to whom Everett had
written. If Frances too had donated the love letters, then surely Stella
or Christopher or Waldo would have known who she was, or would
at least have known her last name.

When asked in 2008 about the Frances letters, Rusho had no answers. He was not aware that the letters had gone missing, or where
they might be. He could not recall how he had gotten hold of them in
the first place, although he thought it likely that Waldo had lent them
to him. When asked how the family could have gained possession of
the letters without knowing who Frances was, he confessed to his
own complete bafflement.

An extremely bizarre theory was advanced around 2003 by the
filmmaker Diane Orr, who in the 1980s began to work on a movie
about Everett. Orr unfolded the scenario to Nathan E. Thompson,
who was writing a master's thesis about Everett. In Thompson's summary, Orr argued "that Frances, the woman Ruess was supposedly in
love with, was actually the young wife of one of Ruess' father's friends.
The love letters, argued Orr, were merely a cover up for Everett Ruess'
sexuality." Orr further argued that Everett had confessed to Waldo,
and to Waldo alone, his homosexual tendencies.

This summary does not explain how Orr came into her special
knowledge of the situation. Nor does it clarify who would have perpetrated the cover-up—Everett himself, or Christopher and Stella, or
Waldo in later years, presumably to hide evidence that Everett was
homosexual. Given that Orr is convinced that Everett was gay, her

theory of fake love letters to the wife of a friend of Christopher must be taken with a healthy dose of salt. What is more, the five letters to Frances that Rusho published, in all their detail and specificity, sound genuine, not the sort of thing one would concoct as a smokescreen to hide a guilty homosexuality.

In January 1934, Everett continued his philosophical discourse with his father in several long letters. From them emerge the first hints that Christopher and Stella may have started to lose patience with their prodigal son's wayward course in life. On January 2, lashing back at criticisms his father had voiced, Everett wrote, "There is no need for fearing that I will be a 'one-sided' freak artist, to use your phrase, for I am interested almost equally in all the arts and in human relations and reactions as well."

Everett's financial dependence on his parents had apparently started to exasperate them. In a defensive voice, in the first paragraph after pleading for yet another money order, Everett rationalized:

> As to the way I've spent my money, I think it *has* done credit to my emotions, and I don't regret it. On occasion, I have calculated things to a very fine point, but you may well cease hoping that I will ever be practical in the accepted sense. I would sooner die.

In his hyperintellectual way, rather than bluntly accuse his son of being a freeloader, Christopher couched his strictures in a cloak of moral responsibility. "What you say is partly true," Everett wrote his father on January 27, "in your remark that I have done what I wanted in spite of the world crisis." Everett rebutted the accusation obliquely, by mentioning three friends who were involved in the "world crisis," only to deride them: "They have been wallowing in the shallows of life this past year—not growing or having new or enlarging experiences."

His father was not the only one who had leveled this charge against Everett. In an earlier letter to Christopher, Everett recalled:

> A year ago my Communist friends were firing it at me when I told them that beauty and friendship were all I asked of life. I am not unconcerned with the crisis of our civilization, but the way of the agitator, the social leader, and the politician is not my way. . . .
>
> So, instead, during this last year, I have continued to seek beauty and friendship, and I think that I have really brought some beauty and delight into the lives of others, and that is at least something.

Whether or not he grudgingly acknowledged the selfishness of his quest, or the entitlement implied in expecting his parents to foot the bills, Everett knew himself. Beauty and friendship were indeed all that he asked of life. It was a credo he would carry to his untimely grave.

Christopher's most aggressive attack, however, focused on trying to persuade Everett to go back to college—and this brought out in the stubborn son some of the angriest and haughtiest remarks he would ever direct against his parents. "As to this half-baked pother about my always feeling inferior in the presence of college graduates," he wrote to his father on January 2, "that fear is groundless too. I am not nonplussed in the presence of anybody, and I am seldom at a loss with anyone I am interested in."

Christopher had apparently badgered Everett with the monetary rewards a college degree would guarantee for the rest of his life. Again Everett lashed back: "As to the million-dollar endowment of going through the college mill, I have three million dollar endowments already, that I am sure of, and I don't have to go begging. I have my very deep sensitivities to beauty, to music, and to nature."

Everett had clearly been stung by his father's complaints. "You can be ashamed of me if you like," he went on, "but you cannot make me feel ashamed of myself." And: "As for me, I have tasted your cake, and I prefer your unbuttered bread. I don't wish to withdraw from life to college, and I have a notion, conceited or not, that I know what I want from life, and can act upon it."

It is a tesimony to the complexity of Everett's relationship with his father that in a letter filled with such proud and sneering rejoinders, he could write on, lapse back into chatty news, and sign off, as always, "Love from Everett."

By January, Everett was at loose ends. Only nine days after announcing to Waldo the existence of "one girl with whom I am intimate," he wrote to his brother, "After various turnings, twistings, and recoils, I still have not been able to find any proper outlet for my feelings. Perhaps there is none and perhaps it is necessary for my feelings to die of weariness and refusal." This may be a veiled confession that already his liaison with Frances had fallen apart, or it may be only a declaration of the existential despair that always lay just beneath the surface of Everett's flights of transport.

On March 2 he bragged to his family that he had sold a painting and spent four dollars on a ticket on a boat that would soon convey him from San Francisco to Los Angeles. Could one of his parents meet him at the dock with the family car? "I will have a great deal of luggage," he warned them.

Everett spent about a month at home on North Kingsley Drive. During that stay, he celebrated his twentieth birthday. In an undated letter to Waldo, he mused, "These last months in the cities have been very strange; there have been many beautiful moments. . . . [M]y relations with people have been riper, with more complete understanding than before."

Waldo had offered to drive his brother to Arizona. Everett could not wait to get started on another journey across the desert Southwest.

For 1934, he had planned a more ambitious expedition than any of his previous jaunts. Sometime in early April he loaded his belongings into the car of a friend who would drive him east to San Bernardino, where he would rendezvous with Waldo. In the undated letter to Waldo, he had closed, "I look forward to the time when we will be going places, together on the road. You are surely a good brother to me."

His gear packed, in a hurry to leave, Everett said goodbye to his parents. Christopher and Stella would never see him again.

FIVE

"I Have Seen More Beauty Than I Can Bear"

WALDO AND EVERETT ARRIVED IN KAYENTA on April 14. From this small town on the Navajo reservation in northeastern Arizona, Everett had launched his first Southwest expedition three years earlier. And here he had met John Wetherill, who had given him his first tips about backcountry ruins in remote canyons such as the Tsegi Canyon system. Kayenta was far more congenial to Everett's spirit than touristy Roosevelt, where he had been stuck for two months in 1932 as he tried to get his journey under way, while Clark dithered and then lost the heart to join Everett on his rugged trek.

In Kayenta, the brothers went on a couple of short walks, taking photographs of each other that they would trade by mail, before Waldo turned around and started back toward Los Angeles. About a week later, Everett made a deal with a local to buy two new burros. He named them Leopard and Cockleburrs.

Everett kept a diary throughout his 1934 wanderings, but the leather-bound book would eventually disappear with him. A few tantalizing paragraphs from the journal that he transcribed into a letter to a Los Angeles friend survive. If they are characteristic of the kinds of entries he was regularly making, then the 1934 diary was utterly different from the 1933 Sierra Nevada journal, which had been so full of quotidian events, so lacking in deep reflection. The 1934 paragraphs soar into a metaphysical realm.

Once more, as with the 1930 and 1931 excursions, it is chiefly from the letters home that we are able to reconstruct the last seven months of Everett's wandering career. These letters, too, are strikingly different from the ones he mailed to family and friends from the Sierra the previous year. They amount, in fact, to a kind of high-wire act, for as never before, in 1934 Everett strove to match the beauty of the landscape with beautiful, crafted prose. The letters neglect the homely but concrete detail of daily life in favor of transcendent statements of spiritual belief, distilling the hard-won insights he had gleaned from his relentless vagabondage since the age of sixteen.

From Kayenta around the beginning of May, Everett headed north toward Monument Valley. At once he suffered a misadventure not unlike others he had undergone with skittish pack animals in the past. In a "raging gale," riding one burro and leading the other, Everett covered twenty-five miles that day. "The seas of purple loco [weed] bloom were buffeted about by the wind," he wrote to Waldo on May 3, "and the sand blew in riffles across our tracks, obscuring them almost at once."

Ten miles north of Kayenta, Everett passed by the soaring plug of volcanic rock the Navajos call Agathla. Despite the wind and the oncoming night, Everett dismounted to make a painting of the imposing pinnacle. By the time he hit the trail again, aiming for a hogan he had discovered in 1931, in which he hoped to camp, it was almost pitch dark. Now he walked, guiding both animals by their leads. Just as he found a rock cairn that served as a landmark near the hogan, the burros "suddenly bolted into the night."

It was a potential disaster, right at the beginning of the trip. In the darkness Everett ran after the burros "until my lungs were afire." He could hear the thumping noise of saddlebags slapping against the burros' flanks, but he could not find Cockleburrs or Leopard. "I thought of the smashed saddles and broken kyaks," he wrote Waldo, "their contents scattered broadcast, of the crushed camera and the paintings lying in the rain."

In despair, Everett found the faint Monument Valley road and headed back toward Kayenta. Two days after the debacle he wrote,

> I started to walk there to ask help of my Mormon friend, but a mile away, I turned about and went back. It was not that I couldn't stand being laughed at by the whole town, for it really was funny, and such things don't bother me. But it would be asking too much of the Mormon, and anyway, for a long time I had flattered myself that I could "take it," and always had, without complaint, so I thought this was a good time to show myself.

At the time, in the windy night, Everett's predicament was decidedly not funny. Returning to the bend in the road where the burros had bolted, Everett found two saddle blankets snagged in the rocks. With these he approached the hogan, got a fire going inside, and slept fitfully through the rest of the night.

In the morning it started to rain, but with first light he found the burros' tracks. It was not long before he came upon his pack animals. Cockleburrs "was standing stock still, looking very foolish. Leopard was nearby, equally sheepish, his saddle under him, but unhurt." A canteen and Everett's camera were missing, but after half an hour of searching in circles, he found both. All was well, the catastrophe avoided. Everett returned to the hogan, where the fire was still blazing. "I felt perfectly delighted with everything," he insisted to Waldo, "gave the burros an extra ration of oats, hobbled them out, and put on the pot to cook my supper and breakfast."

Just how carefully Everett was now structuring the record of his excursion is revealed in the fact that his account of the mishap near Agathla in the letter to Waldo matches almost word for word another telling of the episode in a letter to a family friend, Emily Ormond, even down to the "purple loco bloom buffeted about by the wind." The letters home, no longer merely news dispatches, had become drafts of chapters in a book he might someday write to share his adventures with the world. In this sense, in 1934 Everett had finally become as ambitious a writer as he already was an artist.

Everett had been in Arizona for only a little more than two weeks when he wrote Waldo on May 3. But he claimed that in that short span, "I had many other thrills when I trusted my life to crumbling sandstone and angles little short of the perpendicular, in the search for waterholes and cliff dwellings. Often I was surprised myself when I came out alive and on top." He repeated the formula almost verbatim to Emily Ormond, but added, in his characteristic perfect tense, a grandiloquent boast that has nonetheless become one of Everett's signature mottos: "I have seen almost more beauty than I can bear."

In 1931 and 1932, in pursuit of cliff dwellings that he hoped no other Anglos had ever visited, Everett had done some bold climbing, but now, in 1934, he pushed the margins of safety to a thinner edge than ever before. In these daring scrambles, there may have been a hint of a suicidal impulse. Everett seems to have realized as much, for in a letter to a Los Angeles friend named Edward Gardner, he declared, "Yesterday I did some miraculous climbing on a nearly vertical cliff, and escaped unscathed, too. One way and another, I have been flirting pretty heavily with Death, the old clown."

If Everett reached and explored Monument Valley during early May, it was during a very brief visit, for by May 5 he was in Chilchinbito, a Navajo outpost sixteen miles southeast of Kayenta. There he made his first new friend of the 1934 outing, a Hispanic trader named José Garcia. To his mother, Everett wrote in praise of the man,

When I came here last night, Jose's kindness and courtesy
almost brought tears to my eyes, for there is something very
fine about him, and I have not met many of his kind in this
country. His father, a wizened old pioneer of the Spaniards,
is here too. They are good, simple people without sophisti-
cation, living happily in this at present untroubled part of
the world. Jose speaks four languages—English, Spanish,
Navajo, and Zuni.

Everett offered to paint a geologic wonder on the western
skyline—a triple tower of dark rock called the Three Fingers—for
Garcia. Lingering about Chilchinbito, he noted "some handsome,
lithe young girls among the Navajos." (An undated photograph survives, in which Everett stands beside a Navajo hogan, next to a handsome native woman holding a baby in a cradle. Everett supplied the
caption: "My Navajo Wife.")
    It was a shock a month later when Everett learned that José Gar-
cia had been killed in an accident. The trader, he wrote Bill Jacobs,
"was riding the load on a truck. A wheel came off, and the whole load
fell on him."
    Out of the blue, its provenance undecipherable, emerges a long
letter to Frances, dated May 5 and written in Chilchinbito. At the
Kayenta post office, Everett had received a letter from Frances with
photographic negatives in it, presumably mailed from San Francisco.
Everett's response begins guardedly enough, as he repeats almost
word for word the encomium on José Garcia that he had written to
his mother. Slowly the letter warms toward the personal. "You should
see the glorious color," he tells Frances, "when the first light of dawn
spreads on the golden clifftops and the grey-blue pinyon-clad slopes."
    The impulse to show the Southwestern landscape to the girl with
whom five months earlier he had fallen in love nudges Everett toward
a reflection on "my life in the cities." He concludes a meandering

paragraph, "I do not know if I shall ever return to the cities again, but I cannot complain that I found them empty of beauty."

In the next sentence, Everett's regret (as quoted in the previous chapter) about the dissolution of his linkage with Frances pours forth: "I was sorry, though, that our intimacy, like many things that are and will be, had to die with a dying fall."

Then Everett resumes his guarded pose, as he tells Frances in abstract terms about his first three weeks in the desert—"a life of strange contrasts," as he labels it. "There has been deep peace, vast calm and fury, strange comradeships and intimacies, and many times my life and all my possessions have tottered on the far side of the balance."

The letter closes with a wistful hint of how much Everett misses Frances:

> But much as I love people, the most important thing to me is still the nearly unbearable beauty of what I see. I won't wish that you could see it, for you might not find it easy to bear either, but yet I do sincerely wish for you at least a little of the impossible.
>
> Love from Everett.

*   *   *

So far as we can trace Everett's wanderings during his first few weeks in 1934, they amount to tame Arizona forays out of a base in Kayenta—the first a simple hike up the road (today's U.S. Highway 160) to Dinnehotso, followed by the jaunt past Agathla toward Monument Valley, then the reconnaisance of Chilchinbito ("bitter water" in Navajo, Everett informed his parents) toward the south.

But Everett had an overriding itinerary in mind, which he outlined in a letter to Waldo on May 3. "Today I am starting for Chin Lee [Chinle], Canyon de Chelly, the Lukachukais, and the Carrizos.

I shall probably be gone a month or two. Chin Lee will be my next post office."

So far as we can tell, Everett carried out his program to the letter, making a loop of 170 miles. He was back in Kayenta by mid-June. Most of the terrain he explored through the rest of May and early June, however, was not new to him. He had had memorable experiences in Canyon de Chelly in both 1931 and 1932, finding the Anasazi necklace the first year, having his horse Jonathan collapse and die the second. In 1932 he had pushed on out of Canyon del Muerto to cross the Lukachukais into New Mexico. Shiprock and Mesa Verde had disappointed Everett, so this time he would not extend his journey to the northeast, but would turn straight north from the crest of the high mesas of the Lukachukais to poke through the neighboring maze of canyons and buttes called the Carrizos—the one part of the loop with which he was unfamilar, and still today one of the most unfrequented regions in all the Southwest.

The whole of that itinerary lay within the Navajo reservation. Despite his ambivalence about Indian character, Everett was determined to learn more about Navajo culture, and to teach himself a serviceable vocabulary of Diné words.

Whether or not Everett was truly bipolar, as some analysts would have us believe, he certainly underwent extreme mood swings over short periods of time. On May 5, the same day that he wrote his plaintive letter to Frances, he dashed off another to Bill Jacobs that is full of exuberance and triumph. "Once more I am roaring drunk with the lust of life and adventure and unbearable beauty," it begins.

The letter marks the first time in more than a year (as far as we know) that Everett had written to his best friend. In it there is no hint of lingering resentment about Jacobs having so often stood Everett up, backing out of journeys together at the last minute. No matter how deep his funks, Everett seems never to have nursed a grudge. His gentle forgiveness of parents who scolded him or friends who let him down forms one of his most endearing qualities.

Yet that letter to Jacobs is oddly impersonal. Everett voices no curiosity about what his pal may be doing back in Los Angeles. Instead he makes an oracular declaration of the quest he has chosen to pursue. And once again, comparing his proud independence to the wretched lives of "suffering, struggling, greedy, grumbling humanity," he strikes a tone of Nietzschean arrogance. One of the least attractive aspects of Everett's five-year swagger across California and the Southwest is the way that, surrounded by the detritus of the Depression, he managed for the most part to ignore the hopelessness and poverty he saw at every hand. And when he did not ignore it, he sometimes railed against the stricken men and women whose paths he crossed as if their blighted dreams and everyday misery were their own fault, the natural outcome of failed imagination and sedentary torpor. All this, while Christopher and Stella were subsidizing his endless ramble.

"I shall always be a rover, I know," Everett announces to Bill in the May 5 letter. "Always I'll be able to scorn the worlds I've known like half-burnt candles when the sun is rising, and sally forth to others now unknown." Everett explodes with joy: "Oh, it's a wild, gay time! Life can be rich to overflowing. I've been so happy that I can't think of containing myself." Yet such flights are counterbalanced by a sense of doom. "Finality does not appall me," he tells Bill, "and I seem always to enjoy things the more intensely because of the certainty that they will not last."

The letter closes with the kind of thundering tonic chord Everett cherished in the symphonies of Beethoven or Tchaikovsky: "Alone I shoulder the sky and hurl my defiance and shout the song of the conqueror to the four winds, earth, sea, sun, moon, and stars. I live!"

Anyone interested in retracing Everett's extraordinary 1934 journey in day-by-day or even week-by-week detail will be disappointed, for the surviving letters float on such a high philosophical plateau that ordinary events and chance encounters get lost in the spiritual ether. And yet, on the basis of seven paragraphs transcribed into a May letter from Canyon de Chelly to his Los Angeles friend Edward Gardner, the diary too may have glossed over daily life to focus on the transcendental.

That letter begins with a modicum of detail. Somewhere near Chinle, Everett swears, "I narrowly escaped being gored to death by a wild bull." The letter is headed simply "May," from "East Fork of Canyon de Chelly." "For five days I have been in this canyon," Everett testifies. "I have not seen an Indian, and it is a week since I saw a white skin." The solitude that he had not seemed to miss in the Sierras the year before had reclaimed him in all its splendor, provoking deep thoughts:

> Strange, sad winds sweep down the canyon, roaring in the firs and the tall pines, swaying their crests. . . . I am over-whelmed by the appalling strangeness and intricacy of the curiously tangled knot of life, and at the way that knot un-winds, making everything clear and inevitable, however un-fortunate or wonderful.

This *pensée* prompts Everett to transcribe the passages from his diary. Since his early teenage years, Everett had striven in his writing to compose aphorisms, one- and two-line gems that nailed strikingly original perceptions. There is always the danger in such utterances of sounding an all-knowing *ex cathedra* note—not a comfortable pose for a college dropout who had just turned twenty.

Yet a selection of excerpts from the diary passages copied for Edward Gardner makes a small anthology of some of Everett's lines that are most often quoted today:

> All accomplished works or deeds perish or are forgotten eventually. No love lives forever, and no two can completely understand one another, or if they do, it kills their love.

For to think is the beginning of death.

Beauty isolated is terrible and unbearable, and the unclouded sight of her kills the beholder.

But he who has looked long on naked beauty may never return to the world.

The absorbing passion of any highly sensitive person is to forget himself, whether by drinking or by agonized love, by furious work or play, or by submerging himself in the creative arts. . . . But the pretense cannot endure, and unless he can find another as highly strung as himself with whom to share the murderous pain of living, he will surely go insane.

In 2000, the historian Gary James Bergera would title an essay that argued that Everett had commit suicide " 'The Murderous Pain of Living': Thoughts on the Death of Everett Ruess."

We have almost no idea what adventures Everett had or what discoveries he made in 1934 in Canyon de Chelly, the Lukachukais, or the Carrizos, for only four letters survive from that more than month-long circuit, and they unfold a relentlessly internal narrative. A two-page letter to his parents from the Lukachukais, however, recounts an idyllic night and following day. This, too, is a calculated performance, as Everett strives to write beautiful prose. Yet there is promise in that prose of the attentive nature writer he might have become. Riding Cockleburrs and leading Leopard, Everett set out at twilight for a moonlit jaunt to a high crest. But a thunderstorm threatened to turn the lark into an ordeal.

For awhile the northerly sky was clear, and stars shone brilliantly thru the pine boughs. Then darkness closed upon us,

only to be rent by livid flashes of lightning, and thunder
that seemed to shake the earth. The wind blew no longer,
and we travelled in an ominous, murky calm, occasionally
shattered by more lightning. Finally the clouds broke, and
rain spattered down as I put on my slicker. We halted under
a tall pine.

The storm blew quickly by, gone within an hour of its arrival. The
rain stopped, the stars came out again, and Everett resumed his ride.
"By moonlight we climbed to the rim of the mountain, and looked
over vast silent stretches of desert. Thirty miles away was the dim
hulk of Shiprock—a ghostly galleon in a sea of sand."

The next day, in glorious sunshine, Everett lounged in a meadow
and wrote the letter:

Flowers nod in the breeze, and wild ducks are honking on
the lake. I have just been for a long, leisurely ride on Leopard, skirting the edge of the mountain, riding thru thick-
ets of rustling aspen, past dark mysterious lakes, quiet and
lonely in the afternoon silence.

None of Everett's nature writing the previous year, in either his letters or his diaries, matches the pastoral lyricism of these passages. But
in the Sierras, Everett had not once found himself ensconced in such
trailless wilderness as the Lukachukais offered in abundance, nor had
he been able for days at a time to luxuriate in true solitude.

At the small town of Lukachukai, just west of the aspen- and
pine-thick forests rising toward the New Mexico border, Everett had
picked up a batch of mail, including, to his surprise, another letter
from Frances. Camped alone in a high meadow a few days later, he
wrote a long epistle in response. "It shocked me slightly," he confessed, "when you spoke of my greed for life. That is a harsh word,

but I guess it is true. I am not willing to take anything but the most from life." In defense of that greed, Everett quoted a *memento mori* from FitzGerald's *Rubaiyat:* "You know how little while we have to stay, / And, once departed, may return no more."

Everett was evidently more than slightly shocked by Frances's stricture, for he devoted another long paragraph to justifying why "I . . . don't like to let opportunities for living slip by ungrasped." From this declaration emerges a complaint:

> There are too many uninteresting people—like the trader at Lukachukai. He certainly made me feel like hitting him. He is a typical moron, only interested in food, business, and home. I was telling him about Canyon de Chelly and del Muerto, and with no provocation he remarked that he had lived here a long time and had never been to them and never expected or intended to. Obviously his decision was right for a person like him, because wherever he might go, he would see nothing beautiful or interesting.

Sadly, in the 1934 letters there are all too few such vignettes of Everett's doings on the trail or in the outposts where he resupplied. With his rationale for his "greed for life" off his chest, Everett lapsed into fine nature writing, as he replayed the moonlight ride through the thunderstorm, adding further details. The subtext of these paragraphs is a defiant claim: "I'm doing fine out here all by myself." But love broke through Everett's defenses. "I enjoyed your letter," he interrupts himself, "and I know I did not mistake myself when first I liked you. We did have some moments of beauty together, didn't we?"

And with that, Frances vanishes from the chronicle of Everett's life, slipping away as evanescently as she had suddenly appeared the previous December to disturb him with giddy hope, followed by wistful regret.

From the 1934 journey, a few pages have survived that seem not to have been parts of letters addressed to anyone, but instead resemble set pieces of nature philosophy. Most of them are undated, but they may well have been composed during his month-long loop through the Lukachukais. One recounts a stormy night on a high crest, ending, "Then in wild, whirling fury, the storm rises, boiling and seething until with a furious upward rush, the whole horizon is submerged, and it fills the air with swirling, stinging, blinding snow. With this black dawn I perish."

Another, dated simply "May," announces, "I am drunk with a searing intoxication that liquor could never bring—drunk with the fiery elixir of beauty. . . ." But that intoxication by nature comes at a price: "I am condemned to feel the withering fire of beauty pouring into me. I am condemned to the need of putting this fire outside myself and spreading it somewhere, somehow, and I am torn by the knowledge that what I have felt cannot be given to another."

Whenever Everett tried most earnestly to express the rapture that solitude in the wilderness brought him, he tended to lapse into melodrama. Beneath the passion pulses a vein of self-pity, as he casts himself as a martyr to his own obsession. But this is the writing of a twenty-year-old. Other passages prove that along with a weakness for the grandiose, Everett had a sense of humor, and could poke fun at himself in an ironic mode. Had he lived longer, the melodrama might well have been tempered by wisdom. There was indeed the potential for a John Muir in Everett Ruess, a nature and adventure writer who could at once sing the glory of the natural world and yet keep a sense of proportion about the limits of human endeavor in the wilderness.

Beauty and friendship remained the twin goals of Everett's quest. But the short-lived liaison with Frances seems to have convinced him that he could not have both. And if he had to choose, he would choose beauty.

* * *

Back in Kayenta in mid-June, Everett retrieved another batch of mail as he planned the next leg of his open-ended journey. On June 19 he wrote to his parents, "I am on my way to Navajo Mountain now, and probably will not get back until July or August."

Rising to a summit of 10,388 feet just north of the Arizona-Utah border, Navajo Mountain has long been a sacred location for the Diné. It stands, moreover, in what is still today one of the most remote regions of the Southwest. The sharp, twisting canyons that crease the mountain's western and northern flanks are among the ruggedest in the United States. Near the mouth of one of those tributaries of the Colorado River, hidden in a bend of sandstone, looms Rainbow Bridge, the largest natural geological span in the world.

In previous years, the closest Everett had come to Navajo Mountain was during his solitary prowl through the Tsegi system in 1931. At the ruin of Keet Seel, the largest cliff dwelling in Arizona, Everett had camped only twenty-five miles southeast of the mountain. On other treks across northern Arizona, he had often seen Navajo Mountain in the distance, for it is one of the lordliest landmarks in the Four Corners region.

John Wetherill, the Kayenta trader, would have told Everett all about Navajo Mountain and Rainbow Bridge. In 1909, Wetherill had guided the first party of Anglos to discover the great arch (though some historians dispute this claim). After that, he built the Bridge Trail traversing the northern slopes of Navajo Mountain, one of the most cunning horse-packing routes in the country, which traverses miles of slickrock slabs. Wetherill then guided scores of tourists along the trail to Rainbow Bridge, among them Teddy Roosevelt and Zane Grey. And in 1922, guiding the Bernheimer Expedition, he blazed another trail to the bridge that linked soaring defiles on the southern and western sides of the mountain, solving the crux passage through Redbud Pass with dynamite.

The route by which Everett planned to approach Navajo Mountain was a challenging one, as he intended to pass once more through Monument Valley, then proceed straight north almost to the San Juan River, where he would turn to the west and cross lofty and seldom-visited No Mans Mesa before arriving at the lower slopes of the sacred mountain. Then, instead of riding one of Wetherill's trails, Everett planned to find his own way over a high shoulder of Navajo Mountain before winding down toward Rainbow Bridge.

Never in any of his four previous excursions through California and the Southwest had Everett tackled wilderness quite this remote or difficult. By now, however, "I flattered myself that I could 'take it,' " as he had written to Waldo in early May.

Before leaving Kayenta, on June 17 Everett wrote a long letter to Bill Jacobs. That piece of writing offers some of the most revealing insights into Everett's state of mind during his 1934 expedition. Annoyance about his friend's having backed out of so many trips that Everett had proposed lingers about the opening paragraphs, as he teases Bill, "Do you know, it is in a way rather sad that you cannot have had some of my wild experiences, for you have the desire to use such things, and I do not. Perhaps it is your craving for material security."

Bill himself was evidently an ambitious writer, for Everett further taunts his friend, "I have no desire to bend my efforts to entertaining the bored and blase world. And that's what writing amounts to—or at least your kind, I think. Your stories, if polished and published, would serve to divert various morons and business people."

For Everett, this was an uncharacteristically blunt remark. As if to excuse his peevishness, he went on, "I hope this gets you down, for I feel like puncturing the stupid satisfaction and silly aspirations of the world this morning."

In his disdain for common humanity, for Thoreau's "mass of men lead[ing] lives of quiet desperation," Everett often veered toward the misanthropic. In June 1934, if the letter to Bill Jacobs is any indication, Everett's mood reached a new nadir of antisocial contempt. "Often, alone in an endless open desert, I find it hard to believe that the rest of the world exists," he confessed. And, "Personally I have no least desire for fame. I feel only a stir of distaste when I think of being called 'the well known author' or 'the great artist.' " This comment marks the first time in the surviving 1934 letters that Everett ponders the career that, despite his protestations, he had been aiming at for more than four years—that of the wandering artist supporting himself by selling his work. Perhaps the effort to launch that career via studios and galleries in San Francisco had so discouraged him that he felt he had to turn his back on hopes of fame or recognition.

The same letter rails against the Anglo settlers of the small towns Everett had passed through. "It has come to the point," he swore, "where I no longer like to have anything to do with the white people here, except to get supplies and go on." Traders, in Everett's view, were the worst: "Behind bars in their dirty, dingy, ill-lighted trading posts, they think of nothing but money." Everett had recently bought a Navajo bracelet made of three turquoise stones set in silver. He claimed that he had spent "all my money" on the piece of jewelry "and was broke most of the while since." During the next several months, the bracelet became Everett's favorite personal adornment. He never failed to marvel how the stones reflected the glimmer of a campfire or caught the rays of the sun. "But one of my trader friends," he complained to Bill, "asked as soon as he saw it, 'How much did it cost?' "

In this remarkable, far-ranging letter, Everett made a kinder assessment of Navajos than of white settlers.

> I have often stayed with the Navajos; I've known the best of them, and they were fine people. I have ridden with them on their horses, eaten with them, and even taken part in their

ceremonies. . . . They have many faults; most of them are not very clean, and they will steal anything from a stranger, but never if you approach them with trust as a friend. Their weird, wild chanting as they ride the desert is often magnificent, with a high-pitched, penetrating quality.

Having proclaimed his disdain for fame, Everett abruptly announces, "Beauty has always been my god." Like so many of the utterances in the 1934 letters, this is not news shared with a friend (Bill well knew how Everett felt about beauty), but a declaration for eternity. And so it has served, for that line is one of the most oft-quoted sentences that Everett ever wrote.

It is characteristic, however, that in the same letter Everett climbs down from his lectern in the clouds to chat with his old friend: "Did you get *The Purple Land*?" he asks. "This trip has been longer than I expected. I have wandered over more than 400 miles with the burros these last six weeks, paying no attention to trails, except as they happened to serve me, and finding my water as I went." The mileage total may be a slight exaggeration, but Everett's sense of mastery was well earned. Despite the bad start when his burros got loose near Agathla, by 1934 Everett had come into his own as a wanderer.

He was still, nevertheless, tied to his parents' generous handouts. On June 19, he wrote to thank them for their latest package, which included a bridle, several magazines, and some dried plums: "I had never tasted them before." Everett goes on to place his next order with Christopher and Stella:

There are a couple of things I wish you would send me; *Don Quixote,* a Modern Library book which you can get for 95 cents, and eight of those half-pound chocolate bars which you can get downtown for eight or nine cents each. Get half of them plain, and half with raisins and peanuts.

Despite his contempt for the residents of Kayenta, during his brief stop there in June, Everett made the acquaintance of several young men who would furnish one of the highlights of Everett's 1934 excursion. "There is an archaeological expedition in town now," he wrote Bill Jacobs. "Some pretty likeable and intelligent young fellows are in it, and I expect to visit their camp when I come back from the mountains."

From Everett's daring cross-country jaunt toward Rainbow Bridge, only two letters and a fragment of a third survive. The traverse of No Mans Mesa nearly turned disastrous. A high, elongated butte stretching from north to south, it is guarded on all sides by rimrock cliffs. No trail leads to the top. In late June, Everett led his burros down Copper Canyon, a tributary of the San Juan that runs the length of the east side of the butte, then veered westward to tackle steep slopes soaring more than two thousand feet toward the mesa top. Somehow Everett found a break in the cliffs, but, as he wrote Bill Jacobs a few days later,

> Near the rim it was just a scramble, and Leopard, whom I was packing, in attempting to claw his way over a steep place, lost his balance and fell over backwards. He turned two backward somersaults and a side roll, landing with his feet waving, about six inches from the yawning gulf. I pulled him to his feet. He was a bit groggy at first; he had lost a little fur, and the pack was scratched.

To reach Navajo Mountain, Everett now had to find a way off the west side of No Mans Mesa, then cover twenty-five trailless miles across two more mesas separated by the deep ravines of Nokai and Piute Canyons. This was country almost never traveled by Anglos, inhabited only by a scattering of Navajos and a handful of San Juan Paiutes—the latter people belonging to one of the most marginalized

Native American tribes in the United States. Of this adventure, Everett wrote not a word.

On June 29 he was camped at War God Spring, 8,700 feet up the southeast flank of Navajo Mountain. There he wrote another long letter to Bill Jacobs, containing another rich outpouring of joy. It had not rained in a month, so he had had to search long and hard for water holes, but, he boasted, he and his burros had never gone more than two days without water. It was now high summer. The brown desert in the distance that Everett gazed upon from his lofty perch scorched in the sun, but the glade in which he sat to write his letter was idyllic.

> The beauty of this place is perfect of its kind; I could ask for nothing more. A little spring trickles down under aspens and white fir. By day the marshy hollow is aswarm with gorgeous butterflies. . . . There are a hundred delightful places to sit and dream; friendly rocks to lean against—springy beds of pine needles to lie on and look up at the sky or the tall smooth tree trunks, with spirals of branches and their tufted foliage.

So transported was Everett by this perfect campsite that he waxed lyrical about how much he loved his burros "when they stand up to their knees in wildflowers with blossoms in their lips and look at me with their lustrous, large brown eyes."

His afternoon delight nudged Everett to another Nietzschean pronouncement, in which he couched a further reproof to Jacobs for his unwillingness to stray far from his Los Angeles home:

> The perfection of this place is one reason why I distrust ever returning to the cities. Here I wander in beauty and perfection. There one walks in the midst of ugliness and mistakes. . . .

Here I take my belongings with me. The picturesque gear
of packing, and my gorgeous Navajo saddle blankets make
a place of my own. But when I go, I leave no trace.

Yet the fleeting joy Everett found on Navajo Mountain, he was
increasingly convinced, depended not only on solitude, but on his dif-
ferentness from other people, on the "freakish person" he had confessed himself to be to Bill Jacobs back in 1931. Now he wrote Bill, "I
have some good friends here [i.e., in and around Kayenta], but no one
who really understands why I am here or what I do. I don't know of
anyone, though, who would have more than a partial understanding.
I have gone too far alone."

War God Spring lies on an old trail that leads to the summit of Navajo Mountain. To get from that camp to Rainbow Bridge, Everett had
to traverse a high, trailless forest toward the west and descend 2,500
feet in rugged Horse Canyon to intersect the trail around the mountain
that John Wetherill had blazed in 1922. That was a considerable bush-
whack, but not one Everett bothered to mention in his letters.

The next day at sunset, he wrote a letter to his parents, locating
his camp as "a day's journey from Rainbow Bridge." Awed by the
landscape opening before him, he tried to describe it to his parents:

> [T]he country between here and the San Juan and Colorado
> rivers and beyond them is as rough and impenetrable a terri-
> tory as I have ever seen. Thousands of domes and towers of
> sandstone lift their rounded pink tops from blue and purple
> shadows. To the east, great canyons seam the desert, cutting
> vermilion gashes through the gray-green of the sage-topped
> mesas.

A single line in an August 19 letter to Waldo records Everett's at-
tainment of the goal of this jaunt through true wilderness: "When I

walked to Rainbow Bridge at night I found a six-inch scorpion beside my bed at dawn." Yet Everett never described the colossal arch in his letters, at least in the ones that have survived.

A curious side of Everett's nature worship is that truly grand landscapes left him inarticulate. In Yosemite in both 1930 and 1933, he scarcely mentioned the colossal granite monoliths such as El Capitan. Although he climbed Half Dome, he barely described the ascent in his diary. In the Grand Canyon in 1931, his eye was not on towering buttes and plunging gorges, but on damselflies flitting through the air just above his head as he lay on his back on the bank of the Colorado River. Perhaps the monumental sweep of Rainbow Bridge left him comparably speechless. The "friendly rocks to lean against" and "springy beds of pine needles to lie on" at War God Spring were more congenial to his temperament.

By the end of the first week of July, Everett was back in Kayenta. There he caught up with the archaeological team whose members he had first met and liked three weeks earlier. Rather than simply visit their camp, he persuaded the men to hire him on as a cook and packer.

Everett had had a fascination for the prehistoric past ever since childhood, telling his father at age thirteen that he was deliberating between a career as an archaeologist and one as a naturalist. So far, however, his curiosity had mainly taken the form of pocketing artifacts he found in Indian ruins. Now, for the first time, however briefly, Everett would see what professional archaeology was all about, as he participated in an excavation at as remote and eerie an Anasazi site as his fondest wishes could have fixed upon.

* * *

The team outfitting in Kayenta was part of a massive, multi-year project called the Rainbow Bridge–Monument Valley Expedition. Between 1933 and 1938, researchers undertook an extensive survey of Anasazi ruins ranging (as the title indicates) from Monument Valley through the Tsegi Canyon system, and across the Rainbow Plateau to Rainbow Bridge—all in country that was part of the Navajo reservation. The rationale for the project, run by the National Park Service, was to lay the groundwork for a new national park encompassing those scenic and cultural wonders. Had such a park come into existence, it would have torn out of the reservation some three thousand square miles, or about one-eighth of its total area.

Most aficionados of the backcountry Southwest are heartily glad such a park never got established. Instead, today a tiny square around Rainbow Bridge constitutes Rainbow Bridge National Monument, while three more minuscule squares covering the stunning ruins of Keet Seel, Betatakin, and Inscription House add up to Navajo National Monument. Monument Valley is a Navajo Tribal Park. And the convoluted Tsegi system (minus Keet Seel and Betatakin), the whole of the Rainbow Plateau (across part of which Everett had traveled from No Mans Mesa to War God Spring), and all of Navajo Mountain remain reservation land. For the most part, the magnificent country that the NPS had its eye on in the 1930s remains pristine wilderness.

The director of the RB-MV Expedition (as it is usually abbreviated), was Ansel Hall, a Park Service archaeologist based in Berkeley, California. In Kayenta, Everett had noted, a number of the "likeable young fellows" on the team were UC Berkeley students, who had friends in common with Everett. During its far-ranging six-year study, the RB-MV project surveyed hundreds of remote and mysterious sites. What was more, the teams also spent weeks excavating some of the more interesting sites.

The team that Everett signed on with was led by Lyndon Hargrave, then thirty-eight years old, the field director of the Museum of Northern Arizona in Flagstaff, one of the leading research facilities in the Southwest. But the leader in the field, and the man who hired Everett, was H. Claiborne ("Clay") Lockett. In a letter to his parents, Everett described Lockett as "a grizzled young chap of 28, widely experienced, and a magnificent humorist. He is an ethnologist and something of an artist as well." Also on the team, serving chiefly as a guide, was Ben Wetherill, John's son. As a teenager, Ben had lost an eye when he was kicked in the head by a horse, but he would go on to shape a career as a wilderness guide almost as remarkable as his father's. Given to depression and dark moods, Ben had a loner's disposition the equal of Everett's at his most melancholy.

In July 1934, Lockett's team had returned to Kayenta from the Tsegi Canyon system to resupply before tackling a remote cliff site they had discovered earlier in the summer. In Dowozhiebito Canyon, six hundred feet above a well-known Anasazi ruin called Twin Caves Pueblo, just beneath the rim of Skeleton Mesa, the team had found a Basketmaker burial cave. (The Basketmakers were the phase of Anasazi before AD 750, who built not masoned roomblocks such as their descendants specialized in, but underground pithouses and slab-lined storage cists.) "Its discovery," as Lockett later wrote of the new ruin, "was the result of a Sunday climb by some of the more daring members of the Expedition who worked out two routes up the cliff to the cave. The more hazardous parts of both routes were found to have hand- and toeholds pecked into the cliff, evidence that the trails were used in prehistoric times."

Hand-and-toe trails carved with pounding stones into the surface of sheer cliffs, or "Moqui steps," as the cowboys called them, were an Anasazi staple—treacherous shortcuts to high places that the ancients seem to have used blithely for commuter runs. The trails are especially numerous (and terrifying) in the Tsegi system. But this was the kind of sport that Everett reveled in: the "crumbling sandstone and nearly vertical angles" to which he boasted of trusting his life again and again comprised many a scary Anasazi hand-and-toe trail.

The team eventually named the new site Woodchuck Cave, after they found woodchuck bones in a pair of cists, "probably," Lockett wrote, "the first record of this mammal in Arizona." The official report on the excavation was not published until 1953, or nineteen years after the dig. In it, Lockett (and Hargrave, his nominal coauthor) fail to mention Everett's participation in the expedition, omitting his name from the list of personnel.

Everett, however, was enthralled by the more than two weeks he spent with the team, as he absorbed a crash course in Anasazi prehistory. "We have been in the cave for four days now," he wrote to his parents on July 22.

> There is a very precarious way down the face of the cliff with footholds in the stone hundreds of years old. The only other way is the horse ladder, six miles up the canyon. We came that way with pack burros, passing the carcass of a horse that slipped. After two days of wandering on the mesa top, in the trackless forests, we crossed the bare rock ledges in a heavy cloudburst and came here.

Several photos survive showing a shirtless Clay Lockett and Everett tugging the burros up the horse ladder. They rank among the finest pictures known of Everett in action in the wilderness. The photographer was apparently another member of the team.

Woodchuck Cave was not, on the face of it, a prepossessing site. The small, low-roofed alcove enclosed not a single habitation structure, but only some fifteen slab-lined cists sunk in the earthen floor. It was the contents of those cists that proved astounding and perplexing. Along with animal bones, pieces of woven baskets, yucca sandals, and a few other artifacts, including wooden dice, the team discovered the whole or partial remains of twenty human beings, seven of them infants. These included not only skeletons but naturally mummified bodies. The burials were identified as belonging to the Basketmaker II period, dating between 1200 BC and AD 500. Everett reported that Lockett dated the cave around AD 500, but the 1953 monograph fixes the date as AD 200, plus or minus one hundred years.

Nearly all the bodies had been placed in classic Anasazi burial positions, lying on their backs or sides with knees flexed upward in front of the chest. What stunned the researchers, however, was the discovery that all of the adults had been beheaded. All the skulls were missing, and only four partial mandibles could be found.

In their 1953 report, Lockett and Hargrave did not speculate what the grisly beheading might have signified, except to say that it looked as though later pillagers had ransacked the graves not for jewelry but for the bones themselves. (Along with the skulls, many long leg bones were missing.)

No further excavation of Woodchuck Cave has ever been undertaken, and during the last seven decades it is unlikely that more than a small handful of hikers, if any, have ever found their way into the inaccessible burial chamber.

Digging up dead people didn't bother Everett at all. During his weeks of cooking for the team, as he was paid only in free meals, he got along famously with the crew. "We have great fun up here by ourselves," he wrote his parents, "discovering something new every day, and looking out over everything from our sheltered cave." He retained an admiration for Clay Lockett.

That feeling, evidently, was not reciprocated. Lockett would drift away from field archaeology, the Woodchuck Cave bulletin his only serious publication. He served briefly as director of the Arizona State Museum, then for a longer time was in charge of the gift shop at the Museum of Northern Arizona. He died in 1984. His obituary identified him as an "Indian trader, lecturer, and authority on Southwestern Indian arts."

Two years before Lockett's death, in 1982, researching *A Vagabond for Beauty,* Bud Rusho interviewed the man, then seventy-six years old. Lockett's recollections of Everett were consistently unflattering. In Rusho's paraphrase,

Everett did not impress Lockett with his interest in archaeology, for Ruess spent most of his free time, which was considerable, in gazing out over the landscape. Lockett noticed also that Everett seemed careless about his safety when climbing around cliffs, citing as an example the time Everett wanted to make a watercolor sketch of rain-spawned waterfalls shooting off from several points. According to Lockett, Everett nearly got himself killed finding a vantage point on the wet slickrock. Needless to say, the rain-streaked watercolor sketch was not one of his better efforts.

Lockett is also the sole source for the tradition that John Wetherill was put off by the young vagabond. Again in Rusho's paraphrase, "[I]t has been reported that Wetherill had little respect for Everett, whom he considered a 'pest' who would simply hang around [the trading post] for days seeking information and conversation, but who would buy nothing."

Given that in 1935 Wetherill put considerable effort into guiding searchers as to where to look for the lost wanderer, this judgment seems dubious. Lockett was, as Everett had noted, "something of an artist." He may even have been envious of the twenty-year-old camp cook's talent as a painter.

By the end of the RB-MV dig, in early August, Everett had been in the Southwest for four months. But his 1934 journey was just getting started. From the Tsegi he decided to head south across Black Mesa to visit the Hopi villages, where he had stopped briefly on the way to the Grand Canyon in June 1931.

On that first visit, Everett had not been impressed by the Hopi villages atop the three parallel mesas facing south. All he wrote home about Hotevilla and Oraibi was a complaint about heat and dust, and ancient Walpi, with its incongruous mix of stonemasoned houses and fences made of old bedsteads, had seemed "rather a disillusionment." But in the succeeding three years, Everett had matured as a connoisseur of Native American cultures. His encounter with the Hopi in 1934 would prove far more consequential, both for himself and for the hosts who welcomed him into their villages.

In August, Everett had learned, the Hopi performed their rain dances. By the 1930s a small number of Anglo cognoscenti made journeys to attend these sacred rituals, marveling at the gaudy and esoteric panoramas that unfurled in the courtyards of old villages. And during that era, the Hopi themselves were far more welcoming to outsiders than they are today (most of the sacred dances are now closed to Anglo spectators).

Everett did not write home again until August 25. The day before, he had watched the Snake Dance in Hotevilla, a village on the Third Mesa that had been founded in 1907 by a group of natives who had seceded from Oraibi, resolving a religious schism that had threatened to tear apart what is often called the oldest continuously inhabited settlement in the United States. Hotevilla was thus one of the more "progressive" Hopi towns, in which Everett seemed to have been openly accepted as a guest. "I have been having great fun with the Hopis here," he wrote his parents, "and just finished a painting of the village. The children were clustered all around me, some helping and some hindering."

A week later, in the Hopi village of Mishongnovi on the Second Mesa, Everett not only watched but participated in the Antelope Dance. This was a singular honor for a white visitor, but Everett seems to have taken the privilege almost for granted. "[M]y Hopi friends painted me up and had me in their Antelope Dance," he wrote his parents on September 10. "I was the only white person there." In the next breath, he added, "Killed two rattlers the other day. One struck before I saw him. I caught the other alive. Sold a print yesterday."

As these passages indicate, by this point at the end of summer,

Everett's letters home had grown short and laconic. It was as if he was so caught up in the ceaseless novelty of his adventure that he had little energy or time left to craft the fine writing, the evocations of natural beauty, that he had poured into his correspondence earlier during the journey. At the same time, Everett was growing more independent of his family than ever. It would not be until November that he again made the effort to share his deepest thoughts with Waldo, Christopher, and Stella.

On September 9, Everett arrived at Desert View, the tourist center on the South Rim of the Grand Canyon. A few days before, descending a steep trail into the canyon of the Little Colorado River, he had suffered a mishap that could have spelled the end of his 1934 expedition. Two years before, when his packhorse Jonathan collapsed and died near the head of Canyon del Muerto, Everett had recorded the tragedy in vivid emotional detail in his diary, and also in a letter to Bill Jacobs. It may be that Everett's 1934 diary contained an equally vivid account of the disaster in the Little Colorado. But the only record of it that survives is a single, understated line in a letter to his parents: "Lost a burro (Leopard) down Little Colorado Canyon the other day, with some of the pack, but have already replaced him with a bigger burro."

The new pack animal, which Everett bought from a Navajo woman for nine dollars, he first named Chocolate (presumably for his coloring), later modified to Chocolatero. "He is young, strong, and good natured," he wrote to his mother, "inexperienced, but bound to learn from his experienced comrade."

Thanks to the scarcity of surviving letters, we have no idea what Everett accomplished in the Grand Canyon between the end of August and the middle of October, when he finally pushed on north toward Utah. The only episode he narrates was a visit to Clay Lockett in Flagstaff. Apparently the twenty-eight-year-old archaeologist and his twenty-year-old camp cook were still on good terms, for Lockett had invited Everett to stay at his house. South of Flagstaff, Everett wandered up and down the sinuous bends of Oak Creek Canyon, which inspired him to pull out his watercolor kit. "In Oak Creek Canyon I painted a couple of striking effects of brilliantly lighted buttes against inky storm skies," he wrote his mother sometime in September. "Also a massive tower, calmly beautiful under shadowing clouds."

In 1982, Lockett recalled Everett's visit in ambivalent terms. In Bud Rusho's paraphrase,

> Clay Lockett's income, in 1934, was only about $30 a month, supplemented by his garden and a few chickens. Everett's big appetite was not welcomed, especially by Lockett's wife, Florence, who informed her husband, half in jest, after a week of having Everett as a guest, "Either he leaves or I do!" Lockett then tactfully suggested to Everett that he visit Oak Creek Canyon—immediately.

Yet the archaeologist and his wife were surprised when, on his return from Oak Creek, Everett gave each of them a book.

> Lockett concluded that Everett was not trying to take advantage of them but was simply a "free spirit," who did not worry about the complexities of social behavior, and who simply "loved the Navajos and everybody, loved animals, burros, dogs, kids, and everything." Everett himself, says Lockett, was a "strange kid."

Back at Desert View on the South Rim in late September, Everett was surprised to find a letter from Ned Frisius, one of the two Hollywood High School boys with whom he had climbed Mount Whitney the previous summer. The letter Everett wrote in response on September 27 has survived, no doubt a gift from Frisius to the family after Everett disappeared. In it the vagabond recounts a strange episode in his 1934 travels that is preserved in no other document—nor can we guess where or at what point during the previous six months the episode occurred.

> Evidently you overheard something of my adventures with my friends the Indians. I have a great time with them, especially the Navajos. I once spent three days far up in a desert canyon, assisting and watching a Navajo sing for a sick woman. I drove away countless hordes of evil spirits, but after I went away the girl died. The sand paintings, seldom seen by white men, were gorgeous.

There is no evidence that Everett ever made up imaginary adventures to regale his friends and family with. He may have exaggerated here and there, but he had no trace of the liar about him, or even of the spinner of tall tales. Yet this Navajo scenario is so unusual that it must bespeak a profound trust that Everett had won from natives somewhere in Arizona. For a traditional family—and any Navajos living "far up in a desert canyon" were traditional—to let an Anglo see the sand paintings that a medicine man would have composed on the ground, and then effaced shortly after they were finished, would have been extraordinary. And to let that Anglo not only attend but participate in a sing intended to cure a fatally ill woman would have been even more extraordinary.

From a few summary judgments in Everett's letters written between August and November, we can be certain that the adventures he underwent were dramatic and even dangerous. To Waldo on August 19, he wrote, "I have seen more wild country than on any previous trip. I almost lost one burro in the quicksands—he was in up to his neck. . . ." To Ned Frisius on September 27, "In my wanderings this year I have taken more chances and had more and wilder adventures than ever before. And what magnificent country I have seen."

Maddeningly, though, we have almost no idea what the actual content of those "wild adventures" was. No doubt Everett spelled them out in rich detail in the pages of his diary. But the diary is forever lost.

We cannot even be sure of Everett's itinerary after he left the Grand Canyon in mid-October. In *Vagabond,* Rusho guesses at it, surmising that Everett traveled north along the route of today's U.S. Highway 89, crossed the suspension bridge over the Colorado River at Navajo Bridge, then traversed the Kaibab Plateau into Utah as he made his way to Bryce Canyon National Park. An October 15 letter to his mother lists his next post office as Ruby's Inn, Utah—the nearest lodging to Bryce, just west of its western gateway.

During these weeks of travel, Everett had begun to taste a little success as a commercial artist. Able at last to envision real independence from the financial support of his parents, he proudly tried to push aside the stipends Christopher and Stella unfailingly mailed to their wandering son. Sometime in September, from Flagstaff, Everett wrote to his mother, "I've sold a number of pictures lately, and you won't have to worry about me much longer. In fact you can discontinue m.o.'s [money orders] any time you want to. I received the one for 15 early this month, but nothing since." And then on October 1, to both parents, almost in annoyance, "Evidently you didn't have my last letter. I don't want you to send any more money, as I can get along alright and you really need it. I have twelve dollars due me for a picture I made a while ago."

It was not only his parents' money Everett was pushing away—it was his parents themselves. The glum conclusion he had come to in May, that "I am torn by the knowledge that what I have felt cannot be given to another," that if he had to choose between beauty and friendship he would choose beauty, now had the ring in his ears of triumphant freedom. The solitary wandering artist had at last come into his own. And there is no indication in any of the 1934 letters that Everett envisioned an end to his present expedition.

We know that Everett reached Bryce Canyon and spent time there, for he befriended the chief ranger, Maurice Cope. But as early as August 19, in his letter to Waldo from Kayenta, Everett had imagined a journey stretching beyond Bryce into yet another wilderness that was unknown to him: "My plans are not definite, but I think I shall go to the Grand Canyon from the Hopi country, and maybe spend the winter exploring around Thunder River or the Kaiparowitz [sic] Plateau and Straight Cliffs."

The Thunder River is a short, steep, spectacular canyon tributary to the Colorado on the north side of the Grand Canyon. It is unlikely that Everett ever made his way into it. But when he was last seen by anyone, in November 1934, he was leading his burros southeast along the Hole-in-the-Rock Trail, with the massive Straight Cliffs looming above him on the right as they soared toward the summit of Kaiparowits Plateau.

*   *   *

The last three letters Everett sent home diverge abruptly from the laconic shorthand of his previous efforts. The first, to his parents, was written on November 4 from the Mormon town of Tropic, the first settlement south of Bryce. Maurice Cope, the head ranger, himself a Mormon, had invited Everett to stay for a few days at his home in Tropic, with his wife and nine children. The mood of the letter is ebullient, as Everett admits to having "great fun" with the locals. "This morning I rode out with one of the boys to look for a cow," he elaborates. "We rode all over the hills, and stopped at an orchard to load up with apples. Then I went to church, my first time in a Mormon church. It was an interesting experience."

In a postscipt, Everett revels in "more fun—apple fights, church, and until about morning we amused ourselves with some Navajos who were camped nearby." For his parents, Everett conjured up the beauty of the "grotesque and colorful formations" through which he had ridden on his way south from Bryce, in a way that he had not bothered to in months. "Mother would surely enjoy the trees," he wrote; "they are fascinating, especially the twisted little pines and junipers. I had never seen the foxtail pine before."

He had sold a couple of pictures to an eccentric hermit, Everett reported. With the letter, he also sent home a painting he had made of several houses in the Hopi village of Oraibi.

After Everett's disappearance, some of the searchers held out hope that if they failed to find the young man, they might at least discover the camera he had carried with him throughout his 1934 journey. Developing the last pictures Everett had taken might furnish clues to his fate. But in the November 4 letter, he had dashed such hopes: "I sent back the kodak because it has not been working well and is an extra expense and weight." (The letter was published in *On Desert Trails* in 1940, but with this key sentence omitted. The full text was not published until 1983, in Rusho's *A Vagabond for Beauty*.)

Much as he enjoyed the Copes' hospitality and the social life of Tropic, Everett was eager to push on. With the ranger he discussed in detail his plan to pass through the town of Escalante, thirty-eight miles east of Tropic, then push on down the lonely Hole-in-the-Rock Trail toward the Colorado River. To his parents, he explained, "The weather has been delightful, although I was in one snow flurry on the Paunsagunt Plateau [west of Bryce]. Now I am heading across the pink cliffs toward Escalante and the lower country toward the river."

The logical route would have taken Everett from Tropic along the valley bottom of the Paria River, through the tiny Mormon towns of Cannonville and Henrieville, then northeast over a low divide to the headwaters of the Escalante. Today's State Highway 12 follows this path. Yet it seems unlikely that Everett took that route, for in a letter to his parents mailed from Escalante, Everett described "a truly delightful trip over the mountains, finding my way without any trails."

In Escalante, Everett camped beside the river, rode horseback with the local boys, hunted for arrowheads with them, and treated the boys to his campfire dinner of venison and potatoes. With the ranchers he discussed his plans for the coming weeks, maintaining his insouciant poise in the face of their skepticism. On his last night in town, he took several of the boys to the movie theater. The next day, as he rode away down the Hole-in-the-Rock Trail, he left everyone who had met him in Escalante with indelible memories of his brief visit.

Before he left, Everett mailed his last two letters, one to his parents, one to Waldo. In *Vagabond*, Rusho heads them both "November 11," and calls the letter to Waldo "the last—so far as is known—to be received by anyone." This is the sequence that ought to have been, for the letter to Waldo is one of the deepest Everett ever wrote, and in light of his disappearance, it has a prophetic power.

But Everett actually wrote to his brother a few days before he wrote to his parents. The letter Christopher and Stella received is dated

November 11
Escalante, Utah.

The one to Waldo:

November the ? 1934
Escalante Rim, Utah.

Internal evidence gives us a more precise date. To Waldo, Everett wrote, "Tonight the pale crescent of the new moon appeared for a little while, low on the skyline, at sunset." A new moon in 1934 occurred on November 6. The pale crescent Everett observed would have been visible only from November 8 to 10. His camp on the "Escalante Rim" was probably pitched near the divide separating the Paria and Escalante drainages, at least a dozen miles west of the town.

With the letter to his parents, Everett sent home yet more paintings. His subjects ranged from the volcanic pinnacle of Agathla to the Anasazi ruin of Betatakin. The best of the lot, he wrote, "I . . . mean to frame for my room." In this phrase there is a hint of an anticipated return to Los Angeles. But at the same time, Everett wanted no more handouts from his parents. To the contrary,

> As I have more money than I need now, I am sending you ten dollars, and I want both of you to spend five for something you have been wishing to have—books, or a trip, but not anything connected with any kind of duty. Let this be the first installment on that nickel I promised you when I made my first million.

As he wrote the letter, Everett was sitting by his campfire beside the Escalante River, cooking dinner with two of his youthful new friends. Turning his thoughts to his burros, he recounted a problem that would have a crucial bearing on the search for Everett after he disappeared:

> Chocolatero is a good burro by now. It was hard to get him across the Colorado river suspension bridge, as he was very frightened by it. A packer dragged him across behind his mule, and he left a bloody track all the way across. Later it was hard to teach him to make the fordings where the water was deep and swift, but now he does not mind.

In mid-November, with the leaves mostly dead on the trees, winter was not far away. But Everett had no plans to curtail his journey. In the letter to his parents he outlined various plans for the coming months, in a passage that would be pored over by Ruess partisans for decades:

I am going south towards the [Colorado] river now, through some rather wild country. I am not sure yet whether I will go across Smokey Mountain to Lee's Ferry and south, or whether I will try and cross the river above the San Juan. The water is very low this year. I might even come back through Boulder, so I may not have a post office for a couple of months. I am taking an ample supply of food with me.

The letter to Waldo, to whom Everett had not written since August 29, tries to summarize the doings of his last two months, while at the same time insisting on the impossibility of sharing them with others.

Since I left Desert View, a riot of adventures and curious experiences have befallen me. To remember back, I have to think of hundreds of miles of trails, thru deserts and canyons, under vermilion cliffs and thru dense, nearly impenetrable forests. As my mind traverses that distance, it goes thru a long list of personalities too.

But I think I have not written you since I was in the Navajo country, and the strange times I had there and in the sunswept mesas of the Hopis, would stagger me if I tried to convey them. I think there is much in everyones life that no one else can ever understand or appreciate.

To his brother, Everett confided an intimacy from his visit to Tropic that he had not told his parents about: "I stopped a few days in a little Mormon town and indulged myself in family life, church going, and dances. If I had stayed any longer I would have fallen in love with a Mormon girl, but I think it's a good thing I didn't. I've become a little too different from most of the rest of the world." After the Ruess cult had gathered momentum, locals in Tropic and Escalante would trade speculations as to who the Mormon girl was, but Everett had been too shy in his attentions for an obvious candidate to emerge.

With these declarations, it seems, the wilderness loner emerged full-blown. As he had done several times in the past, Everett turned his pride toward a haughty dismissal of Waldo's way of subsistence: "Even from your scant description, I know that I could not bear the routine and humdrum of the life that you are forced to lead."

Somewhere between Tropic and Escalante, Everett had shared a camp with a pair of Indians:

> I even met a couple of wandering Navajos, and we stayed up most of the night talking, eating roast mutton with black coffee, and singing songs. The songs of the Navajos express for me something that no other songs do. And now that I know enough of it, it is a real delight to speak in another language.

In the 1930s, Navajos from the reservation crossed the Colorado River every autumn to trade for horses in and around Escalante. Everett's fraternization with these indigenes would also play a role in the theories about his fate.

The November letter to Waldo has a valedictory tone throughout, as if he were composing a testament for eternity.

> I don't think I could ever settle down. I have known too much of the depths of life already, and I would prefer anything to an anticlimax. That is one reason why I do not wish to return to the cities. . . .
>
> This has been a full, rich year. I have left no strange or delightful thing undone that I wanted to do.

And it contains the single paragraph that, more than anything else Everett ever wrote, has come to stand as the eloquent manifesto for his vagabond life:

As to when I shall visit civilization; it will not be soon, I
think. I have not tired of the wilderness; rather I enjoy its
beauty and the vagrant life I lead, more keenly all the time.
I prefer the saddle to the street car and the star sprinkled
sky to a roof, the obscure and difficult trail, leading into the
unknown, to any paved highway, and the deep peace of the
wild to the discontent bred by cities.

Everett closed this passionate and oracular letter with a sentence
about his future plans that has haunted his devotees ever since: "It
may be a month or two before I have a post office, for I am exploring
southward to the Colorado, where no one lives."

A week later, more than fifty miles down the Hole-in-the-Rock
Trail, Everett bumped into the sheepherders, Addlin Lay and Clayton
Porter. For two nights he shared their camp near the head of Soda
Gulch. On the morning of November 21, as Everett prepared to push
on, the men offered him a quarter of mutton, which he declined, telling them he had plenty of food. They watched as he ambled away to
the southeast with his burros, Cockleburrs and Chocolatero.

As far as we know—which is not nearly far enough—that was the
last time anyone ever saw Everett Ruess.

PART TWO

———

Say That I Kept My Dream

SIX

Nemo

Two months passed with no word from Everett to his parents or his brother. The family, however, was not troubled, for in his Escalante letters, Everett had warned them, as he had written Waldo, that "It may be a month or two before I have a post office."

As soon as she received the paintings Everett had mailed home with his November 11 letter, Stella had them matted and framed. For her, the act may have had a tinge of wishful magic about it—as if preparing the bedroom she and Christopher kept for their younger son (his artwork hanging on its walls, as Everett had hinted he would like) might hasten his return.

Meanwhile, Waldo had found new employment as a secretary for a religious mission. The posting would take him much farther from Los Angeles than his water company job in San Bernardino had, for the mission was based in China. On December 17 his parents parted with Waldo as he boarded a ship in the Los Angeles harbor. Stella, who kept a five-year diary, with space for only a few sentences each day, wrote, "[W]ent to see W. off, & then went to Krese home [friends of the family] & held candles in the window as the boat went out of the harbor. Good-bye for how long?"

From mid-November through January, Stella and Christopher wrote letters to Everett. They mailed them to Bryce Canyon National Park, probably because Everett had written warmly about his friendship with Maurice Cope, the park's chief ranger, and they hoped that their son might resurface there.

By the end of January, however, still having received no answer from Everett, Christopher and Stella were growing worried. To be sure, during his previous journeys their footloose son had sometimes been out of touch for more than a month at a time. But not for two and a half months, and not in the dead of winter.

Sometime that winter, the letters that had fetched up at Bryce were forwarded to Marble Canyon, Arizona—the nearest post office to Lee's Ferry, one of the possible destinations of his upcoming rambles that Everett had mentioned in his November 11 letter. The postmistress at Marble, Florence Lowry, waited for what she called "a reasonable time" for the letters to be picked up, then, in early February 1935, returned them to their senders. When Christopher and Stella received their own missives, still sealed in their envelopes, their faint malaise burst into full-blown alarm. They wrote at once to Lowry. She replied, "I am sorry I have not seen or heard of your son. I have made inquiry of everyone near here and havent found anyone who has seen him." Lowry added, "The country north of here is very wild and arid and it was ill advised of anyone to start with out a guide but if your son was an experienced camper he will no doubt come through all right."

At the same time as they wrote to Lowry, Everett's parents sent off a query to the postmistress in Escalante. She turned this plea over to her husband, Jennings Allen, a local rancher and county commissioner. He wrote back to the Ruesses, offering to instigate a search, as he vowed, "We will search for him as though he were our son."

Between February 11 and 25, Christopher and Stella wrote letters to the postmasters of every town in the Southwest that they knew their son had visited during his three seasons of vagabondage in the region. They also wrote to the sheriffs of every county Everett had passed through, to Anglo traders on the Navajo reservation, to Indian agents, forest rangers, and newspapers and radio stations. These anguished appeals typically began,

> Dear Sir:
>   Can you help us?
>   Have you seen or heard of our son?

There followed a precise physical description of the missing twenty-year-old.

In these letters, Christopher and Stella tried to balance their fears with faith in their son's wilderness skills:

> Everett is not inexperienced as he has lived this way in the mountains for four seasons, but not during December and January. He may have travelled into great danger, and we hope you can . . . tell us how to find trace of him. Do you send out notices, or is there a plane that searches for lost people?

The responses from agents, sheriffs, traders, and the like were uniformly diligent and compassionate. But the sum total of their information about the vagabond's whereabouts was zero. And so, Christopher and Stella's alarm began to deepen with the edge of grief.

Maurice Cope sent a long letter from Bryce Canyon in which he summarized his discussions with Everett the previous November as to how he planned to pursue his journey beyond Escalante:

> He had with him a gun, plenty of ammunition, a compass etc. We discussed the condition of Fifty Mile Mountain

[Kaiparowits Plateau] during the winter months its height 7000 feet etc. . . .

When he left here, he did not intend going over the mountain, but keep under the mountain near the river where the elevation is only 3500 feet and there is never enough snow to bother.

Christopher and Stella wrote to Waldo in China. The letters took weeks to arrive, but Everett's brother promptly answered each one. At first he strove for an upbeat outlook. On March 12, sixteen days before Everett's twenty-first birthday, Waldo wrote,

First of all, I want to wish Everett a happy "Coming of Age." This will probably arrive a few days after his birthday but the sentiments are there. I do hope that I will hear from him some time this year!

I wish I were there; I would certainly go out to try to find him. But since I have had no word from you and your letter is now 3 weeks old I presume everything is all right.

The word of Everett's having gone missing leaked out to the press. A Los Angeles newspaper picked up the story as early as February 14. Reports of Everett's disappearance eventually spread across the United States, via Associated Press and United Press dispatches.

On February 22, out of the blue, Stella received a telegram from someone signing himself Captain Neal Johnson:

WILL CONDUCT SEARCH YOUR REQUEST. KNOW INDIAN SCOUTS. KNOW REGION WELL. NO WATER EXCEPT SNOW. IF LOST CAN BE FOUND. SNOW MELT SOON. NO WATER, WILL PERISH. SEARCH MUST START IMMEDIATELY. . . . WILL CONDUCT SEARCH FOR EXPENSES FOR INDIAN SCOUTS ONLY.

Since all the letters from Indian traders and forest rangers had produced not a scrap of evidence as to Everett's doings, Christopher and Stella grasped at Captain Johnson's straw. On February 28 the man came to Los Angeles and spent the night at their home on North Kingsley Drive. Johnson claimed his knowledge of the country came from the many years he had prospected through the Southwest in search of gold. He attributed his title of captain to a stint flying planes for the Mexican government. The next day, Stella recorded in her diary, "Went to bank & took out $75.00 to give Capt. Johnson for Indian search."

Meanwhile, starting on March 1, a search out of Escalante had been launched by Jennings Allen. After consulting with Addlin Lay and Clayton Porter, the two sheepherders who were the last men to see Everett the previous November, Allen set out with some dozen local men on horseback down the Hole-in-the-Rock Trail. They began their search where the old trail crossed the head of Soda Gulch, the site of the sheepherders' November campsite.

In Soda Gulch the party found no sign of Everett's passage, nor did they in Willow Gulch, three miles to the northwest. On March 6, however, the men rode down an old livestock trail that offered the only easy entry into Davis Gulch, yet another tributary of the Escalante, located two miles southeast of Soda Gulch. One of the searchers, Walter Allen, carved the date and his name in the sandstone cliff at the foot of the livestock trail (the inscription is still legible today). And here the party struck pay dirt.

Exactly what the searchers found in Davis Gulch that day, however, remains a matter of controversy. In the early 1980s, several of the searchers still alive reported that as soon as they had reached the floor of the narrow canyon, they came upon Everett's two burros. A brushwork fence had been built to confine them in a huge natural corral consisting of the upper three miles of Davis Gulch. Some of the men said the burros were thin and emaciated, but others, including Jennings Allen, swore they were "fat and healthy."

The searchers later testified that they found a bridle, a halter, and a rope draped on the brushwork fence. One of the men, Gail Bailey, herded the burros up the livestock trail and headed with them back to Escalante, while the others searched farther down-canyon.

In a natural alcove not far from the foot of the livestock trail, the searchers also found unmistakable signs of what they presumed was Everett's last camp: footprints on the ground, empty cans that had held condensed milk, candy wrappers, Anasazi potsherds (gathered, presumably, by Everett), and the impression in the dirt of a bedroll.

The searchers were puzzled, however, to find no trace of the young man's camping gear, cooking equipment, food, watercolor painting kit, or cash. Nor was there any sign of the journal he had kept throughout the first seven months of his 1934 expedition.

The searchers also claimed to have found Everett's footprints "leading to the edge of a cliff"—though which cliff, they never clarified. On March 15, Jennings Allen wrote to Christopher and Stella, "We have searched the country good on this side of the Colorado River and haven't been able to find any fresh sign of Everett."

Maurice Cope, the Bryce Canyon head ranger, was deeply puzzled by the findings of the Allen party. On March 21, he wrote Christopher:

> The fact that his burros were fenced in and his camp outfit is not to be found is evident [sic] that he has a permanent camp some where. The most reasonable thing for me to believe is, that he in some way crossed the river to the east side or attempted to cross. . . .
>
> If he did not cross the river, I cannot understand why he left his burros. . . .
>
> Near where his burros were found are deep canyons and in them are signs of cliff dwellings. There is always danger in attempting to climb up to them. . . .

I am very concerned and no doubt there is some need for alarm. If he established a camp some where with the intention of staying until spring every thing will be o. k. . . .

If any thing has happened it would no doubt be some kind of accident.

From far-distant China, Waldo was still trying to stay optimistic. On March 25 he wrote his parents, "And I hope he is found. *He ought to get good publicity out of that & with his writing ability, capitalize on it and write magazine articles.*"

In Los Angeles, however, Christopher and Stella were consumed with anguish. In her diary on March 2, Stella recorded, "About Everett on radio. Calls from Press." And on March 8, "Radio said Everett may be hopelessly lost."

The parents held out hope that someone might organize a search by airplane. In response to their appeals, on April 8 the acting U.S. Secretary of War promised an aerial search "when training flights are made over the area." But Maurice Cope, who knew the intricacy of the Escalante wilderness firsthand, warned Christopher, "The National Park does not have an air plane. In fact an air plane in that part of the country would be of little value." In the end, no attempt to canvass the Escalante country from the air was ever launched.

Throughout the next three months, Stella and Christopher received a steady stream of dispatches from Captain Neal Johnson, detailing the progress of his search with Indian scouts. The reports were handwritten in pencil, the grammar and spelling semi-literate. At the head of each letter, Johnson recorded the town from which he wrote, as he performed a virtuosic crisscrossing of the Southwest: Cortez, Colorado; Holbrook, Arizona; Blanding, Utah; Richfield, Marys Vale, Hanksville, and ultimately Salt Lake City, also in Utah.

From Cortez on March 14, Captain Johnson wrote:

Reached here this evening. . . . I stoped several times to communicate with diferent Indians of diferant trading posts alond up through New Mexico and Arizona also Colorado. There is several that knew of Everet. One Chief told me today. Picture man heap savy wild mountains O.K. never the less I was unable to get any information from them concerning him nothing more than heap O.K. Picture man. He make picture for Indians.

In the same letter, Johnson went on to assert:

I still do not believe that Everet is in danger unless he gets abandoned from more than any one [of the Indians] because they are loyal if they are your friend. Most of the Indians know of the Paint man whitch is Everett they say he is Yabi-toch which means fun, good humor. . . .

In another letter, allegedly mailed from Blanding, Captain John-son named his three Navajo scouts. They were Cidno or Cidney, Bully Chaho, and Buch Nash Chaho. "These Indians are not charging me anything Just expenses," Johnson wrote. "They are friends of myne and they feel Owe It to me for if One or any Navajo is your friend he loves and worships you. I like them for their loyalty to me." Another source of the scouts' loyalty, Johnson let on, was that "I saved one of them from dying with pnemonia."

On April 8, Johnson wrote, again from Blanding:

The latest Report is that it is of their opinion that your son is with two Indians Both Navajos. And that they have headed for the camp of Hostene Buchasia a Navajo Indian that lives near Navajo Mountain. . . . The two Indians and the white man seen to be verry clever in avoiding seeing, or litting any one see them. Hostene Buchasia is an old Indian and

he knows most everything that is known about the Navajo
tribe. . . .

I ask [one of my scouts] what percent of chances did
Everett have of being alive. He held up his hands with only
one finger turned down. 9 to 1.

From the start, Stella and Christopher had had their doubts about
Captain Johnson. As early as March 4, shortly after Jennings Allen and
his fellow Escalante ranchers had headed out the Hole-in-the-Rock
Trail in search of Everett, Christopher and Stella had sent Johnson a
telegram: "PLEASE LET ALLEN CONDUCT SEARCH INSTEAD
RETURN BALANCE OUR MONEY." Yet in the desperation of their
hope that Everett was still alive, his parents clung to the strange and
vivid rumors Johnson fed them. Through the end of May, they continued to send him further infusions of money and even some of Everett's
drawings and typed-out passages from his letters. In return, Johnson
fawned:

> I wish that I could write like Everett it is a Gods Gift what
> a delightful letter to write to a boy friend the wilderness the
> out of dorse is Everetts God his sole and heart is raped up
> in it. . . . I envy him I wish I could take his place and let him
> come home to you.

Among Captain Johnson's schemes for contacting Everett was a
plan to drop handbills from an airplane over every watering hole in
the Southwest. "They will settle to the Earth," Johnson predicted,
"and Everett is bound to pick one up." To this end, on April 19, he
claimed he was heading for the dirt strip that served as the Moab,
Utah, airport, where he hoped to rendezvous with copilots and a
plane the Ruesses might hire. "Don't forget to Instruct the pilots to
bring an Extra Parachute," he urged. "I do not like to fly without

one over a rough country." Three weeks later, writing from Richfield, Utah, Johnson claimed he had performed the flight out of Moab, to no avail because the country was indeed too rough to fly over low to the ground.

As the weeks sped by, one glitch after another kept thwarting Johnson's best-laid plans. On April 29, after claiming to have met his scouts in Bluff, Utah, for an update, Johnson found Cidno, Bully Chaho, and Buch Nash Chaho in a despondent mood. They were "tired of being followed," Johnson said, by other Navajos who were their enemies. Yet even so, the scouts delivered news that must have rent Christopher and Stella's hearts. "I have some news for you," Johnson warned. "I don't know whether to consider It good or bad." Despite the hostility of the other Navajos "following" them, the scouts "did obtain the Information that there is a white man with the two Indians. That he is well and dont want to be bothered."

All spring, Captain Johnson had planned to head for Navajo Mountain himself to verify the substance of his scouts' reports. But week by week, he found reasons to delay this mission. In early June he was ready to go, when he was suddenly stricken with appendicitis. In an apologetic letter to Christopher and Stella, he pleaded that he needed time to recover from the operation to remove his appendix before he could make the arduous trip to Navajo Mountain. He thanked the Ruesses for their latest enclosure, a stipend of fifteen dollars. He claimed that he was still convinced their son was alive.

"The money I spend on this of my own I will do of my own free will and of no obligation to you," Johnson pledged. "I will settle or fix it some way with Everett when I locate him."

In retrospect, it is obvious that Captain Johnson was a complete charlatan, a con man who sucked sizable sums of money—$350, all told—out of trusting parents made frantic by a personal tragedy. As Stella and Christopher would eventually learn, it is doubtful that Johnson performed any of the deeds he claimed to have set in motion, or even that his three Navajo scouts existed. Yet for months after the parents finally confronted Johnson with their suspicions of his duplicity, he continued to sputter protestations of innocence and sincerity.

Nor was Captain Johnson the last of the con men to see in the Ruesses' plight an opportunity for personal gain. For years after Everett's disappearance, a procession of sociopathic and/or delusional informants would surface, offering stunning revelations about Everett's fate or his secret existence. And the tragedy of Christopher and Stella's loss was exacerbated by the dogged hope that compelled them to follow each fugitive path to its bitter dead end.

*   *   *

Around March 21, a second search party set out from Escalante. Though its scope was limited, this team of ranchers on horseback made one important new discovery. "About the first of April," a chief ranger for the National Park Service wrote the Ruesses, "footprints were seen between Davis Gulch and the Hole-in-the-Rock." From the top of the livestock trail leading down into Davis Gulch, an overland hike of some nine miles would take a traveler to the V-notch gap in the cliff above the Colorado River, where the Mormon pioneers in January 1880 had started lowering their wagons down the precipitous nine-hundred-foot chute to the river's edge.

Navajos were known to keep a canoe cached at the Hole-in-the-Rock crossing, to facilitate their trading missions from the reservation to Escalante. If the footprints were Everett's, he might have left his burros in the Davis Gulch "corral" as he headed on foot for the cleft in the plateau. As the NPS ranger speculated, "It is more probable that [Everett] has ferried his camp across the river and taken his burros back to Davis Gulch where there was water and grass."

This hypothesis, however, ran head-on into a cardinal objection. As the leader of yet a third search party wrote to the Ruesses in June,

The consensus of opinion seems to be that Everett did not
cross the Colorado River onto the Navajo Mountain. There
was a man camped at the Hole in the Rock from about December 6 until sometime in April who seems positive that
had anyone come to that place he would have seen them.
In viewing this country you would agree that it is unlikely
anyone could cross the river at that point without being seen
by a party camped there.

By 2009, no one in Escalante recalled the identity of this mysterious winter camper, or the purpose of his mission. But a probable
answer lies carved in the rock. Along the upper third of both walls
bordering the Hole-in-the-Rock cleft, passersby have carved their
names, initials, and dates for more than a century. A handful of the
hundreds of inscriptions derive from the original pioneers in 1880.
Among these "Kilroy was here" notations, faded but still largely legible, one reads:

    Quinn   Dec. 12, 1934
      R
    Roundy   Feb.   35.

Nudged by a transcription of this graffito, local writer Jerry
Roundy (a distant relative of Quinn), the author of an excellent town
history called "*Advised Them to Call the Place Escalante*," supplied
some context: "Quinn would have been herding sheep. He wasn't the
owner—he would have been working for somebody else. Sometimes
they had a sheep wagon, and they'd stay out there all winter.

"If Quinn saw Everett, I never heard him say so."

Dissatisfied by the necessary superficiality of the first two searches
(the ranchers, after all, were taking unpaid leave from their onerous
cattle- and sheep-raising chores to ride down the Hole-in-the-Rock

Portrait of Everett Ruess at age nineteen, shot by Dorothea Lange in San Francisco in late autumn, 1933. *(Dorothea Lange Collection, Oakland Museum of California)*

Everett's mother, Stella Ruess, in front of the family house in Los Angeles. *(Courtesy of the Ruess family)*

Family gathering in Los Angeles, ca. 1924. Left to right: Stella, Waldo, Christopher, Everett. *(Courtesy of the Ruess family)*

Everett (left), Waldo, and Stella pose with the family automobile, a Dodge they named Dorinda, ca. 1929. *(Courtesy of the Ruess family)*

A young Everett receives an art lesson from professional sculptor Edith May. *(Courtesy of the Ruess family)*

Everett reading at home in Los Angeles, ca. 1929. *(Courtesy of the Ruess family)*

Everett with the burro he named after himself and Curly, the rez dog, somewhere in the Southwest, 1931. *(Special Collections, the J. Willard Marriott Library, University of Utah)*

Everett leads Curly and his burro along an exposed trail in Zion National Park, 1931. *(Special Collections, the J. Willard Marriott Library, University of Utah)*

Everett and Waldo with Curly, at home in Los Angeles, late 1931 or early 1932. *(Courtesy of the Ruess family)*

Everett with his burros, Nuflo and Jonathan, in Canyon de Chelly, 1932, shortly before Jonathan's death. *(Courtesy of the Ruess family)*

Everett in front of a hogan on the Navajo reservation, date unknown. *(Courtesy of the Ruess family)*

Everett standing on his burro's back, Sierra Nevada, 1933. *(Courtesy of the Ruess family)*

Opposite: Everett exploring a cliff dwelling, probably in Mesa Verde, 1932. *(Courtesy of the Ruess family)*

Everett at a lake in the high Sierra Nevada, 1933. *(Courtesy of the Ruess family)*

Everett and Clay Lockett (shirtless) pack a burro up the old Navajo trail to Woodchuck Cave, Tsegi Canyon, 1934. *(Courtesy of Fort Lewis College, Center of Southwest Studies, Ansel Hall Photograph Collection)*

The search party emerges from Davis Gulch, spring 1935. *(Special Collections, the J. Willard Marriott Library, University of Utah)*

Trail and look for clues), Ray Carr, the secretary of the Associated Civic Clubs of Southern Utah, organized a third search. It was launched in late May. Pushing down Davis Gulch farther than either of the previous parties had, this team made a pair of discoveries that has haunted Everett Ruess devotees ever since. Hurrying back to Escalante, Carr telegraphed the Ruesses on June 5, "DOES WORD NEMO HAVE ANY SIGNIFICANCE TO YOU FOUND CARVED IN CAVE."

In a follow-up letter, Carr elaborated:

> In one place in the lower part of the Davis Gulch an area which had not been covered before tracks made by a size 9 shoe were found leading from Escalante Creek up the Gulch to an old moquie indian [Anasazi] dwelling where the searchers found an old indian pot and other things neatly piled up by the moquie house entrance. Cattle and sheep men in this vicinity are certain that no one other than Everett was in this vicinity last year. On one of the steps leading to the entrance was found the inscription "NEMO 1934."

Carr's party also found another inscription downstream from the livestock trail, near the base of an ancient Fremont pictograph panel. Drawn with charcoal in small, black characters, it too read:

NEMO
1934.

The discovery set off bells in the parents' heads. Upon receiving Carr's telegram, Stella immediately wired back:

EVERETT READ IN DESERT GREEK POEM ODYSSEY, TRANSLATED BY LAWRENCE OF ARABIAN DESERT. HERE ODYSSEUS GREEK

WORD FOR NOBODY, "NEMO" BEING LATIN WORD FOR
NOBODY. ODYSSEUS TRAPPED BY MAN-EATING GIANT IN CAVE,
SAVES LIFE BY TRICK OF CALLING HIMSELF NEMO. EVERETT
DISLIKES WRITING HIS OWN NAME IN PUBLIC PLACES.

It was true that Everett had never been known to carve or scrawl his name on the walls of canyons he traveled through. But in 1931 he had twice assumed pseudonyms, calling and signing himself first Lan Rameau, then Evert Rulan, before reverting to his given appellation. The taking on of aliases went deeper than mere adolescent wordplay; it had everything to do with a discomfort with his own identity.

None of Everett's 1934 letters had been signed "NEMO." If he had decided to take on yet a third pseudonym, he must have done so only in late autumn, perhaps while he camped alone in Davis Gulch.

In Book Nine of the *Odyssey*, the hero and his men are trapped in the cave of the Cyclops Polyphemus, a one-eyed giant, who casually dashes out the brains of two of the sailors and eats their bodies raw. To save himself and his remaining men, Odysseus gets the monster drunk on good wine from his ship; in gratitude the Cyclops promises the hero a "guest-gift," and asks him his name.

In T. E. Lawrence's translation, Odysseus answers, "My name is No-man: so they have always called me, my mother and my father and all my friends." Polyphemus proffers a cruel guest-gift: "I will eat No-man finally, after all his friends. The others first—that shall be your benefit."

While the Cyclops is drunk, Odysseus sharpens a stake of olive wood in the fire and thrusts it into Polyphemus's eye. Blinded, in pain and rage, the monster calls out to his fellow giants to help him finish off the humans. "What so ails you, Polyphemus," they answer, "that you roar across the heavenly night and keep us from sleep?"

"My friends," Polyphemus answers, "No-man is killing me by sleight."

His fellow Cyclopes only laugh: "If you are alone and no one assaults you," they jibe, "but your pain is some unavoidable malady from Zeus, why then, make appeal to your father King Poseidon." Soon after, Odysseus's men escape the cave by hanging on to the underbellies of the giant's sheep and riding the animals past the furious fumblings of the Cyclops's hands.

To be sure, Homer never uses the word "Nemo" (he wrote, of course, in Greek, not Latin). But Everett would have linked the Latin name with the famous passage from the *Odyssey,* just as his mother did.

Later, Christopher realized that NEMO also echoes Captain Nemo, the misanthropic antihero of Jules Verne's *Twenty Thousand Leagues Under the Sea,* a well-thumbed copy of which Everett had read more than once. In the novel, after hunting what they thought was a giant sea monster all over the oceans of the world, the protagonist, the learned Professor Aronnax, and his two companions are taken captive on the captain's mysterious submarine. There is a vivid moment when the three men first meet their jailer. In all likelihood, Everett felt a deep identification with Captain Nemo's proclamation: "I'm not what you would call a civilized man! I've broken with all of society for reasons which I alone can appreciate. I therefore don't obey its rules."

Two other echoes may help explain Everett's choice of a last pseudonym. In June 1934 he had traversed No Mans Mesa, one of the most remote places on the Navajo Reservation, almost losing his burro Leopard in the process. From a camp just west of the mesa, he had written his declaration to Bill Jacobs, "The perfection of this place is one reason why I distrust ever returning to the cities. Here I wander in beauty and perfection. There one walks in the midst of ugliness and mistakes." And at the end of his letter to Waldo from Escalante, Everett had signed off, "It may be a month or two before I have a post office, for I am exploring southward to the Colorado, where no one lives." ("Nemo" is usually translated as "no one" or "nobody," not the more specific "no man.")

By now, both NEMO inscriptions in Davis Gulch lie under water, drowned after 1957 by the rising waters of Lake Powell following the construction of the Glen Canyon Dam. But nobody seriously doubts that the two signatures were Everett's work. The single Latin name and the date stand, forever enigmatic and portentous, as Everett's last words to the world.

*   *   *

Agonizing in Los Angeles over their missing son, Christopher and Stella Ruess felt the need to act. On June 21, 1935, they set out on a trip by automobile to northern Arizona and southern Utah. They brought with them a number of Everett's paintings. Their aim was not to try to find the lost youth on their own so much as to visit the places that he had cared about so passionately, and to meet some of the people who had crossed Everett's path.

Navigating the Southwest from the Grand Canyon to Bryce Canyon, from Kayenta, Arizona, to Panguitch, Utah, Christopher and Stella conferred with all kinds of men and women with whom Everett had shared his thoughts and plans during the seven months before he disappeared. Stella kept a diary separate from her five-year journal during this trip, and years later wrote a short essay summarizing the pilgrimage. The diary is oddly travelogue-ish, dutifully recording scenery, miles traversed, places camped, meals eaten. But here and there a mother's grief breaks through, as in an entry about a natural formation in Zion National Park that her son had passed by: "We climbed up a steep trail to Weeping Rock & it made me weep thinking of Everett."

The parents' first stop was not Escalante, but Kayenta, where Everett had begun his 1934 expedition. There they met John and Louisa Wetherill and their son, Ben, who had been with Everett on the Rain-

bow Bridge–Monument Valley excavation of Woodchuck Cave. On
June 24, Stella wrote, "Visited Wetherills, who discredited N. Johnson, explained Indian situation & said Everett was very happy last
Sept." (This entry casts further doubt on Clay Lockett's testimony
that John Wetherill "had little respect for Everett.")

The veteran trader and guide recounted how he and Everett had
pored over maps the previous summer, plotting a course for his upcoming months of travel. It was Wetherill's firm belief that after visiting the Escalante region, Everett hoped to cross the Colorado and
explore Wilson Mesa. Had he done so, he might well have followed
the faint trail blazed by the Mormon pioneers in 1880. And so far,
none of the searchers had looked for the missing young man on Wilson Mesa—then as now, one of the more inaccessible regions in all
the Southwest.

The next day Stella and Christopher drove to the Navajo Mountain trading post. Along the way they met Edward Nequatewa, a
Hopi man who had become an ethnologist. "Long talk," Stella noted
dryly. The gist of what Nequatewa had to say is preserved in a letter
he later wrote to the parents:

> What Navajos that I had talked with, from the Navajo
> Mountain, said that they had never seen Everett or any
> white man around there at that time nor there was never
> any searching party came around there, otherwise the Na-
> vajos would be talking about it. They also said that if Ev-
> erett has met his foul play in that region it won't be by an
> Indian. If this Johnson really had sent these Indians out
> on searching party, he certainly would have some reports
> from them.

From Navajo Mountain, Stella and Christopher drove west
through the Kaibab Forest to Zion National Park, then northeast

toward Escalante. Along the way, a number of people who had met Everett the previous autumn offered suggestions as to where he might be found. One of them was George Shakespeare, who lived in Tropic, the little town where Everett had lingered for several days before pushing on to Escalante. About Shakespeare, Stella recorded, "Spent considerable time with E., & would like to go searching. Thinks E. may be with Navajos." Joe Lee, the proprietor of The Gap, a trading post south of Lee's Ferry, had another hunch: "Thought E. would go across Hall's Crossing [on the Colorado River, almost a hundred miles to the north] on a raft, maybe drowned." Bryce Canyon chief ranger Maurice Cope was even more definite: "Set up tent & called on Mr. Cope. E. told him he would stay with the Navajos until July. Navajos do not use burros very often."

Though Stella's diary only laconically records the speculations about Everett's itinerary, one can imagine the mixture of anguish and hope each glimmering insight must have sent coursing through the parents' veins. In and around Escalante, they met most of the members of the first two search parties. Jennings Allen, head of the March 1935 team, drove Christopher and Stella forty-two miles down the Hole-in-the-Rock road, which was as far as he could coax his car—"so that," Stella later wrote, "we realized how difficult was Everett's burro-riding toward Davis Canyon, southeast. We wished that we had wings to fly."

Except for the two-day stopover at the Grand Canyon by Stella in 1923, the journey was the parents' first encounter with the desert Southwest. They were awed by the landscape, but its beauty brought pain:

> From the [Navajo] bridge, we thrilled at the deep gorge of the Colorado. We thought we recognized the very view Everett painted, and which we called "On and On and On" as printed on a folder with his "Wilderness Song"....

We saw many sheltered spots where Everett probably
slept, and the impressive Amphitheatre of great rocks with
a drapery of green foliage and a natural pulpit in a pool of
water. We felt sure that Everett had declaimed some well-
loved lines to the surrounding vermilion cliffs.

In Escalante the parents got an earful of appraisals of Captain
Neal Johnson. The brunt of the testimony was that the gold miner
was a thoroughgoing fraud and scoundrel. As Christopher later wrote
Waldo, "I can't make him out. He may never have sent any Indians at
all—a peculiar character. We are financing him no further."

Johnson got wind of the Escalante scuttlebutt. On June 1, from
Hanksville, Utah, he wrote Everett's father, summoning up all the in-
dignation he could muster:

> I cannot hardly believe you said it. The report was that you
> said you considered what money you had sent me was a loss
> that you considered I had used It for my own use. . . . I do
> not need that kind of money. Blood money. If Everet was
> Dead whitch I believe he is not he would haunt me. If he was
> alive he would haunt me.

Although by temperament inclined to think the best of everyone,
Christopher responded bluntly: "Can you blame us for being entirely
on the fence as to whether you were half right and half wrong or all
wrong? Some suggested that you had not hired or sent out any Indians at all." And yet, despite his resolve to cut off financing Johnson altogether, in the same letter Christopher offered to pay him twenty-five
dollars if he would go to Navajo Mountain and come back with a
short note from Everett. The captain seized on that shred of encour-
agement and continued to pursue his bizarre "search" through the
summer of 1935.

On July 3, Christopher and Stella arrived back in Los Angeles. About a week later, officers found a badly burned corpse in the desert near Gallup, New Mexico. Speculation on whether this might be Everett flared high enough to reach the newspapers. The Gallup chief of police corresponded with Christopher and Stella, asking if any dental records of their son existed. The parents appealed to the College of Dentistry at the University of Southern California, where in December 1932 and January 1933 Everett had had work done on his teeth. On July 16, 1935, the college mailed to Christopher three pages of skimpy and somewhat ambiguous records. They indicated two inlays and one gold foil. Christopher also knew that Everett was missing a tooth from his upper right jaw.

On August 1, the Gallup chief of police wrote back, saying that his men had found "no missing teeth roots" and no metal whatsoever among the ashes of the dead man's skull. On this basis, it was concluded that the corpse in the desert could not be Everett's.

Unwilling to let Christopher's frank accusations sabotage his campaign of feinting and dodging, Captain Neal Johnson wrote from Salt Lake City on August 12:

> I am leaving here in the morning for Navajo Mountain. Where I will stay until Everett is found. . . . Mr. Ruess I hate to say this but there is a boy living with a bunch of Navajos in the vicinity of Navajo Mountain. He has had a tribal wedding. I am most sure this is Everett.

This time, for once, the con man would make good on a promise, at least in terms of actually setting out into the field on the Navajo reservation. The search that unfolded in August 1935 was not, however, of Johnson's creation, but rather that of a far more famous sleuth who aimed at a far more high-profile resolution of the mystery. By the end of the month, the most ambitious search yet prosecuted for Everett Ruess would announce to the world what its author regarded as the definitive answer to the puzzle of the young wanderer's disappearance—an answer that nonetheless left the essential mystery untouched.

*   *   *

John Upton Terrell was a prolific popular Western historian and reporter for the *Salt Lake Tribune.* Before his death in 1988, he would write some forty books, including *Search for the Seven Cities, Apache Chronicle,* and biographies of John Wesley Powell, Zebulon Pike, and Cabeza de Vaca, the lost conquistador who accidentally made the European discovery of the Southwest. Terrell was a flamboyant, even sensationalistic writer in the vein of Zane Grey. By 1935 he was widely credited with discovering the horn-rimmed spectacles that helped solve the Leopold-Loeb murder case, but there is no independent evidence that he had anything to do with solving the "Crime of the Century."

Terrell agreed to undertake the search on assignment for the *Tribune.* The results of the inquiry, in dispatches written by Terrell, were published on the pages of four successive issues of the newspaper between August 25 and 28. The first dispatch, printed at the top of the front page of the Sunday morning edition on August 25, under the headline "S.L. Tribune Expedition into Desert Finds Clues to Fate of Young Artist," opened with a bold proclamation of the team's unshakable conclusion:

> Everett Ruess, 21-year-old missing Los Angeles artist, probably met death at the hands of a renegade bad man or Indian in a lonely canyon near the southern end of the untracked Escalante desert.
>
> This is the united belief of the best Indian and white trackers, traders and wilderness residents of southern Utah

and northern Arizona. Their conclusion is based on several "trails" of evidence, which to the men trained in the ways of remote lands, are almost irrefutable. But also these expressions of opinion have come following an extensive and intensive search by an expedition sent out by The Salt Lake Tribune, and which has practically exhausted other possibilities.

To buttress its claims, the *Tribune* published a map of the terrain traversed by the searchers. It covers an impressive swath of country stretching from Blanding, Utah, to Tuba City, Arizona. From the Navajo Mountain trading post, Terrell's company (including Indian guides) worked its way northwest by pack train through some of the most rugged and seldom-visited canyonlands anywhere in the Southwest, finally crossing the San Juan and Colorado Rivers to arrive at Davis Gulch.

Read at a distance of seventy-five years from their publication, Terrell's dispatches brim with an omniscient arrogance that poorly conceals the scarcity of real evidence the expedition was able to unearth. In 1935, however, the dispatches could well have seemed to give a definitive answer of sorts.

Terrell's ace accomplice was not Captain Johnson (who is all but invisible in the published reports), but one Dougeye, a "famed Navajo trailer." (Dougi, as the name is normally spelled, was actually a Paiute.) Even though more than eight months had passed since the last Escalante men had seen Everett in November 1934, Dougeye claimed (or Terrell claimed for him) that he could tell by tracks still printed in the dried mud on "the only possible trail" that no more than six men on horseback had crossed the San Juan and Colorado into Navajo country during that time. And all six, Dougeye was sure, were Indians. One was Dougeye himself, who the previous autumn had come to trade in Escalante, where he said he had met and spoken to Everett.

Terrell put Dougeye to work on the old footprints in Davis Gulch. The tracker's verdict: "White boy come in, not go out."

To dismiss the romantic idea that Everett might be living peacefully among the Navajos, having turned his back on white civilization, Terrell trotted out his own ethnographic maxims, such as, "A Navajo Indian cannot keep a secret. He reveals all such things to traders and agents."

The mystical climax of Terrell's search came in a hogan near Kayenta, Arizona, where the reporter's guides led him to the camp of a Navajo medicine man. "I have forgotten the Indian's name," Terrell wrote. "It was, for me, unpronounceable. He was, however, Natani, which means 'wise man' or sometimes 'head man.' " The old man's wife was a renowned seer.

After the requisite sharing of cigarettes and gossip about the latest Indian policies of "Washingdon" (as Navajos referred to the federal government), "Natani" suddenly asked, "Why have you waited so long to look for your friend?" And for the first time, the medicine man's wife spoke, almost inaudibly: "Far north."

As Terrell's party watched spellbound in the rainy night, Natani began to chant, while his wife covered her face, then started to sculpt a mound from the sand on the ground. Twice she destroyed and rebuilt the topographic model, which Terrell's guides recognized as Navajo Mountain. Eventually she used a finger to draw a pair of crooked lines enfolding the peak, signifying the San Juan and Colorado Rivers.

> The chant ended abruptly. Natani's wife sat with her head fallen, breathing deeply, as if she were very tired. The rain stopped. . . .
>
> Natani spoke: "Go to the forks of the rivers."
>
> Guide: "He lives there?"

Natani: "He was there. Close by he made a camp. You will find the fire."

Guide: "Have you seen him?" (He meant in a vision.)

Natani: "He has gone away from there."

Guide: "He's dead."

Natani: "He has gone away and does not mean to come back."

Pressed by Terrell's Navajo guide and translator, Natani made a last effort to "see" Everett. At last he spoke:

There is a shadow. Only some of his outfit was moved away. There is more some place. I see him talking with two friends. They are Navajos. Young men like himself. They sing and eat together. Then there is a shadow. He has gone away. The Navajos have left the place. They are no longer with him. She says they may have traveled together. He (Ruess) has given himself to our gods. He has taken us in his arms and wished to come among us.

The vision of Natani and his wife directed Terrell to Navajo Mountain, where he recruited Dougeye, then visited the junction of the Colorado and San Juan Rivers. The tracker scrutinized the riverbanks, then spoke, "White boy not camp here."

Onward to Davis Gulch, and thence to further consultations with Indians and Anglo cattlemen. The cloak-and-dagger melodrama of Terrell's dispatches obscures the fact that the search, for all its "extensive and intensive" apparatus, was little more than a flamboyant wild goose chase. Terrell's conclusion, moreover, was not so much a QED as a grasping at the kind of straw that might sell newspapers. The closing passage of the last dispatch, for all its air of certainty, seems to acknowledge silently that Terrell's party could not identify Everett's alleged killer, or even come up with a convincing motive for such a crime.

> This is the result: Everett Ruess was murdered in the vicinity of Davis canyon. His valuable outfit was stolen. He never reached the Colorado river.
>   "But some day," we said, "pieces of his outfit will turn up."
>   Then we would take the trail again.

The gripping accounts in the *Salt Lake Tribune* made a big splash. A Utah Department of Justice agent prepared to make a case before federal authorities to launch a manhunt for Everett's killer(s). The state governor promised to open an official investigation.

To their credit, however, Christopher, Stella, and Waldo refused to swallow Terrell's detective work whole. As of September 1935, they still held on to the hope that Everett was alive.

SEVEN

Desert Trails

DESPITE THE DELPHIC PROCLAMATION by John Upton Terrell in the *Salt Lake Tribune,* by the autumn of 1935, four different theories about Everett's fate were in currency. During the next seven decades, those four theories continued to hold sway, generating many an impassioned debate in bars and around campfires all over the West.

The possibility that Everett had been murdered could not be ruled out. Terrell's vague formula fingering the killer as a "renegade bad man or Indian" was complemented by dark rumors circulating around Escalante. And though the residents of that insular town tried to keep the gossip away from the ears of outsiders, the gist of it leaked out. Everett could have been murdered by a local rancher. The motive might have been simple robbery, although even in Depression times the goods Everett carried with him were so meager they would not have been likely to tempt even the most hardened thief. But another scenario sprang from the fact that some of the locals were known to be cattle rustlers. If Everett had stumbled upon rustlers in the process of butchering a stolen cow, they might have killed him to forestall the discovery of their crime.

A second theory, the one to which Christopher, Stella, and Waldo clung, was that Everett was still alive, but had chosen to stay indefinitely in hiding. A romantic version of this scenario postulated that Everett had "gone native"—crossed the Colorado River into Navajo country, decided never to return to the hated cities, taken up a secret life among the Indians, and perhaps even married a Navajo girl.

A third theory was that Everett had chosen to end his life. Few beyond the circle of his family and best friends were aware of the despair and depression that lurked just beneath the surface of Everett's exuberance, but a desert suicide was not an unprecedented phenomenon in the Southwest.

The last theory had Everett leaving his burros in Davis Gulch as he took off on a side jaunt, perhaps simply a day hike. He might have been caught in a snowstorm in some remote nook of the canyons and frozen to death. Or he might have drowned trying to swim the Colorado River. Or he might have fallen to his death from some cliff, his body coming to rest in a place almost impossible to find. As he had bragged in his letters home, he had taken many a wild chance as he climbed to inaccessible Anasazi ruins, and to Edward Gardner in May 1934, he had jauntily admitted, "One way and another, I have been flirting pretty heavily with Death, the old clown."

Much as they wanted to believe their son was alive, Christopher and Stella were too realistic to rule out the alternative. Unquenchable hope fought in their hearts against grieving pessimism. On September 24, Christopher wrote to a friend, "If Everett is dead, he has truly lived,—and more than most people do in a century." Five days later he wrote to Waldo in China: "He had a fine feeling for you. You were two brothers, I believe, who never had fights. I do not recall your quarreling when little."

Two months earlier, at about the same time as the dental records proved that the burned corpse found near Gallup could not be Everett's, a certain "Preacher Smith" claimed that Everett was living in

Blanding, Utah. "Everett may have lost his sense of identity through some blow or fall and amnesia; or he may be 'broke' and too proud to communicate," Christopher wrote in his diary on July 20, summarizing Preacher Smith's claim. "I still think he is with the Navajos on the mountain side, and does not communicate lest he break the spell, arouse feeling of suspicion that he is tattling." The alleged Blanding sighting was quickly proven to be erroneous.

In September, fresh off his search with Terrell on the Navajo reservation, Captain Neal Johnson visited the Ruesses in Los Angeles. Despite their loss of all confidence in the quirky gold miner's reports of Everett's alleged doings in the backcountry, Stella and Christopher treated the con man with unfailing hospitality. "He sleeps in Everett's bed and I in your bed right now," Christopher wrote Waldo.

Out of this visit arose the most far-fetched and, to the parents, disturbing of all Captain Johnson's bizarre allegations. "Johnson says that his brother slept with Everett his last night in Escalante," Christopher wrote in his diary on September 24—by "slept with," Christopher meant merely "camped beside"—"and that Everett had nearly $1000 in bills—sounds fishy." Even fishier was Johnson's story about how Everett had come into such a fortune. Christopher summarized this yarn in a letter to Waldo:

> No way of telling what money Everett had; Johnson full
> of fairy tales; had an idea Everett took a package of photo
> plates, really drugs, for drug smugglers from New Mexico
> to Bryce National Park, and was paid $1000 for that; this
> is absurd, for it took Everett weeks to go that distance and
> I think Johnson just told it to me to get me to bribe him to
> keep Everett from being prosecuted.

Absurd the tale may have been, but it only intensified a nagging malaise about the claim in Everett's last letter home that he had "more money than I need" and his unprecedented act of sending ten dollars to his parents to spend on something special.

Waldo had already wondered on September 21, "Have you ever learned the exact source of Everett's money—it seems to me he never did tell us just how or when he got it." Christopher's answer: "[I] believe Everett must have met some well-to-do people who paid generously for his pictures."

Another of Everett's odd comments haunted Christopher and Stella. Even though Everett had insisted that the correspondence between himself and his brother remain confidential—"Of course our letters should be strictly personal," he had written in 1931—Waldo had shared the letters with his parents. On October 9, 1931, from the Grand Canyon, Everett had confided to his brother, "What I would have missed if I had ended everything last summer!"

Now, on November 24, 1935, in a letter to Waldo, Christopher voiced an excruciating surmise:

> Tell me some thing about Everett. In one place . . . he says that if he had shuffled off his mortal coil a year previously as he discussed with you, he would be missing all the great experiences and beauty that at that moment he was recording. We have wondered whether he might have died by suicide. He could have tied stones or the like to his body and his goods and have sunk in the swift Colorado without trace at that point. But he was so cheerful in all his later letters that that seems unthinkable.

Waldo's answer was not as reassuring as his parents had hoped:

> From what he had said, I might believe that he would commit suicide in that he would drive himself on in a stoical manner not always being considerate of his bodily needs

until he starved to death or from not caring for wounds properly but I doubt if he took life in such a way as to be willing to hang a rock around his neck and jump in the Colorado. I might think that he fell down some chasm but that is not certain because if that was so his belongings should be around somewhere at least. It certainly seems like someone might have "done him in."

The alternating currents of hope and sorrow wormed their way into the parents' dreams. On November 13, Christopher wrote in his diary, "Dreamed of Everett, saw his skeleton; Mother dreamed of him and saw him stalking into the kitchen the other day, tall, healthy, with sweater with Indian symbols on it, saying, Well, here I am!"

Onto the void left by a near-total absence of hard evidence about Everett's fate, however, the parents could not help projecting the kinds of scenarios only wishfulness at its wildest could concoct. During his teenage years, Everett had occasionally expressed a desire to explore Mexico, Latin America, and South America. On October 30, 1935, Christopher wrote to Waldo:

> I think he was influenced by the Odyssey reading; and thought of himself as a wanderer like Ulysses, else he would not have carved NEMO in two caves, revealing his thoughts. Many boys run away from home because misunderstood or mistreated at that time of life; others have just the wanderlust and can't restrain themselves. . . . If he has gone this way, he may go to Mexico, then South America, then elsewhere. He may even get to China, working his way on a boat. In any case I think he will eventually communicate with us again.

Waldo, however, could not imagine his brother making his way to China to reunite with him; the previous March, he had doubted that Everett even knew he was headed off to that distant country. On Thanksgiving Day he wrote his parents, dismissing the China fantasy, and adding,

> As many of his poems and writings lead one to think [that] might happen sometime, he has undoubtedly driven himself beyond his physical endurance and died, beautifully and alone in the desert. Whether he suffered or not at the time is a moot question but it was a beautiful death because he was living a life of beauty, a life of doing what he wanted to do.

Yet strangely, if perhaps inevitably, Waldo's brave effort to imagine his brother meeting with "a beautiful death" brought out the most abject sense of unworthiness: "As I think about him I begin to realize what a poor excuse for a person I am. What a shallow empty life I am leading as compared to him."

*   *   *

An unsolved mystery such as a young man's disappearance in the desert attracts all kinds of cranks and self-styled experts. Everett's vanishing did so in spades, not least because his parents vigorously pursued every possible lead, no matter how unlikely. From the distance of seven decades, it is hard to judge the sincerity of each of the strangers who made overtures to Stella and Christopher about their missing son. Few of these interlopers were outright charlatans like Captain Johnson, but few had the keen analytical talents of a good detective. Most lay somewhere along the slippery continuum between the plausible and the downright crazy. Taken all together, however, the hints and hopes these problem-solvers threw across the parents' path created a gauntlet of heartbreak that would last for the rest of Christopher's and Stella's lives.

In September 1935, a man named Sparks, hailing from Wolf Hole,

Arizona (by 1935 already a ghost town), "came to Escalante" (as Christopher wrote to Waldo), "inspired confidence, and said he would search for two months if someone would provide a horse or two and food supply." It is unclear what Sparks actually accomplished, but by mid-October, Christopher had become convinced the man was a fraud. Sparks claimed to have undertaken a sixty-day solo search, but, wrote Christopher, "left his grubstake carelessly behind."

A trader from Tuba City, Arizona, wrote to the parents on March 4, 1935, while Jennings Allen's initial search party was still in the field, and averred that "a young man came through here driving two burros. . . . As far as I can remember it was around two months ago and I believe that he was headed for Kayenta, seventy-five miles north of here." Two months prior to the trader's writing would date the young man's passage around the beginning of January 1935, or six weeks after Everett's last contact with ranchers out on the Escalante Desert. It is hard to know what to make of the trader's sighting. The young man may have been someone other than Everett, who coincidentally happened to have two burros of his own. Or the trader's sense of time was badly off, for Everett had in fact passed close to Tuba City in October 1934, as he made his way from Flagstaff to southern Utah—five months before the trader's letter, not two.

As the seasons passed, Christopher and Stella brooded daily about their lost son. On April 2, 1936, Christopher wrote to Waldo, still in China, "If Everett has disappeared and married an Indian, we would feel shock that he had cut himself off from the whites and perhaps cut his wife off from the Indians, and his children from both races." The next day he lamented to his diary, "I think we all poorly understood Everett."

The months stretched into years. For all their faith in reason, the parents sought the help of astrologers, fortune-tellers, and other "seers." On June 18, 1937, an astrologer in Berkeley, California, wrote to Stella and Christopher:

You need not worry about him. He never suffered—not even at the time of his death, for he is dead, and I would judge he passed away soon after you last heard from him. Death undoubtedly occured [*sic*] through drowning. That was written in the stars at the time of his birth.

A handwriting analyst determined, "He has conflicts with regard to his mother-father attitudes having both marked unconscious mother and unconscious father attachments. These keep him in almost constant turmoil." In October 1938, a woman in Moab, Utah, used a "cycle-graph" to discern Everett's fate: "I claim that the boy was—or is—temporarily controlled by an entity which makes him do what he is now doing. When *IT* leaves he will be himself. And try to find his way back to civilization again."

Perhaps the cruelest purported sighting came from a woman named Caradonna, who may have been a close friend of the family. In an undated letter, she wrote to Stella:

> Just before we moved, in 1936, Everett came to visit us a couple of times. He acted differently and often spoke of going back to Mexico . . . [her ellipses] and at one thing he said to us I chided him and said . . . "Everett Ruess!" Then I noticed something strange about him . . . he asked us . . . "Is that who I am?"
>
> I do know that when we asked him of his parents he always said "I HAVE NO FAMILY."

The sybilline Caradonna closed her message of woe as follows:

> Bless you . . . I do hope this helps ease your dear mind . . . and do give up now . . . Release your sweet loving mind from this double thinking . . . for really Stella, darling . . . wherever

your boy is he is IN GODS LOVING CARE . . . and that's
all we need to know isn't it?

In early 1938, buoyed by hints or clues now lost to the record, Christopher and Stella believed they were closing in on the whereabouts of
their missing son, even though it had been more than three years since
his disappearance. That February, Christopher sent off a flurry of more
than thirty letters to bus depot agents, newspaper editors, and the like
in many different towns near the Four Corners. The parents had become convinced that Everett was living somewhere in that region, but
that he was not using his real name—whether because he had suffered
amnesia or had deliberately chosen to conceal his identity, they could
not be sure, although they leaned toward the latter explanation.

The plea that Christopher and Stella asked their recipients to pass
along makes for poignant reading today. From a February 2 letter to
the editor of the *Herald Democrat* in Durango, Colorado:

> Now we are not interested in urging him to come home,
> unless he should so desire. We are not interested in telling
> the world he is found. We feel that he has a right to live his
> own life to his own ends in his own individual way. He is
> no doubt getting in his experiences more education for his
> future work. He may become a nature writer like Thoreau
> or Burroughs, illustrating his own writings. . . .
>
> Tell him we often see him in our dreams, that he is in our
> words daily, that his watercolors are on the walls, that many
> of his friends write to us, but that if he wishes to reveal
> himself to us and not to them, it shall be as he desires.

Each of these letters begged Everett to consent to a brief, once-only
meeting with his parents somewhere in Colorado or Utah. But nothing came of this campaign of last-ditch hope.

*   *   *

As early as August 1935, even before Terrell's search, Christopher and Stella were already thinking about trying to publish "some kind of book of Everett's letters and poems in memory of him." For three years they struggled in vain to find a press interested in such a project. In 1937 they typed up a miscellany of passages from Everett's letters, poems, and essays, titled it "Youth Is for Adventure," and distributed it to friends.

With their homemade anthology, Stella and Christopher kept Everett's words alive, even if the audience for them was small and local. Then, in September 1938, a writer named Hugh Lacy wrote an essay about Everett that appeared in *Desert* magazine, a widely read monthly out of Palm Desert, California. Lacy's essay was titled "Say That I Kept My Dream . . . ," an allusion to the best stanza in Everett's best poem, "Wilderness Song":

> *Say that I starved; that I was lost and weary;*
> *That I was burned and blinded by the desert sun;*
> *Footsore, thirsty, sick with strange diseases;*
> *Lonely and wet and cold . . . but that I kept my dream.*

Lacy opened his essay with a bold claim for Everett's enduring legend: "Wherever poets, adventurers and wanderers of the Southwest gather, the story of Everett Ruess will be told. His name, like woodsmoke, conjures far horizons."

The piece, which was accompanied by photos of Everett and reproductions of some of his paintings, garnered widespread attention. Lacy followed it in December 1939 with another essay for *Desert,* titled "What Became of Everett Ruess? . . ." Its opening was equally bold: " 'NEMO.' After five years that cryptic clue seems to summarize the desert mystery of Everett Ruess, young Los Angeles artist-adventurer who disappeared at 20 in the wasteland of South-east Utah." Lacy skillfully summarized the phantom bits of evidence the various searches had come up with, thereby reviving the contro-versy over Everett's ultimate fate.

Lacy's essays also unleashed a spate of new "sightings." The first—to which Lacy gave enough credence to urge its publication as a first-person account in the December 1939 issue of *Desert*—was by one Cora L. Keagle. In "Is Everett Ruess in Mexico?" Keagle recalled an April 1937 auto trip with her husband to Mexico City. On the way home, near Monterrey, the couple stopped to offer assistance to two young American men tinkering with a broken car. One of them insisted on showing the Keagles his "portfolio." "I never let this out of sight," he explained. "It's the source of my living." The artist went on to display the kinds of watercolor landscapes he said he traded for food and lodging. He "also said he had been living among the Indians in Arizona painting and writing."

At the time, the Keagles thought little of the encounter. But when Cora read Lacy's "Say That I Kept My Dream . . . ," she was instantly convinced that the youth they had met by the Mexican wayside was Everett. At once she rushed out to the garden where her husband was working and asked him if he remembered the face of the artist they had met near Monterrey. When he said he did, Cora opened the issue of *Desert* to a photograph of the lost wanderer. "That's the very fel-low," said Mr. Keagle at once.

"We are convinced that we saw Everett Ruess," Cora Keagle closed her piece. "And if it was Everett he was tanned, healthy and happy and several pounds heavier than when he disappeared."

At the time, Christopher and Stella had no way of evaluating the Mexican story, but it did dovetail with their conviction that Everett might have headed south toward Latin America to explore new wil-dernesses.

Most false sightings, as FBI agents and police officers wearily conclude, are well-meaning, the by-products of the vagaries of memory and an all-too-human propensity to ignore discrepancies and seize upon coincidences. Yet some of the testimonies elicited by Lacy's articles can be attributed only to something far more sinister than the desire to unravel a mystery. The authors of these all-knowing screeds seemed to derive a dark pleasure in the laying out of details that they must have known were acutely painful for Everett's grieving parents.

On November 27, 1939, a man named Burton Bowen, a former Floridian now living in New York State, wrote to Christopher. With the dry dispassion of a self-appointed sleuth, Bowen wrote:

> About May 1935 Everett Ruess registered under an assumed name at Disston Lodge, St. Petersburg, Florida, a federal transient camp, after walking from Lake City, Fla. with the dog Curly. He and the dog had hitch-hiked from Arizona taking several weeks as it was difficult to obtain a ride with the dog.

The inclusion of Curly in the story was meant by Bowen to be a brilliant piece of insider knowledge. But in its September 1938 issue, *Desert* had published a photo of Everett at home in the winter of 1931–32, playing in the front yard with the "rez dog" he had adopted. What Bowen had no way of knowing was that Curly had disappeared in May 1932 after Everett, in a fit of anger, beat his dog because Curly had eaten his owner's supper.

Bowen offered to send the parents photographs of the boy and his dog, though he never followed through on this promise. In the same letter he recounted his initial conversation with Everett:

> He told me how he had left the burros loose in the canyon. . . . He thought his parents might be looking for him but didn't warm up to the suggestion to drop them a

postcard. It appears that he wanted to be free to live the life
of a hermit philosopher. . . .

He wanted no companion other than the dog.

He disappeared without saying anything.

One wonders why Christopher tolerated the chicanery of Bowen's bogus revelations, corresponding with the man for another four years. Perhaps any contact with his lost son, however phantasmal, was better than the eternal silence from the desert.

Christopher and Stella had dwelt on the implied allusion to Odysseus represented by the NEMO inscriptions. By the late 1930s they had begun to speculate that Everett, still alive, was acting out his "Ulysses years." Ulysses (or Odysseus), Christopher argued, had wandered for seven years before returning to his home in Ithaca, reclaiming his beloved Penelope, and slaying her suitors. So the parents would wait for seven years, until 1941, before giving up hope of Everett's return. (Christopher's calculation of seven years' wandering is curious, for in Homer's epic, it is clear that Odysseus is away from home for twenty years—ten of them fighting the Trojan War and ten returning to Ithaca.)

Indeed, however, in 1941, an apparent solution to the mystery dramatically surfaced, though it was hardly the denouement Christopher and Stella could have wished for. A Navajo "renegade" named Jack Crank was arrested near Monument Valley for murdering an elderly white man who had passed through the Oljato trading post northwest of the valley. According to one source, as reported by Bud Rusho in *A Vagabond for Beauty,* "Crank's motives were that he needed the scalp of a 'blood enemy' for ceremonial use, and that he simply hated white men." While in detention in a Phoenix jail, he bragged that he had murdered Everett Ruess.

Crank may have been mentally ill. Although the authorities cautioned the Ruesses that the Navajo's testimony was shaky at best, and though the man was never prosecuted for Everett's murder, Christopher and Stella clung for years to this possible solution of their son's disappearance. In 1952, Crank was released from prison after serving a ten-year sentence. That August—nearly eighteen years after their last contact with Everett—Christopher wrote to a friend of their son's who had briefly traveled with him in 1931: "[Crank] was a sort of outlaw among his people even. He was probably drunk when he did the deed. . . . For us, this seems to solve the riddle."

*   *   *

With Lacy's articles, the cult of Everett Ruess was born. As Randall Henderson, editor of the monthly, wrote in 1940, "Readers of the Desert Magazine—literally hundreds of them—wrote letters to the publishing office. They wanted to know more about Everett Ruess. Some of them volunteered to renew the search for him."

Under Henderson's stewardship, the miscellany the parents had envisioned finally saw light in book form, as *On Desert Trails with Everett Ruess,* published in 1940 by Desert Magazine Press. A slender, large-format volume, the book reproduced some of Everett's paintings and woodcuts, interspersed with choice passages from his writings. For the first time, readers beyond the circle of friends and family were exposed to Everett's aphoristic utterances. Proclamations such as "Once more I am roaring drunk with the lust of life and adventure and unbearable beauty" and "I am overwhelmed by the appalling strangeness and intricacy of the curiously tangled knot of life" and "I have left no strange or delightful thing undone that I wanted to do" began to acquire a canonic resonance.

In the foreword to *On Desert Trails,* Henderson articulated for the first time the siren appeal of the vagabond's vision:

[This book] is offered, not merely as entertainment, but as an intimate picture of a very intelligent young man who sought in his own way to find the solution to some of the most difficult of the problems which confront all human beings in this highly complex age. We cannot all be wanderers, nor writers nor painters. But from the philosophy of Everett Ruess we may all draw something that will contribute to our understanding of the basic values of the universe in which we live.

A lofty claim, perhaps, for the productions of an artist and writer who had not yet reached his twenty-first birthday. But the book struck a nerve with readers, quickly becoming a minor classic. Republished in different formats in 1950 and again in 2000, it is still in print.

Christopher and Stella did everything they could to make the book a success. They bought scores of copies and sent them to friends, as well as to strangers who might be influential advocates for their son's legacy. They pressed a copy on Orville Prescott, head book reviewer for the *New York Times,* who sent back a polite thank-you note, but warned that he couldn't promise to review the book. (The *Times* never did.)

For the rest of his life, Christopher kept a kind of log book in which he typed out transcriptions of letters he and Stella had received from readers of *On Desert Trails.* Some of the encomiums predated the book, for both Stella and Christopher had sent copies of "Youth Is for Adventure" to all kinds of people who had either known Everett or might become interested in him posthumously. In 1938, Edward Weston, whose door Everett had first knocked on in 1930, at the age of sixteen, sent a heartfelt note:

> Your remembrance reached me in Santa Fe. I don't forget Everett—it was kind of you to include me as one of his friends. The way of his going, I feel, is the way I would like to depart—close to the soil. But he was so young—

The year before, Hamlin Garland, the Pulitzer Prize–winning author of many books of Western history and fiction, wrote to Christopher and Stella: "Your son was a most unusual spirit. I have never known a youth of like endowment and predilection. He is a most interesting character. If he should ever come out of hiding he will bring a noble book in his knapsack!" (Garland may have met Everett, as this note seems to imply, for he had moved to Hollywood in 1929.)

Others made their first acquaintance with Everett in the pages of *On Desert Trails*. Some were profoundly moved. In 1940, Edward Howard Griggs, author of such educational and inspirational tomes as *Moral Leaders* and *The Soul of Democracy*, praised Everett's writing to the skies in a note to Stella and Christopher: "It is unique in American, indeed, in all literature, carrying as it does, Henry D. Thoreau and John Muir to the nth power. Walt Whitman would have said Everett's joyous, free life was his great, rhythmically cadenced poem."

It was only a matter of time before the saga of Everett Ruess caught the attention of a major American writer. Such a collision of sensibilities came in 1942, when Wallace Stegner published *Mormon Country*. In that beguiling meditation on the Southwest, Stegner devoted a whole chapter, titled "Artist in Residence," to the Ruess saga. Those pages contain the first nuanced, judicious appraisal of Everett, not only as an artist and writer but as a wilderness visionary. Stegner's chapter remains one of the best things ever written about the lost wanderer.

EIGHT

Cult and Conundrum

STEGNER WAS NOT AS IMPRESSED as others were by Everett's artistic and literary talents. "He was not a good writer and he was only a mediocre painter," he wrote, "but give him credit, he knew it, and he was learning. It didn't matter greatly that he was not in command of his tools. He was only eighteen [actually sixteen] when he started traveling by horse and burro and on foot through the canyons and plateaus."

Stegner fixed the vagabond in a tradition dating back to the Spanish conquistadors of "spiritual and artistic athletes who die young." He elaborated, "Everett was one of those, a callow romantic, an adolescent aesthete, an atavistic wanderer of the wastelands, but one of the few who died—if he died—with the dream intact."

At the outset of his chapter, Stegner delivered a memorable précis of Everett's quest; it remains today the most oft-quoted summation of his accomplishment:

> What Everett was after was beauty, and he conceived beauty
> in pretty romantic terms. We might be inclined to laugh at
> the extravagance of his beauty-worship if there was not

something almost magnificent in his single-minded dedication to it. Esthetics as a parlor affectation is ludicrous and sometimes a little obscene; as a way of life it sometimes attains dignity. If we laugh at Everett Ruess we shall have to laugh at John Muir, because there was little difference between them except age.

The "Artist in Residence" chapter teeters throughout on the divide between mature condescension and sincere praise, but in the end, Stegner "gets" what Everett was about.

Deliberately he punished his body, strained his endurance, tested his capacity for strenuousness. He took out deliberately over trails that Indians and old timers warned him against. He tackled cliffs that more than once left him dangling halfway between talus and rim. With his burros he disappeared into the wild canyons and emerged weeks later, hundreds of miles away, with a new pack of sketches and paintings and a whole new section in his journal and a new batch of poems.

Whether or not the writing was very good, Stegner saw Everett's performance in his letters to friends and family as "chanting his barbaric adolescent yawp into the teeth of the world." (The allusion to Whitman's "Song of Myself" was apt.)

In Stegner's view, the journeys themselves were Everett's real work of art: "The peculiar thing about Everett Ruess was that he went out and did the things he dreamed about, not simply for a two weeks' vacation in the civilized and trimmed wonderlands, but for months and years in the very midst of wonder."

As he summarized what was known by 1942 about the Ruess saga, Stegner spun a clever riff on the NEMO inscriptions: "No one in the [search] party knew what Nemo meant. Was it an Indian word?

The Navajo didn't recognize it. Did it have some cryptic significance? Was it a message of some kind?" Then, after summarizing Christopher and Stella's gloss on the name, Stegner mused,

> The explanation that it meant "no one" was both useless and tantalizing. Trust a boy with his head full of poetry and his eye full of cyclopean scenery to carve that word on the sandstone. But did he carve it just because the cave he was in reminded him of the Cyclops episode in the Odyssey, or had he been reading *Twenty Thousand Leagues under the Sea* until he fancied himself the same sort of lone-wolf pioneer as Captain Nemo, or was this scrawl a cryptic notice to the world that he intended to disappear, to cast off his identity?

Despite his tendency to hold Everett at arm's length, like some geological specimen, and despite the sophisticated irony that suffuses the chapter, by the end Stegner comes around to admiration, even to empathic identification:

> So there we leave it. Many people in that country believe Everett Ruess to be still alive. . . . The Mormon boys with whom he hunted horses and went to the Ward House in Tropic and Escalante have a sneaking suspicion that he lives, wandering in a gorgeous errant way around the world, painting and writing poetry. Except for the painting and the poems, they can conceive that life, because it is close to their own adventurous dreams. Because they will never themselves go, they would much rather not have Everett Ruess dead. It is a nice thing to think about, that maybe tonight he is sitting under the shadow of some cliff watching the light race upward on the mountain slope facing him, trying to get it into water colors before the light leaves him entirely.

Stegner's ending is as memorable and affirmative as the précis with which he opened:

> It is just possible that the loss of identity is the price of immortality.
> Because Everett Ruess is immortal, as all romantic and adventurous dreams are immortal. He is, and will be for a long time, Artist in Residence in the San Juan country.

*   *   *

Neither *On Desert Trails* nor Stegner's encomium brought Everett true fame. The cult that would eventually solidify around his meteoric passage and mysterious vanishing would take decades to grow. Yet over the years, all kinds of bystanders took the Ruess puzzle passionately to heart, refusing to believe that what happened to Everett was a mystery that could never be solved. Some of these devotees were themselves savvy explorers of the Southwest. None of them was more dogged and resourceful than Harry Aleson.

Although he would become one of the leading river-running guides in the West, Aleson came to the country relatively late. Born in Iowa in 1899, he served in World War I, then kicked around the Midwest as he took a series of jobs ranging from fire lookout to oil company surveyor. In 1939, at the age of forty, Aleson rented a motorboat on Lake Mead, the reservoir on the Colorado River above Hoover Dam, and spent five days puttering around its bays and inlets. Smitten by the grandeur of the place, he moved to the Southwest, where his first home was a shack at the western end of the Grand Canyon.

By 1941, Aleson was leading tame commercial trips on Lake Mead. But the wilder water upstream captivated him, and he began making reconnaissances, often solo, through the rapids of the Colorado River and up the mouths of its many tributaries, including the Escalante. Aleson's exploratory itch drove him away from his boat into the canyons

and up onto the mesas that bordered the riverine systems. Routinely
he would cache his craft on shore, set off on a grueling loop hike, and
return hours or even days later to resume his river run.

On one such hike in 1946, Aleson headed up Davis Gulch from
the Escalante. He climbed a hand-and-toe trail to a high alcove sheltering an Anasazi structure and discovered, purely by accident, Everett's
"NEMO 1934" inscription carved in the doorsill. The find galvanized
his curiosity. By 1948 a reporter from the *Deseret News* could write of
him, "Perhaps no man living has spent as much time in searching for
traces of the lost young man as has Harry Aleson of Richfield, Utah."

Aleson had ambitions as a writer, but one rejection after another
by regional newspapers and magazines soured him on professional
journalism. A pack rat by nature, he kept every scrap of paper that
had anything to do with his career—the food and equipment lists
he sent to his clients, the funky brochures he cranked out by mim-
eograph, even the rejection slips editors wounded him with. He be-
queathed these massive piles of paper to the Utah State Historical
Society in Salt Lake City, where they were archived after his death
in 1972. Those boxes full of letters, first drafts, and random jottings
amount to a treasure trove for scholars of the Southwest, for almost
no self-taught sleuth ever probed so deeply into the arcane mysteries
and controversies of the region.

Aleson's fascination with Everett Ruess drew him into a correspondence with Stella and Christopher. In 1948 he offered to guide
them into Davis Gulch. Christopher was too busy at work to go, but
Stella gamely signed on for what Aleson made clear would be an arduous journey. By then she was sixty-eight years old.

Stella later wrote an account of that pilgrimage. Like her narrative
of the June 1935 auto trip to the Southwest, it is oddly travelogue-ish,
revealing little of the emotions the journey must have brought to the
surface. Stella and a friend from Pasadena named Lou Fetzner drove
to Richfield, where they met Aleson. After a whirlwind, several-day

tour of scenic wonders, on April 15 the river guide, with his assistant, Sterling Larson, drove the women in a pickup truck sixty-six miles down the Hole-in-the-Rock Trail. The next day, leaving their vehicle, the foursome hiked for several hours across slickrock domes and sandy washes until they came to the hidden upper end of the old livestock trail into Davis Gulch.

As Stella later wrote:

> We got down into Davis Canyon to the willows & box elders before noon & then had sandwiches & juice in beer cans.
>
> Then we started down grade to the canyon bed, struggling through young willows that were dense & scratchy. Finally we turned & came upon a circle of red mountains with a high window [i.e., arch], & below it were about 30 Indian pictographs—dancing man, lizard, etc. Harry's name & some of the first searching party were written in the wall with charcoal, so Lou and I added ours.

From this rock art panel, Aleson then led the party to the hand-and-toe trail he had first climbed in 1946.

> Finally we saw the Moqui house high up the canyon wall with an arched overhang. Lou & Sterling stayed below, because he had leather shoes. Harry climbed up first, then came back & said I could make it. He stayed below me & pointed out each crevice (Moqui toe-holds) where I could put one foot after the other while bracing my hands against the sharp slanting wall. By the time I reached the shelf, 15 feet wide perhaps, I felt pretty shaky, because I thought it would be much harder to get down. Here there were quite dim pictographs, & the one Moqui ruin without a roof. . . . Two steps lead up to the door sill where Nemo & 1934 are scratch [sic]. Harry & some one else added their

dates. . . . I took 2 small pottery pieces, & Harry cached below several pieces from a good sized cooking bowl.

Strange it may have been, but characteristic of Stella, to describe her fear on the hand-and-toe trail, but not a word about her feelings on seeing her son's cryptic inscription in such an inaccessible eyrie.

She managed to descend the "Moqui steps," coached and spotted by Aleson and Larson. "The path back to our lunch spot," Stella wrote, "seemed a long long way so we decided to sleep there instead of trying to get back to the cowboy cabin [on the Hole-in-the-Rock Trail]." To the *Deseret News* reporter, Aleson later hailed Stella as the "bravest of courageous women."

In camp, Stella wrote, "Harry and Sterling kept the fire going all night, & Harry talked about Everett until 11:30. He discounts every theory except that Everett fell from a cliff."

During the following years, Aleson latched on to some startling clues about Everett's fate. The scenario they outlined was so incendiary that Aleson never shared it with Stella and Christopher. He may have first committed it to print in November 1951, in a letter to Olive Burt, a friend and former client who worked for the *Deseret News*. In a postscript headed "NOT FOR PUBLICATION," Aleson wrote,

During the past four to five years I have been hearing rumors on the disappearance of young Ruess. I have heard some very bold statements. Names have been named. Certain persons living in the area today are not only suspected, but practically accused of the murder of Ruess. With no substantial proof, of course nothing can be done. I have all the names. . . . For the present, I am waiting, hoping for a death-bed confession. For some years I have known the men most concerned or suspicioned. Have talked to them often . . . I have good reason to continue the suspicion.

It was not until 1953 that anyone in the family was made privy to the Escalante gossip about Everett's possibly having been murdered by locals. On September 12 of that year, Randall Henderson, the editor and publisher of *On Desert Trails,* wrote not to Stella or Christopher, but to Waldo, who had returned to California from postings in El Salvador and Indonesia.

> Two years ago, camping on the Kaiparowitz mesa overlooking the Escalante river basin I listened to the story of a couple of Mormon cowboys—a story that while not conclusive, was an acceptable solution of the mystery. They believe Everett was killed by a couple of cattle rustlers whose names they know. Their story was entirely plausible—and as far as I am concerned it is the solution to the mystery.

It is not clear whether Waldo shared Henderson's revelation with his parents. By 1953, Everett had been missing for nineteen years. Not a month had gone by, however, without his parents brooding upon their younger son's fate. And they still held on to a glimmer of hope that Everett might somehow be alive. In March 1948, having had to decline Aleson's invitation to the trip into Davis Gulch, Christopher wrote to the river guide, summing up the possible scenarios. A number of backcountry veterans who had met Everett, including John Wetherill, thought that the most likely cause of death was a fall from a cliff in some obscure canyon. Wrote Christopher,

> It may be that Everett met his end in such a fall, it may be he drowned crossing the Colorado (as Mr. Henderson of the Desert Magazine came to believe), it may be that he was killed by the Indians for his gear (unlikely), he may have fallen and suffered amnesia, forgetting his identity, or it may be he planned to disappear without a trace and lose him-

self among the natives and he may be in Central or South America or Mexico now. For all these theories there have been believers.

In March 1953, the Salt Lake City newspapers ran several articles about the recent finding of an old camp with a "year's supply" of canned food lying about. The spot was about fifty miles south of the town of Tropic. The headlines toyed with the idea that this could have been Everett's last camp: "Clue to Murder?" and "20-Year-Old Mystery Revived. Discovery of Old Hideout Gives Clue to Lost Artist."

Aleson forwarded the clippings to Stella and Christopher, even while he doubted that the camp could have been Everett's—"[H]e would not have stocked up on a 'year's supply of food.' " The authorities soon agreed. But in the exchange with Stella and Christopher, Aleson hinted obliquely at the secret he was keeping close to his vest: "Assuming that someday we do learn the facts of Everett's disappearance, possibly through a death-bed confession,—to what extent would you, Christopher and Stella, want to know the details? For some years now, I've had the thought that we are going to learn."

Christopher may have thought Aleson was hinting at Jack Crank, the possibly insane Navajo who had bragged about killing Everett, and who had been released from prison in 1952 after serving a ten-year sentence for his actual murder of an elderly Anglo near Oljato. Or he may have harked back to John Upton Terrell's formula of a "renegade bad man or Indian." He answered Aleson, "We would want to know everything, but we hate the idea of general publicity, though it might be desirable to influence others not to venture on the Indian lands without realizing what risks they take. An Indian drunk or sober . . . might well get the idea of vengeance on any white man. . . . Everett probably realized that he was taking his life in his hands."

On April 14, 1954, after suffering complications from a pair of abdominal operations, Christopher died at the age of seventy-five.

Five hundred "loving friends" (in Stella's phrase) attended his memorial service. Despite the vicissitudes that had forced him to take one job after another just to keep his family afloat, the common thread of Christopher's life's work had been service to others in need. His forty-nine years of marriage to Stella had amounted to a seamless continuum of love and loyalty. And by 1954 he was extremely proud of Waldo, who had launched a successful career as an international diplomat and businessman.

The great hole in Christopher's life, however, the dark sorrow that he took with him to his grave, was the loss of Everett, compounded by the impossibility of ever learning what had happened to his son after he had carved his NEMOs on the canyon walls of Davis Gulch.

*   *   *

Meanwhile, Harry Aleson was closing in on what he was sure was the answer. Yet he was loath to commit his knowledge to print. His closest confidant was another river guide and Southwest historian, Otis R. "Dock" Marston. (The Utah State Historical Society holds reams of fascinating correspondence between these two would-be writers and wilderness sleuths.) On December 14, 1952, Aleson wrote Marston "in strictest confidence,"

> I heard firsthand on Pearl Harbor Day this year, some startling statements—from a man of that area, pretty much "in his cups."
>
> The boy was shot. Killer was named to me. Killer died seven years later. Two others threw the body in the Colorado R. Both are living. One served time in Utah Pen for rustling. I've been seeing and talking to him off and on for several years. For some weeks now, he has kept a room here [in Richfield, Utah]. Not more than 20 feet between our beds. Nothing re the murder could be proved in court.

While the parents, whom I know, are living, I'm inclined
to say nothing—let the secret of the disappearance die with
them.

What would you do with this knowledge.

On Marston's advice, Aleson shared his revelations with Randall
Henderson the next March, in yet another letter headed CONFIDEN-
TIAL. As was his wont when dealing with top-secret material, Aleson
reverted to a telegraphic prose, almost like a spy sending a coded
message. The key sentences are doubly indented, each line a new
paragraph:

> This past winter I learned RE disappearance of ER.
> Much of the details of the final hours.
> The names of the men involved.
> The way the murder was committed.
> The disposal of the body in the river.
>
> But, there is no evidence or proof to bring into court.
>
> One of the men is dead.
> One of the other two would have to testify against the other.
>
> Perhaps a death-bed confession will come.

It may be that when Henderson wrote to Waldo six months later,
sharing the cowboy gossip about rustlers he said he had heard on top
of Kaiparowits Plateau, he was camouflaging the information Aleson
had passed to him in March. Or it may be that in 1951, Henderson
had indeed listened in on the cowboys telling a macabre story that
dovetailed closely with what Aleson had wrung from his inebriated
Richfield neighbor.

Aleson had vowed to Marston that he would indeed make a written record of everything he knew about Everett's murder, but would somehow keep it "in confidence." The piece of paper on which he did so may be the most bizarre document in all the annals of Everett Ruess's life and death.

Aleson recorded his solution to the mystery in the form of a Western Union telegram from an anonymous soothsayer to Aleson himself. His almost boyish effort at codifying the message took the form of reversing people's names and stringing words together without spaces. The homemade cryptogram is, however, easily deciphered. The first line dates it: "RECDNIGHTOF   DECSIX   1952." The second line records its arrival: "ATUTAHRICHFIELD   BY ALESONHARRY." The text spells out everything Aleson had learned from his informant:

TOWARD SOLVING OF MYSTERY

LAYADALIN   ONEOFLAST   TOSEEERALIVE

TOLDTOHLABY   BAILEYHUGH

KILLEDBYSHOT   ALVEYEMERON   MANONCE   KICKEDBY

HORSEAND   DEVELOPEDSPOT   ONLUNG   ANDMAY   HAVEDIED

ASARESULT   TBDEVELOPED   DECEASEDWTR   194243

RIDDLEKEITH   ANDPOLLOCKJOE   THRWEBODY   INTHERIVER

PROBABLYOFF   JACKASSBENCH   NEARHOLEINTHEROCK.

Addlin (not Adalin) Lay, Hugh Bailey, Emmorn (not Emeron) Alvey, Keith Riddle, and Joe Pollock were all Escalante ranchers. Lay had been one of the two sheepherders with whom Everett had camped on the nights of November 19 and 20 at the head of Soda Gulch; he was indeed one of the last to see Everett ("ER") alive. What he had to do with alleged murder, however, is completely unclear. The man "in his cups" was Hugh Bailey, for TOLDTOHLABY means "told to HLA—Harry L. Aleson—by." And Bailey apparently fingered Emmorn

Alvey, who had died in 1944, not in the winter of 1942–43, as Everett's killer. His accomplices, Keith Riddle and Joe Pollock, Bailey asserted, had disposed of the body by throwing it into the Colorado River.

Aleson's telegram languished for almost three decades, apparently unnoticed, in the archives of the USHS. No part of it was published anywhere until 1999, twenty-seven years after Aleson's death. The original copy was still in the USHS files in that year. It has since vanished, apparently stolen by a Ruess aficionado.

As to whether Aleson had indeed unraveled the mystery of Everett's fate, or at least come close to the solution—that remains in 2011 a vexed and perhaps insoluble question.

Aleson himself had later thoughts that complicated the question. To Dock Marston in 1956, four years after he had typed out his Western Union cryptogram, he wrote, "Yes, I have a few names of persons suspicioned of murdering Everett. I have two stories, from opposite factions, which attempt to cast blame on the other. The ruggedest of the stories was told to me while the narrator was fairly much 'in his cups.' I am not yet ready to give these names."

Seven years later, in 1963, in a letter to another Ruess devotee, Aleson seemed to retreat further from his certainty of 1952:

> I have only "hear-say" on cattle rustling in the thirties, when Everett dropped out of sight. There are rumors around Escalante town. No one dares speak up because of lack of proof. I do have the names of three men suspicioned of murdering Everett and accused of throwing his body into the Colorado River a short way upstream from Hole in the Rock. One of the three has been dead several years. Perhaps, one must await a deathbed confession—from one or the other of the two still living.

*   *   *

After Christopher's death, Waldo took up the ceaseless quest to figure out what might have happened to Everett. Together with Stella, he chased down every hint of a lead that might trace a path back to 1934 and Davis Gulch. And in the late 1950s, a pair of accidental finds gave Everett's mother and brother surges of hope. In November or December 1956, some prospectors exploring far out on the Escalante Desert came across a skeleton on the west bank of the Colorado River, not far from the Hole-in-the-Rock. Harry Aleson got wind of the discovery and wrote about it to Stella. Without having seen the skeleton, he speculated, "At this time there is a fifty-fifty possibility that the remains of Everett have been found." But an investigation led by the Garfield County sheriff ruled out such a match—on what grounds, the surviving record does not disclose.

In the summer of 1957 an archaeologist working as part of a massive survey of Anasazi ruins along the Colorado River, as teams tried to document those sites before Lake Powell would swallow them for good, came across an old camp near the mouth of Cottonwood Canyon. The scholar and his two assistants, both Escalante men, found an assemblage of utensils and cooking gear—spoon, fork, cup, pans, and a canteen—as well as a box of razor blades made by the Owl Drug Company, which was based in Los Angeles. An eastern tributary of the Colorado, Cottonwood flows directly opposite the Hole-in-the-Rock; the 1880 Mormon pioneers rode up its streambed after they had floated their wagons across the great river. Had Everett crossed the Colorado at Hole-in-the-Rock, he would have emerged at the mouth of Cottonwood Canyon.

The same Garfield County sheriff ultimately shipped some of these belongings to Stella. She and Waldo perused them carefully, deciding in the end that they could not have been part of Everett's gear. (On previous expeditions, Everett had never made any mention of shaving his beard, while at least twice he sought out barbers who gave him both a haircut and a professional shave.)

In a letter to the Garfield sheriff written in 1960, Waldo ran through the various theories about Everett's demise. Stella, Waldo claimed, "prefers optimistically to think that he is alive but an amnesia victim." Waldo himself inclined to the idea, shared by such experts as John Wetherill and Harry Goulding, who had founded Goulding's Trading Post in Monument Valley in 1921, that Everett had fallen to his death from some cliff. "[E]ven if he only broke an arm or a leg," Waldo imagined, "in a remote canyon no one would have known of it and he could have starved to death and eventually been covered over by the shifting sands."

But Waldo could not dismiss the alternate theory that rustlers around Escalante had murdered Everett. "I certainly wish someone could get to the bottom of all this," he wrote to the sheriff. "If my brother met with foul play, by this time whoever did it must have suffered plenty from remorse, over the years; there would be no need or use of punishing them now, after all these years."

Another river guide who become fascinated with the Ruess saga was Ken Sleight. A good friend of Harry Aleson, Sleight was also the model for the character Seldom Seen Smith in Edward Abbey's rollicking novel, *The Monkey Wrench Gang*. Like Abbey, Sleight deplored the creation of Lake Powell—"Powell's Puddle," he nicknamed it. Both men later toyed with the fantasy of blowing up the dam at Page, Arizona, that had created the sprawling reservoir—the guerrilla strike that supplies the plot for Abbey's novel, which in turn inspired the eco-radical group Earth First!

In 1964, Sleight guided Waldo down the Escalante River and into Davis Gulch, after convincing him that he needed to make the visit before the lower gulch (including the NEMO inscriptions) was drowned by Lake Powell. By the summer of 1963, Sleight wrote to Waldo, the reservoir was rising at the rate of one inch per hour. Another reason for the trip was that Sleight was convinced that Everett's body might still be found in or near Davis Gulch. On June 6, 1963, he wrote to Waldo, "[L]et me say that I don't think Everett left the Davis and Escalante drainages. I am sure in my mind that he lost his life in this region. . . . I do not believe there was foul play."

Waldo never wrote about the 1964 trip, but it was clearly a powerful experience for him. Many years later he would say to others, "Ken Sleight told me I could count myself among the first 150 white-skins to go down the Escalante." Somewhere near one of the NEMO inscriptions, Waldo found a prehistoric metate—a stone basin the Anasazi had used for grinding corn. He wanted to take it home as a keepsake of the journey, but the metate was too heavy to pack out. Sleight promised he would pick it up on a return journey, but may never have followed through on this vow.

Sometime in the late 1960s (in later years he could never recall the precise date), Sleight was leading a horse-packing trip down Grand Gulch, a sinuous fifty-five-mile-long northern tributary of the San Juan River that is loaded with Anasazi ruins and rock art. Over campfires in the Gulch, Sleight told his clients all about the mystery of Everett Ruess. One evening, shortly before dark, one of the clients scrambled up to a pair of granaries tucked under an overhang on a ledge some eighty feet above the canyon floor. He returned to report that he had found an inscription carved in the mud wall of one of the granaries, and that it looked like it read "NEMO." Incredulous, Sleight made the climb himself and verified the find.

In 1998, Sleight recalled, "There was also a bunch of colored zigzags painted on the rock wall just left of the granary. Some kind of design or landscape. Looked like watercolor paints to me. I wanted to take a sample to see if it *was* watercolor, but I never got around to it."

The NEMO was plainly legible, though no date was attached to it. It could, Sleight realized, have been a copycat inscription, carved by some later passerby in homage to the lost vagabond. What argued against that explanation, however, was that the shape of the capital letters seemed to match perfectly those of the two inscriptions in Davis Gulch, which Sleight had seen on several occasions. By the late 1960s, however, no photograph of the Davis Gulch NEMOs had ever been published. How could a copycat have gotten the orthography of a faked inscription exactly right?

But this new NEMO raised a host of complicated problems. So far as we know, Everett had never been in Grand Gulch, although he may have intended to make such a trip, for John Wetherill would have told him about the rich excavations he and his brothers had carried out there in the 1890s. But by the easiest hiking route, Grand Gulch lies at least forty miles east of Davis Gulch. If Everett indeed had carved the NEMO in the mud of the ancient storage bin, how had he gotten there without his burros? And when had he made the inscription? Since he had never signed himself NEMO before late 1934, the Grand Gulch visit must have come after he had camped in Davis Gulch in November.

Sleight puzzled over this conundrum for decades, in part because it contradicted his earlier conviction that Everett must have died in or near Davis Gulch. By the early 1980s, Sleight favored the theory that Everett had set out on an arduous hike, intending to visit Monument Valley, where he had spent time both in 1931 and earlier in 1934. He might have left his burros behind because of the difficulty of getting them to cross the Colorado River. In all likelihood, Sleight speculated, after exploring Grand Gulch, Everett had descended the canyon to its mouth, then drowned trying to swim the San Juan River, as he attempted to move from Cedar Mesa onto the Navajo Reservation. The crossing at the mouth of Grand Gulch is a notoriously treacherous one.

Other students of the Ruess enigma were at least as puzzled as Ken Sleight. Because the river guide was so possessive of his discovery that he did not readily disclose the location of the NEMO granary, others wondered whether Sleight had made up the whole story, or had scratched the copycat inscription himself. But to those who knew him well, such an act was unthinkable. It would be very unlikely that a man who had spent decades searching for any trace of Everett Ruess, and who had guided Waldo into Davis Gulch, would have tarnished the legend by fabricating false evidence.

*   *   *

Over the years, fans of Everett Ruess were moved to poetic evocations that tried to capture the essence of his spirit and his quest. One of the finest appreciations came from Hugh Lacy, whose articles in *Desert* magazine had first brought the vagabond's story to a larger audience. In "Say That I Kept My Dream . . ." Lacy wrote,

> He was one of earth's oddlings—one of the wandering few
> who deny restraint and scorn inhibition. His life was a quest
> for the new and the fresh. Beauty was a dream. He pursued
> his dream into desert solitudes—there with the singing wind
> to chant his final song.

A newspaper journalist and friend of the family, Paul Wilhelm, wrote a ballad about Everett, which cleverly if sentimentally imagined his last days in Davis Gulch from the point of view of Cockleburrs and Chocolatero. It begins,

> *At winter dusk they stand and wait—*
> *Two burros by a broken gate . . .*

The poem traces Everett's journeys through late summer and early autumn of 1934, and finally down the Hole-in-the-Rock Trail.

But that was long before we knew
That he corralled the burros two,
Showed them the grass and water near
Enough to keep them for a year.
He'd be away, "O not as long
As you could bray," he said, "your song . . .
Just round the bend, up scarped pine belt,
A cliff cave hangs, where Indians dwelt,
Now wait for me, I'll not be long."
He swung away and sang his song:
"Say that I starved, was lost
On some cold starlit trail agleam—
But that I kept my desert dream!"

And every winter dusk they wait—
Two burros by a broken gate,
For one who was their trail friend
But vanished round the canyon bend
When autumn snows swirled off plateaus
Where Escalante River flows.

The publication of *On Desert Trails* in 1940, and its reprinting in 1950, served handsomely to fulfill Christopher, Stella, and Waldo's desire to keep Everett's memory alive in word and woodcut. But by the 1950s, the family yearned for some additional monument—a fuller anthology of Everett's work, perhaps, or even a biography. It was thus with high expectations that Waldo and Stella reacted to a letter written to Stella in April 1958 by a man named Larry Kellner.

A ranger at Wupatki National Monument near Flagstaff, and a friend of Clay Lockett (the leader of the 1934 excavation of Woodchuck Cave who had hired Everett as camp cook), Kellner also had high ambitions as a writer. As Waldo later summarized the letter's contents, Kellner suggested that he would produce a screenplay about

Everett for "a top rate TV program such as 'Climax' or 'Playhouse 90.' Says can construct a dialogue such as between E and others and between E & Indians by talking to Clay Lockett and to various Indians. Mentions a Navajo about 70 years old who lives on the edge of the Painted Desert and has been there all his life and should know E." Kellner went on to declare a deep sense of identification with Stella's lost son: "Everett's feelings are parallel to mine about this vast country and the Indian people."

Thus began a long correspondence among Stella, Waldo, and Kellner. In February 1959, Kellner apologized to Stella for a protracted silence, occasioned, he said, by attending college in Omaha and suffering from a recurring kidney ailment. Back as a ranger at Sunset Crater, just south of Wupatki, he was eager to get started on the screenplay. He asked, "I was wondering if you might have a spare picture of Everett that I might have, showing a close-up of him. Also, if possible, do you have one of him with his burros, or one similar?" Kellner wanted to show the photos to various Navajo and Hopi elders to see if they recognized Everett. The pictures, he promised, "will be returned to you as soon as possible."

Kellner added an intriguing datum: "I have one Indian name by which he was known—Yabitoch." Almost twenty-four years earlier, on March 14, 1935, Captain Neal Johnson had written Stella and Christopher, "Most of the Indians know of the Paint man whitch is Everett they say he is Yabitoch which means fun, good humor." Although the parents later discounted virtually everything Johnson told them, this striking allusion to "Yabitoch" must have convinced Stella that Kellner was onto a new clue to Everett's fate. Since Johnson's letters had never been published, the Navajo appellation for the "Paint man," it seemed, must have been genuine.

A trusting woman, Stella promptly mailed Kellner a batch of photos of Everett. Some of them were apparently the only prints from negatives that had long been lost. In May, Kellner wrote Stella again, saying that he needed to hold on to the photos a while longer, and asking if she minded if he made copies of them. Once more he tossed out provocative details from his research in the field.

> I have a trader friend (now 47 years old and a white man) who, as a lad, helped on occasion at Gouldings Trading Post from about 1928 to 1934. I showed him the pictures of Everett, and asked if he knew the lad. The first picture he did not recognize Everett, but when I showed him one with Everett and the burros, he replied "Sure—this is Everett Ruess. We were both about the same age. We packed into Monument Valley once, and had a great time. Everett knew how to camp well, but the one thing I showed him was how to use a Dutch oven. Yes, I knew him well. We used to sit and talk by the hours."

Kellner never disclosed the name of this trader friend. He added, "I am still of the opinion, however, that the key to the entire situation lies with the old Navajos whom I will contact, as well as some of the older Hopis."

At some point in 1959 or 1960, Kellner briefly visited Stella and Waldo in Los Angeles. Many years later, Waldo would recall the "fine impression" the man had made.

Meanwhile, however, there was no further talk from Kellner about a screenplay for some television show. Instead, by April 1961 the man had decided to write a book about Everett. As Waldo paraphrased a Kellner letter, "Says wants to do E's complete life, in one good-sized book. Can do more justice that way. Also, believes he would be able to get better TV and/or movie rights from this book." Later in 1961, he wrote Stella to ask what percentage of the royalties she wanted.

Through 1960 and 1961, sporadic letters from Kellner dropped more tantalizing tidbits from his research. A sample, again in Waldo's paraphrase: "Says in Oct. he is going to stop at Polacca when he goes to Canyon de Chelly in search of things E left in cliff dwelling. Says 2 Hopis told him they think E wrote Nema, not Nemo, and Nema is a Hopi word meaning 'I am going home.' "

Three years after first making contact with Stella, Kellner had still not returned the photos of Everett. Nor had the biographer made a second visit to the family. By now, reasonable skepticism ought to have set in. Something was clearly amiss with Larry Kellner, and in some ways he was beginning to resemble the second coming of Captain Neal Johnson. It was not cash that Kellner wanted, but, as it were, pieces of Everett himself.

Half a century later, it is hard to judge how sincere Kellner was, or just how much research he actually undertook. In July 1960 he wrote to Harry Aleson, describing an encounter with some Hopi firefighters with whom he had worked at Saguaro National Monument near Tucson.

> They did not know Everett, although one of them vaguely recalled the young wanderer. I showed him pictures of Everett, but he could not readily recall him to[o] well. He did, however, tell me that there is a white man, about forty-five years old, living among the Hopis. He dresses like a Hopi, complete with long hair.

In 1960, if he were still living, Everett would have been forty-six years old. Kellner added that the firefighters "are going to try to uncover for me information on Everett from among the older Hopi people."

Far from reigning in their collaboration with Kellner in 1961, however, Waldo (who was as trusting as his mother) and Stella kept sending the man original documents, including what Waldo later described as "many letters, papers, etc." And somehow, in early 1961, they offered to lend Kellner one of Everett's trail diaries. The part-time ranger wrote back on March 3, "As to Everett's diary! Nothing would please me more than to read it, document it, and have it published."

In the age before copy machines, Stella and Waldo could think of no alternative to sending Kellner the original diary. By August it was in his hands. The thank-you letter Kellner wrote to Stella on August 5 makes the modern partisan of Everett Ruess want to weep with frustration:

> I received the diary you sent me about Everett's Arizona travels. I have read and reread it many times—I never tire of it. . . . I will, with your permission, keep the diary for a while longer, until I have an opportunity to either copy it and extract from it what I need for the book. Then, with all my fervent prayers, I hope that I can then return it to you in person.

The reference to "Everett's Arizona travels" makes it all but certain that the diary Kellner borrowed was the journal Everett kept during his spectacularly rich ten-month odyssey in the Southwest in 1931. That diary may still exist somewhere, but no disinterested student of the Ruess saga or member of his family has seen it in the last fifty years.

In 1961, Kellner began excusing his delays in getting on with the book project by complaining to Stella about an endless series of physical ailments and job crises that forestalled writing about Everett. In June, after an illness, Kellner claimed that a dentist in Globe, Arizona, had had to take out all his teeth. Later the same month he had to fight a forest fire "raging out of control" in the Chiricahua National Monument in southeastern Arizona. By the next May, his recurring kidney ailment had forced him to quit his job as a ranger. He had planned, he said, to go into Davis Gulch with Ken Sleight, but had to cancel the trip. In January 1963 he was further distracted by his mother's undergoing two lung surgeries and his father's struggling with a "heart condition."

In March 1963, Kellner brazenly asked Stella "if there are any more letters, diaries, photos, etc., which can be made available." It was now five years since Kellner had first contacted her, and neither she nor Waldo had seen a word of the purported book about Everett. Yet Kellner claimed to have had an encouraging response from the venerable Philadelphia publisher J. B. Lippincott & Co. Ever trusting, Stella and Waldo sent Kellner yet more materials, including some letters that Everett had written to his best friend, Bill Jacobs.

By now, Kellner was writing to Waldo with the air of one accomplice in biography confiding in another. On May 24, 1963, he mused,

> As for not finding a romance in Everett's life, I think it is only more intriguing and interesting. I wanted to be sure before writing the book, however, so that it can be written as accurately as possible. . . . [T]he fact that there apparently is no love affair does not make the story more difficult by any means, Waldo. I think this is probably all the more the true Everett.

It was not until April 1963 that Waldo first voiced impatience about the return of the precious original materials he and Stella had lent the biographer. In Waldo's résumé of the Kellner connection, he wrote, "I ask if he has extracted data from the diaries & other written material sent to him so that he can return it soon or now." On May 15, Kellner wrote back, "I have not copied the diaries but only excerpts from them." He asked if he could hang on to the materials "until such time as a publisher is lined up."

Nine days later, Kellner wrote Waldo, "With each passing day, I am more confident in Lippincott." But, "If that does not work out, I have now established contact with an agent in Beverly Hills and one in New York, and they will help fight the way to the publishing house."

The Kellner charade lasted through September 1964. More personal crises—job changes, the continued ill health of his parents, and the like—forced Kellner (or so he claimed) to declare bankruptcy. In March 1964 he wrote to Waldo, insisting that he had submitted a finished book, not to Lippincott, but to a New York publisher, which rejected it. Kellner turned to the Sierra Club, whose large-format picture books about the Southwest (most notably, Eliot Porter and David Brower's *The Place No One Knew*, about Glen Canyon on the Colorado River) were in the process of galvanizing an environmental movement nationwide. But Sierra Club Books, Kellner claimed, narrowly rejected the work.

On June 8, 1964, Kellner wrote Waldo again, giving him news of a family tragedy. Waldo recorded, "Sister ran into another car head-on and 4 of 8 occupants of other car were killed; sister critically injured but after 3 surgeries is making a comeback. . . . This hard on his parents—still alive."

On September 6, Waldo received another letter, with the return address general delivery in Santa Fe. Kellner had changed jobs again: he was now working, he said, for the Institute of American Indian Arts. "He mentions 'deaths in the family,'" Waldo noted, "(but parents still alive)."

Then Larry Kellner simply disappeared.

*   *   *

In the spring of 1964, Stella was eighty-four years old, Waldo fifty-four. During his twenties and thirties, as he crafted his career as an international diplomat, Waldo had spent more time abroad than in the United States, as he took positions in business and government in China, Japan, India, and Russia. He also traveled widely, making extended excursions to Morocco, Algeria, Sudan, Norway, France, Burma, Cambodia, Mexico, Canada, and other countries ("100 foreign lands," he would reckon in 1974). Waldo was also an accomplished polyglot, who became fluent in Mandarin Chinese, Spanish, Russian, and French, and he could converse in yet other languages.

Unlike Everett, Waldo was never shy with women. He had had a series of girlfriends both at home and abroad, but did not marry until he was forty-eight years old. Vacationing on the island of Mallorca in February 1957, Waldo came upon a Spanish woman making her way carefully down a sea cliff toward the beach. Waldo gave her a helping hand. Conchita was a surgical nurse at a local hospital. It was classical love at first sight. Waldo and Conchita were married on Columbus Day, 1957. For a short while they lived in the Andalusian town of Jerez de la Frontera, before the couple came to the United States, settling down close to Stella in Los Angeles. By 1964, Waldo and Conchita had three children, two daughters and a son.

On Mother's Day, May 10, 1964, Stella was resting in a hospital bed installed in her home, as she recuperated from a stroke. Waldo was off in the Escalante country with Ken Sleight, looking for traces of Everett. As he wrote to Harry Aleson a month later:

> Conchita had given Mother a good bkfst, which she enjoyed, and then the children came in and sang, "Happy Mother's Day to you, dear Grandma," she the while waving her arms as if conducting a choir. Then she dropped her arms and slowly faded away. Thus her passing was as sweet and poetic as the manner in which she lived.

Six weeks after Stella died, Waldo, Conchita, and the children moved to Santa Barbara, where Waldo would live for the rest of his life. That summer, his grief about his mother's death was compounded by the growing suspicion that Larry Kellner would never produce the book about Everett he had promised for half a decade. After September 1964, when Kellner stopped answering Waldo's letters, the sense of having been robbed of Everett's irreplaceable manuscripts burgeoned in Waldo (temperamentally the least angry of men) to a quiet but constant outrage.

Waldo would spend the next eighteen years trying to hunt down the shadowy Kellner. It would not be until November 1973—nine years after the man had dropped out of sight—that Waldo was able to obtain an address for him, a post office box in Tucson that the superintendent of Saguaro National Monument had supplied.

On February 9, 1974, Waldo wrote a forceful letter to Kellner. It read in part,

> Larry, could you *please* return to me the correspondence and diaries, etc., re Everett which we had loaned to you? This is part of my remembrance of my brother,—part of my heritage. Our children are growing and they want to read and know more about him. If it is a matter of the cost of sending them, even though we are a family of six [a fourth child had been born in 1965] living on less than $12,000 a year, I will find a way to reimburse you.

Kellner never replied. The Tucson post office box may have been a defunct or bogus address, or perhaps Kellner was simply ignoring Waldo's pleas. Waldo redoubled his efforts to track down the fugitive biographer. But it would take another eight years before he again made contact with Kellner.

The breakthrough came in May 1982, after Waldo had enlisted a friend named Tom Wright, who lived in Scottsdale, Arizona, to aid in the search. Wright managed to get a phone number in Globe, Arizona, and left a message asking Kellner to call him back. As Wright wrote to Waldo,

> Fortunately, when he called me back . . . he called collect, so the number he called from was listed on my phone bill. I called that number back today—I was afraid it might be a pay phone in a drugstore or a gas station, but it turned out

to be his mother's home. She told me that Larry has been out of town for several weeks, trying to find a job. . . . She says he writes or calls at least once a week with a temporary address as he goes from town to town, and she promised to give him the message to contact me just as soon as possible.

By now, in his desperation, Waldo was prepared to try to buy back Everett's original work from Kellner. Wright was sanguine about the propect of this coming to pass: "It shouldn't be too hard to talk a man who is unemployed and prone to bad luck into accepting $200 for a bundle of old papers." The publisher Gibbs Smith had recently commissioned the book that would become *Everett Ruess: A Vagabond for Beauty,* and Waldo was anxious to make all of his brother's letters and diaries available to the author, Bud Rusho.

In May, Waldo finally received his first letter from Kellner in almost eighteen years. Hand-written all in capitals, it listed general delivery in Globe as a return address. The short note is a masterpiece of feigned innocence.

Dear Waldo:

A friend of yours, Tom Wright of Phoenix, made contact with me last week and asked me to get in touch with you. He briefed me on the upcoming expanded book on Everett.

My father passed away in December after a long illness and my mother was hospitalized in March. If I do not reply to your letter immediately, please understand.

I am interested in your endeavor and will be awaiting your letter.

Hope this finds you all well.

Sincerely,

Larry.

On May 21, Kellner sent Waldo a longer, typed letter in response to one from Waldo that he finally acknowledged he had received. But the claims in this new letter were mind-boggling. Kellner insisted that he had never met Waldo or Stella. He also maintained that he had never received *any* of Everett's original writings or artwork from Waldo or his mother, either in person or by mail. He claimed instead that Stella had written him lamenting the loss of some of Everett's manuscripts "after your mothers move to your home."

What Kellner would admit to possessing was material "from people who knew Everett, or in some way were involved in the search for him, or who later became deeply interested in his story, such as Randall Henderson, Harry Aleson, etc. In addition, I [have] information from Indians, government people, traders, etc., who passed over to me what they knew."

Kellner was indeed interested in selling Waldo his files: "At this time, Waldo, I would be willing to consider a cash offer for *all* of the material I have, with acknowledgment in any publication, movie, and/or TV programming. I have a wealth of material, and still have contacts with people, which I am confident has not been disclosed."

All of these obfuscations were couched in the friendliest of blandishments elsewhere in the letter: "[I]t was good hearing from you again"; "I very much appreciate your interest in Everetts life—it was an exception, especially during those times"; "[C]onvey my best to Conchita and the family. I look forward to one day meeting all of you."

Waldo wrote back and offered Kellner $200 for his material, in hopes of making the papers available to Bud Rusho. In his answering letter, Kellner fawned once more: "Believe me, Waldo, I commend you highly for this undertaking. It is a fine tribute to Everett, and the entire story needs to be told." But then he wrote,

> The majority of the material I have is in the form of letters
> and interviews with people who knew Everett, and spans

about a 20-year period on my behalf. Considering the $200 offer, this would amount to $10.00 a year, or less than $1.00 a month. I feel, personally, that the offer is not realistic, not only from the stand point of my continued efforts, but also for the safe-guarding of the material I have.

Yet, like a fisherman playing a hooked trout, Kellner added, "However, this is not closing the door, Waldo. It is my opinion, and that of other authors and historians, that this material would greatly expound [*sic*] on Everett's life."

On August 24, 1982, Tom Wright managed to meet Kellner in person in Tucson. The next day he summarized this "very good visit" in a letter to Waldo. Kellner must have turned on the charm, for Wright concluded, "I think he is fair and honest and will make a real attempt to cooperate." But what Kellner told Wright did not exactly match what he had written to Waldo. As Wright reported:

Concerning Everett's letters, photos, diaries, etc., Larry says he has a mixture of originals and typewritten copies. . . . [H]e says that everything that came from your family was either a copy or an original of which you kept a copy. He says that the material is either labelled with words to the effect of "duplicate—you may keep this" or that the letters accompanying the material when it was sent to him said the same thing.

Now, however, Kellner told Wright that he was willing to "make his collection of Everett's material available to Peregrine Smith" (Gibbs Smith's imprint), but not "the research he's done over the years or his own writing about Everett's life." Even though Wright never saw a single page of Kellner's putative research or writing, the former park ranger somehow won Wright's sympathy: "He is, understandably, reluctant to give away or even sell the results of a 25-year involvement in Everett's story."

In exasperation, Waldo turned over the negotiations to Gibbs Smith. The next April, Waldo wrote to an acquaintance, "Gibbs offered Kellner $500 or $1000 for all of his E papers and data collected since the early 1960s or so, I believe, but I guess he wanted more than that."

In the end, Bud Rusho wrote *A Vagabond for Beauty* without the benefit of a single glance at the Kellner collection. Five more years passed. On November 16, 1987, after visiting Kellner in Globe, Tom Wright wrote Waldo with the news he dreaded to hear:

> He told me . . . that he had sold all his material on Everett. It was sold through a dealer in Santa Fe to a private collector, "an author," living in Richfield, Utah, for $3000. I told Larry that, in the interest of keeping track of the material for the benefit of future historians, I'd be very interested in having the name and address of this "author." Larry replied that he couldn't remember the man's name but that he could get it for me. . . . That was on August 6th, and I haven't heard from him since.

Twenty-nine years after he had first contacted Stella, Larry Kellner was still holding to his story. But the Richfield "author" did not exist. Kellner had, however, sold the collection to a Santa Fe book dealer.

In 1988, the final chapter of this dismal saga was written. On September 14 of that year, Waldo wrote a last letter to Kellner:

> I had heard that a half year ago or maybe a year ago you sold all the things re Everett to someone and have wondered about this because it seems to me my Mother and I sent you so many Everett things which you promised to guard with

your life and return to us,—original letters, diaries, etc. Can you comment on this?

Did you give up on publishing a book about E?

Kellner never responded.

Meanwhile, the Santa Fe dealer had contacted Ken Sanders, founder and owner of a legendary used bookstore in Salt Lake City, and one of the most ardent guardians of the Ruess flame. In 1984 and again in 1985, Sanders had published an "Everett Ruess Calendar," the squares for various days adorned with pithy quotes from Everett's letters and diaries. (March 15: "I go to make my destiny." March 23: "Beauty has always been my god.")

The Santa Fe dealer asked Sanders if he was interested in buying the Kellner collection. In 2009, Sanders recalled the tumult of emotions the offer stirred up. "The Santa Fe guy wanted big money. I called Ken Sleight and asked, 'What should I do?' He said, 'Ken, you have to buy this collection. Otherwise it will disappear forever.' So I made an offer to the Santa Fe dealer, and he took it. He overnighted the stuff in a big silver box. It was full of Kellner's quest to track down Everett. Letters to all kinds of people, even J. Edgar Hoover. Correspondence with the Ruesses. It was obsessive."

Waldo got wind of Sanders's purchase. On February 10, 1988, he wrote to the Salt Lake City bookstore owner. After detailing all the materials he and Stella had shipped to Kellner in the late 1950s and early 1960s, Waldo pleaded, "So, Ken, it certainly seems to me you should return any photos and original papers you bought from Kellner, as being stolen property he sent you."

But Sanders wrote back, "I sincerely doubt that there are any letters I have that you don't already have. They are all copies. . . . The only original correspondence is that which Kelner [sic] sent off to various people and agencies trying to find out information on Everett." As for diaries, according to Sanders, the only thing in the collection was a copy—not the original—of an apparently youthful journal in Everett's hand.

If this is true, there may be two possible explanations. One is that Kellner sold off the original letters and diaries piecemeal over the years. The other is that he kept them separate from the collection that he sold to the Santa Fe dealer, and that they remained in his possession after 1987. It is not possible that Waldo's memory of having sent precious originals to Kellner almost thirty years earlier was faulty, for Kellner's own letters express fulsome gratitude for the "loan" of those documents.

In 2009, Ken Sanders told this writer what happened next. "In a moment of weakness, during a period of poverty, I sold the Kellner materials to a certain individual from Indiana. He considers himself the caretaker of the collection. He thinks it should eventually be donated to a museum or library in Indiana [where Everett lived for several years as an adolescent]. He's another Everett Ruess fanatic."

Sanders would not reveal the private collector's name or address. He promised to forward a letter I wrote to the man, beseeching him to donate or sell the Kellner collection to the University of Utah, so that it could be united with the Ruess Family Papers archived there and accessible to the public. I never got a response.

In 2004, however, at the age of ninety-five, Waldo attended the first Everett Ruess Days festival in Escalante, a celebration that would become an annual event. With him were his wife, Conchita, and three of their adult children. There the family met the Indiana collector—whose name, unfortunately, none of the Ruesses can remember. The man greeted Waldo warmly and posed for some photographs with him. According to Waldo's daughter Michèle Ruess, "He came across to me as awkward and shy. He felt he had obtained the papers in an honest manner. He learned from us that they included stolen property, but he didn't feel any compulsion whatsoever to right the wrong. Apparently he had paid dearly for them. After meeting him I felt that future endeavors to have our property returned to us would be futile."

Waldo's son Brian Ruess adds, "At one point, he indicated a willingness to donate the papers to the University of Utah. But he had some kind of plan to use the materials first—for a book, or a movie, or both. He coyly refused to give our family any access to the materials until after he had finished his project."

Seven years later, the Kellner papers remain in the hands of the Indiana collector. What lost letters, diaries, and artwork of Everett's may be among them, only he, Ken Sanders, and perhaps a handful of other people know.

NINE

"No Least Desire for Fame"

AFTER WALLACE STEGNER, the next major writer to salute Everett was Edward Abbey, in his 1968 book, *Desert Solitaire,* which many Abbey fans consider his finest work. In a characteristic passage, the self-styled "desert rat" complained that while "the majority of the world's great spirits," from Homer to Joseph Conrad, had responded deeply to the open sea, relatively few good writers had hymned the desert. To a short list ranging from C. M. Doughty (*Travels in Arabia Deserta*) to Joseph Wood Krutch (*The Voice of the Desert*), Abbey appended "such obscure figures as the lad Everett Reuss, author of *On Desert Trails.*" Summing up Everett's story in a single sentence, Abbey added a whimsical conceit: "For all we know he is still down in there somewhere, living on prickly pear and wild onions, communing with the gods of river, canyon and cliff."

When this passage was brought to Waldo's attention, he wrote Abbey a letter scolding him for misspelling Everett's last name and for calling him "an obscure literary figure." Abbey wrote back, "I think if you will read my passages about Everett over again you will find that underneath the perhaps over-facetious or sardonic style there is genuine admiration. If I did not admire him so much I would never have mentioned him at all."

It was Abbey who, in 1980, directed Gibbs Smith's attention to Everett. In 1998, Smith wrote,

> [Abbey] viewed Everett as a kindred spirit and urged me to try to find out more about him. After some detective work, I located Everett's brother, who entrusted me with Everett's letters, other writings, and artwork. We both hoped that a new book would result. . . . I worked with the material for two years in my spare time, then asked my good friend W. L. Rusho to help organize a book. Bud and I worked together, and the book *Everett Ruess: A Vagabond for Beauty,* published in 1983, was the result.

In 2009, Smith elaborated on his first contact with Waldo during a visit to Santa Barbara. "Waldo had a garden shed full of Everett's stuff," Smith reminisced, "all of it in boxes and old orange crates. He let me take the letters back to Utah. I had them by my bed for two years. I'd read a few at a time. I slowly realized, these letters are really important. That's when I went to Bud."

On a meager advance, Rusho conducted a great deal of original research, much of it in Escalante, where he interviewed old-timers who had met Everett in 1934. The bulk of *Vagabond* is a selective anthology of some of Everett's letters from 1930 through 1934, interspersed with excerpts from his essays, a few passages from the 1932 and 1933 diaries, reproductions of some of his best blockprints, and photos of Everett in the field.

For continuity, Rusho inserted paragraphs of boldface text in his own voice summarizing Everett's doings between trips. And he bookended the anthology with a prefatory chapter called "The Beauty

and the Tragedy of Everett Ruess" and four short closing chapters
summarizing the decades of search for the lost wanderer, the theories
about his fate, and the lasting import of his legacy.

The book was not an immediate success. Within the first year, *Vagabond* sold only 1,700 copies of the ten thousand in print. But slowly
and steadily the book gained the status of a cult classic. By 2002,
more than 100,000 copies of *Vagabond* and the 1998 follow-up, *Wilderness Journals of Everett Ruess,* had been sold.

In 2009, speaking at a conference in Escalante, Gibbs Smith said,
"I've been in publishing for forty years, and this is one of the most interesting books I've ever published. It's had a life of its own. It's been
carried almost entirely by word of mouth.

"Everett, in my opinion, was the first unscientific appreciator of
this land. His letters are still the best expression of why we so appreciate the beauty of this landscape."

In his closing chapters, Rusho judiciously weighed the four leading theories about what happened to Everett, but committed to none
of them. Each of the four, he concluded, was plausible, but each raised
fundamental problems. The theory that Everett had deliberately disappeared or gone native was tempting (especially in view of the numerous "sightings" of Everett in later years, ranging from Florida to
Mexico), but the chances of this story being true, Rusho concluded,
were "small to the point of being remote." Moreover, wrote Rusho,
"From his letters, it appears that he remained too close to his parents and to his brother, Waldo, to suddenly and deliberately cut all
communication—forever."

The idea that Everett might have committed suicide, in Rusho's
analysis, was linked to the hypothesis of a deliberate escape from the
world. But "He was not a recluse; he liked to converse with everyone he met. . . ." And "Whatever his feelings upon leaving the cities,
his letters indicate a gradual return of confidence and good humor"
through the summer and early fall of 1934. Stella and Christopher

had come to the same conclusion: the last letters home had been too full of joy and enthusiasm to spring from a youth contemplating suicide.

The widely held belief that Everett might have fallen to his death from one of his daring climbs into prehistoric ruins, leaving his body lodged in some inaccessible canyon nook or crevice, ran up against the odd fact that the 1935 searchers found evidence of his last camp-site, but not his cooking and camping equipment, food, or painting kit. Everett would not, Rusho argued, have been likely to carry all that gear with him on a climb to a ruin.

Rusho devoted his most serious attention to the theory that rus-tlers had murdered Everett. In Escalante, he learned that rustling had become so widespread in 1934 that the Cattlemen's Association had spread the false rumor that a government investigator had been dis-patched to the region, traveling through it incognito as he hoped to catch the lawbreakers red-handed. Rustlers startled by the sudden ad-vent of a stranger leading his burros might have thought Everett was the government spy.

"It was into this atmosphere of deceit and suspicion that Everett innocently rode his burros south from Escalante," Rusho wrote. "Of course, Everett must have looked about as dangerous as a puppy dog, but who can account for the possible reaction to him in the mind of a petty thief?"

As Rusho conducted his research in Escalante in 1982, he learned that one local rancher, some years before, had actually bragged about killing Everett. Rusho managed to interview the man in his home, but "found his memory was suffering from old age. He did remember that a young artist had disappeared near Davis Gulch, yet he said that he knew absolutely nothing about the incident." Rather than leap to a facile conclusion, and out of compassion for the alleged confessor in his confused state of mind, Rusho did not name him in *Vagabond,* and left the whole rustler theory unresolved.

Rusho's conclusion about Everett's fate was, "We are left without a final answer, only riddles within riddles."

The legend of Everett Ruess is inextricably tied up with the mystery of his vanishing. But Gibbs Smith has often said, "I was never interested in the mystery. It didn't matter to me." In the closing pages of *Vagabond*, Rusho agreed, making the case that it was Everett's vision, not his disappearance, that accounted for his lasting appeal:

> His love of wilderness, his sense of kinship with the living earth, his acute sensitivity to every facet of nature's displays—all of these, because of their intensity in one young man, gave Everett rare qualities. What made him unique were his reactions to the striking and dramatic landscapes of the American West.

By the time *Vagabond* was published, Waldo was seventy-three years old. Although Christopher and Stella had not lived to see it, in Rusho's book the family finally had the solid monument to Everett's legacy that that they had desired, of which *On Desert Trails* had been only a preliminary sketch. Waldo was involved in every aspect of the new book's production, and he had placed such complete trust in Gibbs Smith that it had led him—despite the Kellner debacle—to hand over all of Everett's original letters that he still possessed.

By now, however, Waldo had become a sometimes crotchety caretaker of his brother's flame. The preparation of Rusho's book caused much friction among the author, the publisher, and the brother (who was executor of Everett's estate). Waldo dearly hoped that Wallace Stegner would write an introduction to the book, but Stegner declined, saying he was "too busy on a book." Stegner's assertion in *Mormon Country* that Everett "was not a good writer" had stuck in Waldo's craw ever since 1942. In April 1983 he complained about the judgment in a letter to Stegner, adding, "Of course he had much to learn; if his 1934 journal can ever be found it will represent his most mature writing."

Stegner responded generously. *On Desert Trails,* he wrote Waldo, was "a sort of classic of its kind—It is the original lone nature-lover's journal, the original adventure of a sensitive young man into country then known only to a few Indians and a few Mormons in the oaseis [*sic*] towns." To counter Waldo's disappointment about his declining to write the introduction to *Vagabond,* Stegner advised, "Forewords go by like water. The book remains."

Waldo and Gibbs Smith turned next to Edward Abbey for the introduction, but he too declined, citing the pressure of other writing. Yet at Smith's behest, Abbey wrote a sonnet for Everett that was published as an afterword in *Vagabond.* In 2009, Smith called it the best poem Abbey ever wrote, while noting that the author of *Desert Solitaire* and *The Monkey Wrench Gang* was not renowned for his efforts in verse. The sonnet is indeed a fervent, mystical evocation:

> *You walked into the radiance of death*
> *through passageways of stillness, stone, and light,*
> *gold coin of cottonwoods, the spangled shade,*
> *cascading song of canyon wrens, the flight*
> *of scarlet dragonflies at pools, the stain*
> *of water on a curve of sand, the art*
> *of roots that crack the monolith of time.*
>
> *You knew the crazy lust to probe the heart*
> *of that which has no heart that we could know,*
> *toward the source, deep in the core, the maze,*
> *the secret center where there are no bounds.*
>
> *Hunter, brother, companion of our days:*
> *that blessing which you hunted, hunted too,*
> *what you were seeking, this is what found you.*

In the end, for the introduction Gibbs Smith secured the services of New Mexico writer John Nichols, author of *The Milagro Beanfield War.* Waldo so hated Nichols's first draft that he prevailed upon Smith to force Nichols to make massive revisions. In the midst of these unpleasant negotiations, Waldo wrote a friend about Nichols's introduction, claiming to be "quite depressed and discouraged (haven't even slept at all a couple of nights due to thinking about it)."

What so upset Waldo was Nichols's celebration of Everett as a half-mad desert mystic. Though the introduction is highly laudatory, much of his take on the young wanderer survives even in the relatively sanitized version Smith published. Excerpts:

> By the time Everett Ruess disappeared, he had fashioned a magnificent obsession that probably killed him.

> At times his writing seems pompous; often it is truly beautiful.

> It would be easy to make fun of Ruess, conjecturing that in the end he must have literally exploded, his slight body incapable of containing all the melodramatic sensations he tirelessly ladled into it. But I picture him simply expiring on the edge of a sandstone cliff, in the shadow of some high circling buzzard, convinced that he could never again return to civilization.

Even in this much-revised final version, Nichols's appreciation of Everett is one of the most nuanced and perceptive that any devotee ever produced. One can imagine that Everett himself would have liked it. But Waldo brooked no criticism of his beloved brother, no matter how balanced by praise. Intimations of madness and suicidal leanings, which Nichols was not the first to suggest, pushed one of Waldo's most sensitive buttons.

The very word "vagabond" in Rusho's subtitle disturbed Waldo. "It has negative or bad connotations to many people," he wrote a friend.

For Waldo, an even touchier subject than suicide was homosexuality. As Gibbs Smith's editor was putting together the selections for *Vagabond,* Waldo tried to persuade him to omit the letter Everett wrote to Bill Jacobs on May 10, 1931, with its closing "Love and kisses, / Desperately yours," but he was overruled.

In 1984, Waldo befriended Diane Orr, a documentary filmmaker who wanted to make a movie about Everett. As the sales of *Vagabond* in the first year after publication hovered in skimpy numbers, Waldo wrote Orr on July 24, speculating, "Maybe many don't want to buy it because they think by the Jacobs letters E was a homo." Orr, who became one of Waldo's closest confidantes, revealed to him that Bud Rusho himself had wondered about Everett's possible homosexual leanings.

Waldo adamantly rejected such inferences. As he wrote Orr, "[W]henever E was at home, we had beds in the same bedroom and often talked together before going to sleep. And I think I knew him pretty well. And I think my parents did too. He definitely was not a homo, or homo-inclined."

Waldo's liberal temperament was evidently at odds with an unmistakable (if perhaps latent) homophobia. To Orr, he went on:

In my late teens and early 20's around Hollywood, being very good looking in those days, a number of "queers" tried to make advances, but I had too many pretty girls I was interested in to have any interest at all. I know what queers are like, having seen plenty in Hollywood. Then in our embassies we had problems with quite a few of them, and they are considered security risks. Some were so flagrant that all of us knew about their "persuasion."

Yet in another letter to Orr, Waldo backtracked a step or two: "It's no crime to be a homo. But my brother was not one so I don't want people thinking or saying he was one, even if such a good person as Christ was one."

For all his discomfort with various aspects of *A Vagabond for Beauty,* Waldo was keen to see the book succeed in winning a wider audience for Everett's artwork and writings. The hints that that was starting to happen heartily gratified him. As early as October 1983, Waldo told bookseller Ken Sanders, "I have even had people write me that they wanted to memorize all of E's writings!"

*　*　*

One sign of the gathering mystique around Everett came in 1984 from the small Mormon town of Kanab, Utah, just north of the Arizona border. A press release for the "First Annual Desert Vagabond Days" announced, "Everett lives! This is the theme of a unique festival of Western arts to be held in Kanab, Utah, June 15 and 16."

Invited as an honorary guest, Waldo rode in the opening parade. The festivities, mixing rodeo and art festival, included a square dance, a doll show, a horse show, a "Special Everett Ruess Exhibit," a "Kaibab Squirrel Celebration," and a "Highway Sign Shooting Competition." The festival was repeated in June 1985, again centered around Everett, but adding such events as a horseshoe pitching contest, "Jackpot Team Roping," a "Western Cooking Contest," and a "Fun Shoot."

In 1985, fifty years after the Escalante ranchers had started searching for the lost youth, Gibbs Smith commissioned a friend to make a pair of bronze plaques commemorating Everett. His intention was to mount one on Dance Hall Rock, a small but prominent sandstone dome forty miles out the Hole-in-the-Rock Road from Escalante, the other in Davis Gulch, fourteen miles farther southeast. (In the flat hollow on the south side of Dance Hall Rock, the Mormon pioneers had organized square dances in November 1879, to boost morale in the face of oncoming winter and the difficulty of the trail ahead.)

Dance Hall Rock lies on Bureau of Land Management land, while Davis Gulch is wholly within Glen Canyon National Recreation Area. The former authority granted permission for the plaque placing, but the latter refused. Smith nonetheless organized a mini-expedition of some twenty Ruess partisans. They included Waldo, now seventy-five years old, Bud Rusho, and Pat Jenks, one of the two teenage boys who had picked up a bedraggled Everett near the Grand Canyon in June 1931 and driven him and his burro to the Jenks family ranch near Flagstaff, where Everett spent several weeks recuperating.

On May 11, the ceremony at Dance Hall Rock went off as planned. Within a short time thereafter, however, some relic collector stole the bronze plaque.

Gibbs's entourage drove on to the head of Davis Gulch, where they camped. Gathered around a fire, the devotees listened as first Jenks, then Waldo, then Rusho spoke about Everett and his legacy. In the morning the party hiked along the rim of Davis Gulch, which in its upper two miles is a very narrow slot canyon. Permission or no, the team had determined to install the plaque. As Waldo later wrote to Diane Orr, "Someone had made a rope ladder maybe 50 or 60 ft. long and many younger people went down it and . . . set a plaque I guess in some crevice where only very unusual hikers might ever see it." The plaque is still in place.

With the publication of *Vagabond*, Everett began to move from the realm of romantic cult figure into the more rarefied circles of academe. In 1989, for instance, Bruce Berger hailed Everett in an essay for *The North American Review* titled "Genius of the Canyons." (Berger meant "genius" in the classical sense of *genius loci*—a spirit inhabiting a place.) Like Gibbs Smith, Berger felt that Everett's cardinal achievement was to see the Southwest in a new way: "Ruess was almost the first to travel that country not to prospect, to herd cattle, to scheme a railroad or escape from the law, but simply to relish it, to absorb it, and to shape that love in the arts."

Other critical evaluations of Everett's achievement followed, including a judicious essay by the Pulitzer Prize–winning novelist N. Scott Momaday, who wrote:

> Of all the myths that pervade the American landscape, none is more pervasive than that of the solitary man whose destiny it is to achieve a communion with nature so nearly absolute as to be irrevocable. It is the act of dying into the wilderness, actually or metaphorically. When Everett Ruess disappeared in the Escalante wilderness of Utah in November 1934, he succeeded to that mythic ideal; he became one with the wild earth.

These commentators all pointed out that Everett had been only twenty years old when he disappeared. Very few painters or poets have made their mark at a comparable age. In the Western tradition, only two writers who died younger than Everett come to mind: Anne Frank, exterminated by the Nazis at fifteen, whose diary made her posthumously famous; and Thomas Chatterton, the eccentric eighteenth-century poet and forger of medieval documents, who committed suicide at seventeen. Among painters, it is hard to name one whose works live on but who died before the age of thirty. The Austrian Expressionist Egon Schiele, dying at twenty-eight, is a notable exception.

Give Everett only five or ten more years of life and writing and painting, and his literary and artistic output might have been far more significant.

Stimulated by *Vagabond*, the Salt Lake City–based filmmaker Diane Orr determined to make a movie about Everett. In 1984 she began a long correspondence with Waldo, which grew into a close friendship. Trusting as ever, Waldo lent Orr many original documents of Everett's, including his 1932 and 1933 diaries.

Early on, Orr communicated to Waldo her high expectations for the work. At one point, she said, Robert Redford was interested in helping finance the project. And Kevin Costner, she claimed, was in line to play the role of Everett.

Yet the project languished for more than a decade, as Orr had trouble raising funds. By 1990, a note of vexation had crept into Waldo's correspondence with the filmmaker: "There has been a great deal of stress and strain on me over these many years re my brother and talking about him so much to you and other people. This has been very hard on me and hard on my family."

In the same letter, Waldo confessed, "I am aged 80 and really 'slipping' lately and don't know how much longer *I'll* last. I seem to remember hardly anything anymore."

As it would turn out, Waldo lasted another seventeen years, dying on September 6, 2007, the day after his ninety-eighth birthday. During his last years he suffered from some kind of dementia. Friends attributed it simply to old age, but his daughter, Michèle Ruess, is convinced that his mental decline dated from a single accident that occurred in July 1987, when, working in his garden in Santa Barbara, he was stung by a horde of yellow jackets. Waldo went into anaphylactic shock and nearly died. According to Michèle, he was never the same after that.

Orr's movie was finally released in 2000, sixteen years after she had started work on it. Titled *Lost Forever: Everett Ruess,* the movie mixes documentary artifacts such as newspaper clippings and Everett's paintings and woodcuts with reconstructed scenes. In the latter, Everett is played not by Kevin Costner but by a young actor named Mark Larson. And those scenes take considerable license with the known truth. In particular, Orr portrays Everett as homosexual, and she dramatizes a final rupture with his parents that never took place.

Waldo was not happy with *Lost Forever*. According to Michèle, "My father was very upset by Diane Orr's film. He saw it once and never wanted to see it again."

It took Orr so long to make *Lost Forever* that her film was preceded a year earlier by a Turner Broadcasting System documentary about Everett called *Vanished!* The director of this effort was Dianna Taylor, daughter from the second marriage of Dorothea Lange (who had taken the memorable black-and-white photographic portraits of Everett in 1933). A feeble production, *Vanished!* strays even further from the historical record than Orr's semi-documentary did.

Vanished! aired on TBS in 1999, then dropped out of sight. It is unavailable today, while Orr's *Lost Forever* still sells steadily on DVD.

*   *   *

In 1987, Waldo sold the rights to Everett's woodblock engravings and prints to the Southern Utah Wilderness Alliance (SUWA) for $8,000. Three years later he complained to Diane Orr, "The last I heard they were selling for $2200 a set but I heard they were raising the price." SUWA adopted Everett's print of a youth leading two burros in silhouette as the alliance's logo. During the first eleven years of merchandising the artwork, SUWA took in $88,214 from sales of the prints.

In 1998, Bud Rusho and Gibbs Smith collaborated to publish Everett's 1932 and 1933 diaries as *Wilderness Journals of Everett Ruess*. As he had in editing Everett's letters, Rusho omitted many passages from the diaries, without indicating their excision even by ellipses.

Vagabond was still selling well, fifteen years after it was first issued. In 2002, Gibbs Smith brought out a "combined edition" of both *Vagabond* and *Wilderness Journals*, adding many photographs that had never been published before, including a generous selection of pictures of Everett in his childhood and early adolescence. Two years earlier, in 2000, Smith had also published a new edition of the 1940 *On Desert Trails with Everett Ruess,* adding a provocative afterword by the Utah historian Gary James Bergera.

No single event, however, ratcheted up the megawatt power of the Everett Ruess cult like the publication in 1996 of *Into the Wild.* In a long feature article for *Outside* magazine, Jon Krakauer had first written about Chris McCandless, the alienated and idealistic young man who had graduated from college, fled his family, hitchhiked and driven all over the West, then made his way to Alaska, where he hiked into the wilderness north of Denali, intending to live off the land. After 113 days on his own, McCandless had succumbed in August 1992 either to starvation or to accidental poisoning from a wild potato plant. He was twenty-four when he died.

Fascinated by this passionate loner and vagabond, with whom he closely identified, Krakauer expanded the article into a book. To research McCandless's zigzag peregrinations, he performed a tour de force by retracing the young man's path over two years, locating and interviewing many of the otherwise obscure men and women who had befriended the wanderer as he ranged from Texas to California, Washington State to South Dakota. And in Alaska, Krakauer back-packed down the Stampede Trail to the abandoned Fairbanks city bus in which McCandless's body had been found three weeks after he died.

As he set out on the trail of Chris McCandless, Krakauer had never heard of Everett Ruess. Tipped off by this writer to the parallels between the two romantic adventurers, Krakauer devoured *A Vaga-bond for Beauty,* then made his own trip into Davis Gulch. In *Into the Wild,* he devoted an eleven-page chapter to Everett. The book became a surprise success, eventually spending 119 weeks on the *New York Times* best-seller list. By now it has been translated into more than twenty-two languages, including Korean, Finnish, and Catalan. And in 2007 it was made into a feature film directed by Sean Penn.

With the publication of the book, an instant Chris McCandless cult was born. Over the years, hundreds of devotees have made their own pilgrimages to the derelict bus in the wilderness, which has gained the numen of a holy shrine.

The success of *Into the Wild* brought Everett Ruess a huge new audience. Readers who admired the mystic flights embodied in McCandless's letters and the makeshift diary he kept in the Alaskan wilderness found in Everett a true kindred soul. Like Everett scorning Waldo's humdrum life, McCandless wrote a long letter to an eighty-year-old friend he had met hitchhiking in southern California, all but ordering him to hit the road and "adopt a helter-skelter style of life." Amazingly, the octogenarian, swayed by his young friend's ultimatum, did just that. Like Everett, McCandless adopted a pseudonym, calling himself Alexander Supertramp, before reverting to his given name in a last, desperate SOS note taped to the bus. Like some of Everett's letters, several of the last ones McCandless mailed to friends have the resonance of farewell notes, including the postcard he wrote, just days before starting down the Stampede Trail, to a man who had given him a temporary job in South Dakota: "If this adventure proves fatal and you don't ever hear from me again I want you to know you're a great man. I now walk into the wild."

In the chapter titled "Davis Gulch," Krakauer noted the "uncanny parallels" between McCandless and Ruess, the "incendiary passion" they shared. " 'NEMO 1934,' [Everett] scrawled, no doubt moved by the same impulse that compelled Chris McCandless to inscribe 'Alexander Supertramp/May 1992' on the wall of the Sushana bus—an impulse not so different, perhaps, from that which inspired the Anasazi to embellish the rock with their now-indecipherable symbols."

Ranging across the Southwest on McCandless's trail in 1993,

Krakauer heard echoes of the romantic myth that Everett was still alive decades after his disappearance. As he later wrote:

> A year ago, while filling my truck with gas in Kingman, Arizona, I happened to strike up a conversation about Ruess with the middle-aged pump attendant, a small, twitchy man with flecks of Skoal staining the corners of his mouth. Speaking with persuasive conviction, he swore that "he knew of a fella who'd definitely bumped into Ruess" in the late 1960s at a remote hogan on the Navajo Indian Reservation. According to the attendant's friend, Ruess was married to a Navajo woman, with whom he'd raised at least one child.

Krakauer tracked down Ken Sleight, with whom he discussed the significance of the enigmatic NEMO inscription on the granary in Grand Gulch. Sleight offered his theory that Everett might have drowned trying to swim the San Juan River at the mouth of Grand Gulch. Then he mused,

> "Everett was a loner, but he liked people too damn much to stay down there and live in secret the rest of his life. A lot of us are like that—I'm like that, Ed Abbey was like that, and it sounds like this McCandless kid was like that: We like companionship, see, but we can't stand to be around people for very long. So we go get ourselves lost, come back for a while, then get the hell out again. And that's what Everett was doing.
>
> "Everett was strange," Sleight concedes. "Kind of different. But him and McCandless, at least they tried to follow their dream. That's what was great about them. They tried. Not many do."

*   *   *

Gary James Bergera's " 'The Murderous Pain of Living': Thoughts on the Death of Everett Ruess," published as an afterword to the 2000 reprint of *On Desert Trails,* makes the most thoughtful case to date that Everett may have committed suicide. "For many readers of Everett Ruess's remarkable letters home," Bergera begins, "a terrible melancholy permeates almost every line." The essay assembles a small anthology of the gloomiest and most despairing quotations from those letters, including the ones in which Everett anticipates his own death. Bergera freely admits that "I focus on particular aspects of Everett's character at the exclusion of others." Yet he is convinced that "what emerges from a careful review of Everett's writings is a portrait of a gifted yet depressive young artist whose tortured engagement with life both powered his creative expression and propelled him toward his own self-destruction."

Bergera does not go so far as to label Everett as bipolar. Instead he sees him as hypomanic—a psychiatric diagnosis that indicates a milder form of bipolar affective disorder. According to one source, hypomania is "characterized by optimism, pressure of speech and activity, and decreased need for sleep. Some people have increased creativity while others demonstrate poor judgment and irritability." All these symptoms closely match some of Everett's recurrent states and moods.

Another of Bergera's medical speculations makes the distinction between pernicious anemia and folic anemia. On July 21, 1932, Everett wrote in his diary, "Physically I feel very weak. I would not be surprised to learn that pernicious anaemia has set in again. A slight bruise has taken three weeks to heal." During one of his stays at home in Los Angeles, Everett may well have been diagnosed as suffering from pernicious anemia. In the 1930s, the cause of the malady—a deficiency of vitamin B_{12}—had not yet been identified. Bergera notes that this form of anemia "affects people primarily over age fifty." It is more likely, he believes, that Everett suffered from folic anemia, caused by a dietary shortage of raw leafy vegetables. (During his travels, Everett seldom if ever mentions eating vegetables of any kind.) In the 1930s, doctors made no distinctions among the various anemias—they were all lumped under the quaint heading of "tired blood."

Although anemia might explain Everett's bouts of lethargy, fatigue, and sore muscles and joints, particularly during his 1932 journey, it would have had nothing to do with his possible hypomania, whose causes remain unknown today. But both, Bergera believes, could have contributed to suicidal inclinations.

Bergera briefly discusses Everett's sexuality, citing both passages in which he writes about being attracted to girls (Frances, the Mormon girl in Tropic, the Indian woman whose photograph he jokingly captioned "My Navajo Wife") and to men and boys whose good looks he found appealing, as well as the sign-off in the Bill Jacobs letter, "Love and kisses, / Desperately yours." But he stops short of labeling Everett as bisexual. Instead, Bergera gathers all these inklings under the rubric of Everett's "attempt to understand his own sexuality."

At the end of " 'The Murderous Pain of Living,' " Bergera spins out a possible scenario covering Everett's last days. He admits that there is no hard evidence for this chain of events—they amount at best to a what-might-have-been. The virtue of this narrative is that it dovetails neatly with the puzzle of what the searchers found—and didn't find—in Davis Gulch in March 1935.

In Bergera's telling, Everett led Cockleburrs and Chocolatero into the gulch by the livestock trail. From a camp on the canyon floor, "he explored nearby side canyons, cliffs and buttes, until he found a wild, lonely spot that reminded him of a place he had been before." Back at his camp, he loaded up one of the burros with his camping gear, food, diary, and painting kit, led the animal to his special spot, and unloaded the baggage. Then he led the burro back to the Davis Gulch camp and constructed the brushwork corral to confine the two animals in the upper part of the canyon, where they had plenty of grass to feed on.

Returning to his special place, Bergera imagines, Everett "gathered up his gear, all the beauty he had carried with him, and secured it in a recess he knew no one would ever find." Then,

> Slowly with the setting sun, the misery and anguish of the past four years began to wash away and Everett felt life loosen its grip. From this altar of beauty, he gazed one last time across the horizon. Content that he had kept his dream, Everett knew he was now going to make his destiny.

What the actual agent of Everett's suicide might have been, Bergera does not venture to guess. In the end, the scenario is simply a romantic fantasy, to which few of the partisans who make up the Ruess cult subscribe.

Along with well-thought-out and sensitive commentaries such as Bergera's, the enigma of Everett's disappearance has elicited responses from clairvoyants and mystics just this side of the lunatic fringe. The most ambitious and curious work in this vein is a slender book by Mark A. Taylor called *Sandstone Sunsets: In Search of Everett Ruess,* published in 1997 by Gibbs Smith.

The problem with *Sandstone Sunsets* is that it's really about Mark Taylor, not Everett Ruess. On the very first page the author announces, "This year marks the tenth anniversary of my quest to find Everett." Yet near the end of his 116-page meditation, he admits, "I had not solved the mystery of Everett's disappearance." His consolation: "I know much more than when I began, especially about my own undefined quest or journey."

The pity is that here and there, Taylor may actually have been on the trail of important new evidence about Everett's fate. In Escalante, he heard a rumor that one of the 1935 searchers had stolen and kept hidden for decades all of Everett's camping gear, perhaps even his journal. Taylor goes so far as to contemplate breaking and entering the houses of one or two of these "suspects," but manages to restrain himself.

One is tempted to dismiss this whole line of inquiry as Taylor's fantasy, but for some odd facts. In *A Vagabond for Beauty*, Rusho unambiguously claimed that the first 1935 search party had come upon Everett's burros in their brushwork corral, and that "[o]n the fence were a bridle, a halter, and a rope." According to Rusho, Gail Bailey, a member of the search team, took the gear and burros back to Escalante, kept the animals there for a while, where they were "ridden occasionally by the village children," then removed them to a sheep camp in the high country.

In his 1939 article in *Desert* magazine, however, Hugh Lacy, whose own Escalante research was conducted only a few years after the Davis Gulch discovery, reported, "The burros were in a natural corral large enough in good season for several months' grazing, but the weather was backward and they were thin and starved. Their halters had been found weeks before, it later appeared, by an Escalantan who thought nothing of their significance."

Indeed, for six decades after the search, until his death in the 1990s, Gail Bailey was suspected by some of his neighbors of having come across Everett's last camp on a solo outing sometime before the March 1935 search, and of having appropriated Everett's belongings. In that most xenophobic of Mormon towns, however, such scuttlebutt was rarely shared with outsiders.

Scrambling for a dramatic climax to his quest narrative, Taylor decides to hike to the top of Kaiparowits Plateau. That gigantic, convoluted tableland overlooking the Hole-in-the-Rock Trail, he argues (as have other commentators), has never been thoroughly searched for signs of Everett's passage.

From his camp, at sunset, Taylor gazes at the horizon.

Out on the line between heaven and earth, the silhouette of a
face began to form. One by one, each facial feature appeared
like magic; they were perfect to the minutest detail. It was my
friend Everett Ruess! I had been waiting and watching for
this moment for a long time. Everett was smiling, and his lips
seemed to reach up, tenderly kissing the heavens above. The
wind swirled around my head, and I felt almost giddy.

"Good night, Everett," says Taylor out loud, before returning to
his campfire.

*　　*　　*

In one sense, the proof that a cult has staying power comes when
its iconography enters the realm of kitsch. In 1994 Waldo made a
deal with a Utah-based designer and artist, Steve Jerman, licensing
him to produce and sell memorabilia incorporating some of Everett's
best blockprints. On the website everettruess.net, today's customer
can buy numbered prints, postcards, journals, T-shirts, coffee mugs,
water bottles, and refrigerator magnets (eight dollars apiece, shipping
free) decorated with prints given arbitrary titles after Everett's disappearance such as "Granite Towers," "Fishing Shack," "Junipers,"
and "Tree No. 1." Escalante Outfitters, a restaurant and outdoor gear
shop in Escalante, sells Vagabond Ale, with a Dorothea Lange portrait of Everett on the label.

Two bad detective novels, Jenny Kilb's *Pilgrim Fool* (2003) and
Jack Nelson's *To Die in Kanab* (2006), spin their plots around mod-
ern sleuths solving the mystery of Everett's fate. Debora L. Threedy, a
University of Utah law professor, wrote a full-length play called *The
End of the Horizon* that premiered in 2008 at Salt Lake City's Plan-B
Theater Company. The play dramatizes the anguish of the family's
loss after Everett's disappearance (in the premiere, Threedy herself
played Stella Ruess).

It was perhaps inevitable that pop and folk song writers would take up the Ruess legend. A number of ballads about the lost vagabond are regularly played at festivals, and can be downloaded on the Internet. Perhaps the best of them are "The Wild Escalante" by Walkin' Jim Stoltz and "Everett Ruess" by Dave Alvin. The latter song memorably ends,

> *You give your dreams away as you get older*
> *Oh, but I never gave up mine*
> *And they'll never find my body, boys*
> *Or understand my mind.*

PART THREE

What Aneth Saw

TEN

Jackass Bar

I FIRST CAME UNDER THE SPELL of Everett Ruess in the late 1980s, when I read Rusho's *A Vagabond for Beauty*. The mystical passion of Everett's response to the wilderness, blazoned again and again in the letters he had sent to friends and family, impressed but also disconcerted me. The oracular intensity of such pronouncements as "I have seen almost more beauty than I can bear" or "Beauty isolated is terrible and unbearable, and the unclouded sight of her kills the beholder" seemed too dramatic to have issued from any experience on the trail. Like Wallace Stegner, I was bemused by "the extravagance of [Everett's] beauty-worship." But like Stegner, I also thought at once of the parallel of John Muir. What won me over to Everett was the simple realization that everything of his that I read had been written before the age of twenty-one.

The sense of doom that haunted other passages in the letters counterbalanced the ecstasy. In light of Everett's disappearance, some of these declarations had an eerie power. The most resonant of them came in the postscript to the letter to Waldo in July 1932: "I'll never stop wandering. And when the time comes to die, I'll find the wildest, loneliest, most desolate spot there is."

About the blockprints reproduced in Rusho's book, I had no reservations. The prints were strikingly simple and vivid, condensing the landscape into a few bold elements with a Japanese economy. By the age of twenty, it seemed to me, Everett was already an accomplished artist.

What I most admired about Everett Ruess, however, was his journeys themselves. Many of the places he had hiked to I knew from my own exploration of the Southwest, which had become—after two decades spent in rapt devotion to unclimbed peaks and routes in Alaska—my favorite wilderness. Yet Everett had crisscrossed Arizona, Utah, and the corners of Colorado and New Mexico when those regions were far less known and explored than they were by the 1990s. The four hundred miles in six weeks that Everett had covered on foot in 1934 far surpassed any continuous jaunt I had ever made, whether in Alaska or the Southwest. And Everett had performed so much of his traveling alone, with only pack animals for companions. I had done plenty of solo hiking and backpacking in the wilderness, always with an acute awareness that a simple misstep or fall could spell disaster. But my longest solitary outing had stretched across a paltry five days.

Finally, the mystery of Everett's fate held me, like all other Ruess partisans, in thrall. In the twentieth century, among English-speaking explorers, only the disappearances of Amelia Earhart over the Pacific in 1937 and of George Mallory and Andrew Irvine on Everest in 1924 seemed to me to outweigh as legends the vanishing of Everett Ruess. Was there a chance that his remains would someday be found, as Mallory's were in 1999, seventy-five years after his death?

In 1998, on assignment for the premiere issue of *National Geographic Adventure,* I set out to see if there was anything new to be learned about Everett's demise. Reading *Vagabond,* I pondered the four leading theories as to how he had met his end. The one most plausible to me (perhaps because I was a climber myself, and had often scared myself silly trying to get into inaccessible Anasazi ruins) was that Everett had fallen off a cliff, and that his bones lay wedged in some obscure cleft or had been scattered by predators.

I started my research in Escalante. I had hiked, backpacked, and llama-packed among the magnificent canyons of the Escalante River and its serpentine tributaries—Harris Wash, Little Death Hollow, Wolverine Creek, Dry Fork Coyote Gulch, and the like—both before and after the region's inclusion in Grand Staircase–Escalante National Monument in 1996. But I had always treated the town of Escalante as a mere motel stop. Now it seemed logical to look up Escalante's old-timers and see if they would talk to me about the stranger who had passed through in November 1934.

This was not an easy task. The town had been founded in 1875 by Mormons from Panguitch, seventy miles to the west. In search of a milder climate, those pioneers had decided to investigate what was then called Potato Valley. Once there, they had laid out a grid of streets just south of an upper stretch of the Escalante River. The town occupies a blissful setting, surrounded by hills, open basins, and the stern escarpment of Kaiparowits Plateau. But life has always been hard in Escalante. By 1998 the settlement was still almost one hundred percent Mormon. Among the residents, the decades of wringing a living from its fields and pastures had bred a fierce distrust of outsiders.

The insularity of the town emerged in a historical irony I had come across in my reading. In 1875, Almon H. Thompson was in charge of a small team of government surveyors exploring this little-known part of Utah, at the behest of Thompson's brother-in-law, John Wesley Powell, who six years earlier had led the first descent of the Colorado River through the Grand Canyon. Thompson's diary for August 5, 1875, notes,

> Came from camp on Last Chance to camp on Pine Creek
> about a mile above its junction with the Escalante. Saw four
> Mormons from Panguitch who are talking about making a
> settlement here. Advised them to call the place Escalante.

Presumably, Thompson told the Mormons all about the great
Spanish friar, Silvestre Vélez de Escalante, who, with his fellow cleric
Francisco Atanasio Domínguez, had accomplished an extraordinary
six-month exploratory loop through the Southwest in 1776, starting
and finishing in Santa Fe. Escalante's journal from that trip remains
one of the classic expedition narratives in western North America.

By the first decade of the twentieth century, the locals were pro-
nouncing the town "ESK-a-LANT," with the accent on the first and
third syllables, the latter rhyming with "slant." (So the townsfolk pro-
nounce it today.) One day during that decade another government
explorer came through Escalante. He asked the residents about the
source of the town's name, only to be told that it was an old Indian
word whose meaning had been lost to memory.

In 1998, as I phoned up old-timers or knocked on their doors and
told them I was interested in Everett Ruess, I got brushed off regularly. One man, greeting me on his front porch but declining to invite
me inside his house, said, "I don't know what you want, but you're
wastin' your time and mine."

I realized, of course, that the inhabitants of Escalante had been
peppered with questions about Everett ever since 1935. And the persistent rumor that it might have been local men who murdered the
young artist stuck in the collective Escalante craw. Rusho's dogged
interviews in 1982 and the more recent probes of filmmakers Diane
Orr and Dianna Taylor had simply stirred up the old resentment of
nosy outsiders.

Gradually, however, I gained entrée to the homes and thoughts of
several locals who had spent time with Everett in November 1934.

They included ninety-year-old Melvin Alvey and seventy-four-year-old Norm Christensen. Yet when these informants talked about the search launched by Jennings Allen's party in March 1935, the story they told me could not be reconciled with Rusho's account. According to them, it was not the searchers who found Everett's burros in Davis Gulch, but Gail Bailey, weeks or even months before the search commenced.

Said Melvin Alvey, "Gail Bailey usually put his bucks down in Davis Gulch in the spring. He went in there to look, and saw the two burros. Brought 'em back to town. There was lots of excitement. Everybody wanted to go in there and look for [Everett]."

But Norm Christensen commented, "It was Gail Bailey that found his pack outfit. I believe Everett's camping gear was there, too. I believe Gail Bailey took the stuff."

Seventy-five-year-old DeLane Griffin was even more censorious: "I think Gail found Everett's camp. He'd say he didn't, 'cause whatever was there, he took. Didn't want anybody to know he had the stuff. I'm sure whoever found the camp, found the journal."

Other informants placed the timing of Bailey's discovery not in the spring, but as early as November or December 1934. As I listened to these accounts, I puzzled over Rusho's certainty that it was the March 1935 search party, of whom Gail Bailey was merely one member, that had discovered the burros. If Bailey had found the animals earlier and on his own, why didn't that alarming discovery instantly trigger a search for Everett? But Rusho was sure that it took Christopher and Stella's letter to the Escalante postmistress, Jennings Allen's wife, to galvanize the ranchers into launching a search.

It didn't take long for me to uncover the likely cause of the discrepancy between Rusho's findings and my own. In 1982, when Rusho did his research, Gail Bailey was still alive. In fact, when Rusho interviewed him, Bailey related the burro discovery as part of the March search party's team effort, though he admitted that it was he who led the pack animals out of Davis Gulch and back to Escalante. While

Bailey was still living, the town's distrust of outsiders apparently out-weighed any regard for the truth. Rusho's informants chose not to contradict their neighbor's story, however suspect it was.

Escalante might present a united front to journalists such as Rusho and myself. But I had already come across hints of long-standing feuds and antagonisms among the residents. One old-timer told me that whether you grew up on the north or south side of Main Street dic-tated which other kids you played with, which in turn cemented life-long alliances and grudges. It wasn't quite the Crips and the Bloods, but the schism was apparently intense. This in a town of a mere eight hundred people!

Gail Bailey died in 1997. By the next year, when I interviewed the old-timers, they no longer felt the need to cover up the rancher's prevarications—nor did they stint on judging his character. One local, Dan Pollock, told me, "Gail Bailey was a nasty little son of a bitch." But DeLane Griffin, who was sure that Bailey had appropriated Ev-erett's belongings, told me, "Gail Bailey couldn't have killed Everett. No way."

All this left me wondering just what had really happened, in terms of the discovery of the burros, and possibly of Everett's camping gear, painting kit, and journal. Later I would hear the same persistent rumor that had reached the ears of Mark Taylor two years before me—that Everett's belongings were still kept inside the house of a longtime Escalantan, and that others had seen the "stuff." Whether or not the alleged thief was Gail Bailey, I could only guess. It was clear, however, that there was a limit to how deeply any outsider would ever be able to penetrate the workings of Escalante society.

*   *   *

After interviewing the old-timers who agreed to talk to me, I made a three-day backpacking trip into Davis Gulch. There was no hope of visiting the two NEMO inscriptions, which I knew the waters of Lake

Powell had long since swallowed. After rim-walking for four miles and descending the livestock trail down which Everett had led his burros sixty-four years earlier, I set up camp beside a stately cottonwood. That night, a full moon rose over the canyon's southeast rim. Frogs croaked noisily from the pool beneath a fern-hung seep.

During the next day and a half, I poked as far up- and downstream as I could. The narrow canyon seemed a sandstone paradise. In early May, the prickly pears were in bloom, bursting with waxy magenta flowers. Globe mallow and primrose sprouted from benches of fine sand. I could see at once why Everett had lingered here, the high rims of the gulch sheltering him from late autumn winds.

As I pushed upstream, every bend in the canyon revealed new wonders. In one alcove I found a masterly pictograph, one of the largest I had ever seen: six and a half feet tall, painted in red ocher, it limned what archaeologists surmise may be that mythical being, the thunderbird—an eagle-like creature that dispenses lightning and thunder. After widening into a green oasis, the gulch squeezed down to its headwaters slot, barely navigable by chimneying across stagnant pools of water.

Except for the stock trail and that headwaters slot, in the whole length of Davis Gulch, I could find only three routes out. These were "Moqui steps"—ladders of hand- and toeholds gouged by some Anasazi daredevil with a quartzite pounding stone. I switched to rock-climbing shoes and started up one of these trails. Sixty feet up, I lost my nerve: yet above me, the holds continued on a parabolic wall that grew steeper every step, then made a wild traverse left before topping out on a vertical headwall. I thought of Everett's boast: "Many times . . . I trusted my life to crumbling sandstone and angles little short of the perpendicular."

Davis Gulch taught me one thing, and only one thing, about Ruess's fate. He had not fallen to his death in this canyon. The three sets of Moqui steps were, I believed, the only routes that even the boldest scrambler would have been tempted to climb. Had Everett died in a plunge from one of these lines, the searchers, even on horseback, would have found his bones in plain sight on the ground.

Before entering the gulch, I had imagined arcane side canyons where a body could stay lost. There were simply none in Davis, not even in the headwaters slot. As I hiked out on the third day, I was convinced for the first time that if Everett had died in Davis Gulch, it was not in a natural accident.

*   *   *

I shared some of my 1998 outings with Vaughn Hadenfeldt, a wilderness guide based in Bluff, Utah, who had become my regular hiking partner in the Southwest. Together we arranged a meeting with Ken Sleight, who greeted us at his Pack Creek Ranch, a sylvan refuge southeast of Moab. We knew that the old desert rat only grudgingly shared the secrets he had won from a lifetime of river-running and horse-packing. Somehow he warmed to us, and now he told us exactly where to find the granary in Grand Gulch where he had found the NEMO inscription in the late 1960s. (Earlier, Sleight had deflected Vaughn's inquiry as to its location.) The inscription, Sleight insisted, was fairly legible when he had first seen it. On a subsequent visit he deduced that some overzealous eco-tourist had tried to rub it out, presumably as a graffito that marred the pristine beauty of the Gulch. Sleight also told us about the panel of "colored zigzags" painted on the rock wall just to the left of the granary.

"Do you think the inscription could have been made by a copy-cat?" I asked.

Sleight scratched his grizzled chin. "I think a copycat," he answered, "would have put it where you could see it better."

Now Sleight spun out his rambling meditation on what might have brought Everett to Grand Gulch. "He couldn't cross the Colorado River with the burros," he mused. "So he decided to take a side

Aneth Nez and his wife at his Enemy Way curing ceremony, 1971.
(Daisey Johnson)

Denny Belson and Daisey Johnson. *(Dawn Kish)*

Comb Ridge, near where Denny Belson found the anomalous crevice grave.
(Dawn Kish)

The crevice grave, after it was disturbed by the FBI team. *(David Roberts)*

A button, found in the crevice grave, made by the Zions Cooperative Mercantile Institution, a Salt Lake City–based manufacturer of clothing goods. *(David Roberts)*

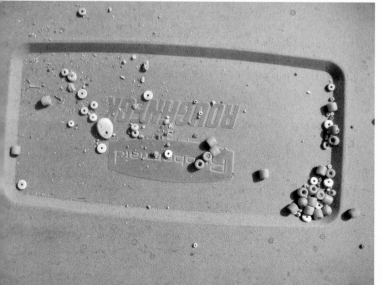

Beads and pendants from the grave site. *(David Roberts)*

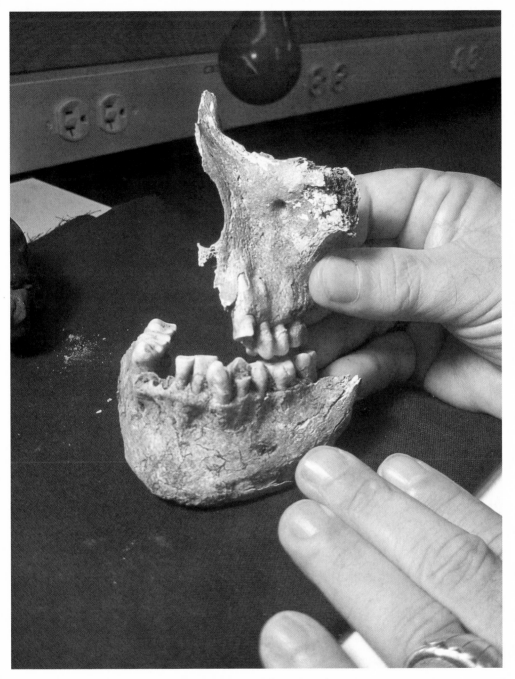

The upper and lower jaws of the skull found in the crevice grave, prepared for study by Dennis Van Gerven in his University of Colorado lab. *(David Roberts)*

Daisey Johnson (left) and Michèle Ruess, Everett's niece, near the grave site on Comb Ridge. *(David Roberts)*

A sketch by inscription expert Fred Blackburn of the faded "NEMO" found in Grand Gulch. *(David Roberts)*

The NEMO inscription found by Greg Funseth in 2001 on the Escalante Desert. *(David Roberts)*

Davis Gulch from the rim. *(David Roberts)*

trip. I think he wanted to make a round trip back to Davis, but he underestimated the distances. He wanted to see Grand Gulch. John Wetherill would have told him all about it, the mummies they took out and all.

"I think Everett made it over to Grand Gulch," Sleight went on, "but by then he was real tired and hungry, and he didn't make it back. I'm not so sure about him drowning in the San Juan anymore. There's lots of ways he could've died.

"I don't know if he had it in him to really explore. I think he was playing Captain Nemo, going down with his ship."

"What do think about Everett as a person?" I asked. "Do you admire him?"

Sleight paused before he spoke. "I see a young fellow, he says, 'Dad, I gotta go find myself.' Had to play out the whole thing. I did that myself with the river"—the Colorado, down which Sleight had made countless rafting trips—"left a wife and kids behind." The man's voice trailed off.

"But Everett did it," Sleight resumed. "And because he did it, that puts him on the top rung. Like John Wesley Powell—he did it."

A few days after meeting with Sleight, Vaughn and I hiked into Grand Gulch to look for the inscription on the granary. It was a beautiful late-spring day, with lazy cumulus clouds sailing across the azure sky. Everywhere white primrose, red penstemon, and scarlet paintbrush were bursting into bloom.

In less than two hours we reached the site. A tricky approach via benches upstream got us onto the ledge of the twin granaries, eighty feet above the canyon floor. Squashed beneath a massive gray brow of sandstone, the two little storehouses sat.

At the wall of the left-hand granary, where Sleight had told us to look, we stared and stared. I could not see the inscription at first, but Vaughn—an expert at reading historic signatures—found the four block capitals in the mud. After we swept the surface with raking headlamp light, I too could make out the NEMO. And in that moment, any vestige of the copycat explanation was put to rest. The shapes of the letters perfectly matched those of the NEMO inscriptions in Davis Gulch, of which no photos had been published before 1983—long after Sleight's discovery.

Vaughn and I, however, could find no trace whatsoever of the watercolor zigzags on the cliff wall to the left of the granary. Whatever Sleight had seen there in the 1960s had vanished, perhaps washed away by the seepage of the decades.

From the granary, we headed upstream several miles to take a look at the Music Note panel, which Vaughn and I had each visited several times before. At the far bend of a seldom-hiked oxbow in the Gulch, on the left end of an enigmatic cavalcade of Anasazi pictographs, someone had etched, in what looked like India ink, a perfect treble clef followed by a pair of joined sixteenth-notes and two neat, separated eighth-notes. The most veteran Grand Gulch aficionados swore that the Music Note panel had been there when they first hiked the oxbow decades earlier. It was not a new inscription.

Over the years, Vaughn and I and our Cedar Mesa friends had speculated wildly about who might have inked those notes on the wall, and when. Now I suddenly wondered whether the artwork had sprung from the same hand as the NEMO downstream. I had also noticed that the notes seemed to replicate the chromatic descending tones of the canyon wren's call—the most plaintive of all Southwestern birdsongs.

On the trail, of course, Everett had had music in his head all the time, singing and humming Beethoven and Dvořák and Tchaikovsky to the surrounding walls. He had played the piano and flute as a young man, and in Los Angeles and San Francisco he had been transported at live concerts. After hearing Sergei Rachmaninoff play in L.A. in 1932, he had written his brazen fan letter to the Russian pianist and composer.

Once more, Vaughn and I stared at the treble clef and the descending tones. Could these indeed be another kind of signature Everett had left behind—a pseudonym in music notes? There was no way of knowing, but as far as we could tell, Vaughn and I were the first ones ever to venture such a surmise.

* * *

At the Utah State Historical Society in Salt Lake City, I pored through the Harry Aleson papers. Among reams of letters, unpublished manuscripts, and scraps of guiding miscellany, I finally found the coded telegram Aleson had written to himself in December 1952, recording the claim that "Emeron" Alvey had killed Everett, and that Joe Pollock and Keith Riddle had dumped his body in the Colorado River. I also found the correspondence in which Aleson had confided his discovery to his crony Dock Marston and to Randall Henderson, publisher of *On Desert Trails*.

Back in Escalante, without revealing the source of my suspicions, I started asking around. Norm Christensen remembered that Emmorn (not Emeron) Alvey had died in 1944. (Aleson's coded telegram had him "DECEASEDWTR 194243.") But to the suggestion that Alvey could have killed Everett, Christensen responded bluntly, "That's an outright lie." Another old-timer had the same view: "Somebody's got their wires crossed. Emmorn didn't even run cattle with Pollock and Riddle. And Emmorn wouldn't have killed anybody."

Still, the supposition that Everett might have been murdered by Escalante men—perhaps rustlers—could not be discounted. Yet how to plumb it? Several times, talking to residents, I felt that I had crept to the edge of some great secret that the town fiercely guarded. One man, Doyle Cottam, who had seen Everett come through Escalante in 1934, changed his mind overnight about talking to me. In the morning, in a hoarse, halting voice, he said, "Too many of the folks that might be incriminated, they still got kids and family around. It don't do nobody any good. I just can't help you."

Thus I had given up hope of pursuing this tack when, as I was wrapping up my second interview with Norm Christensen, he dropped a bombshell at my feet. "So what do you think happened to Everett?" I asked. Oddly, to that point I had failed to put the question so directly.

Christensen's dark eyes held mine, as his face clouded. "I know what happened to him," he said quietly. "He was shot. The man who did it told me."

I was stunned. In measured tones, Christensen went on to recall an afternoon, sometime around 1949 or 1950. Several young men had gathered in Christensen's barn to drink. One of them was Keith Riddle, nine years Norm's senior.

Riddle and Christensen sat on a plank in one corner of the barn, out of earshot of the others. Drink had loosened the older man's tongue.

"We were talkin' about old cowboy stuff," Christensen recalled. "I said, 'Keith, just between you and me, what do you think happened to Everett?'

"He looked at me and said, 'I killed the son of a bitch, and if I had to do it over, I'd do it again.'

"I didn't say another word. I figured I'd pushed it as hard as I could. Keith was a very strong-willed man. He'd fight you at the drop of a hat, and drop the hat himself. If he liked you, he'd do anything for you. If he didn't, he'd have liked to knock you down and kick the guts out of you."

I drew a long breath. "Could it just have been a drunken boast?"

"No," said Christensen. "It wasn't said in a bragging manner. I believe Keith told the truth."

A flashbulb of corroboration was going off in my head. Rusho had claimed the last men to have seen Everett alive were the two sheepherders at Soda Gulch. But Melvin Alvey had insisted that after parting from Clayton Porter and Addlin Lay, Everett had met and camped overnight with two cattle ranchers, Keith Riddle and Joe Pollock.

I asked Christensen why he hadn't gone to the authorities with Riddle's confession. "There was nothing to be gained by telling on Keith," he answered. "He'd served his country well in World War II. And he'd herded sheep and cattle all his life."

In Panguitch, the county seat, I pored over old records. And in Escalante, the simple phrase "Some people think Keith Riddle killed Everett" now opened doors that had previously been shut to me.

Gradually I pieced together a sketch of Riddle's life. Born in Escalante in 1915, one of eight siblings, Keith had seen his father desert the family, leaving his mother to care for her numerous offspring. "Lordy," said Della Christianson, ninety years old in 1998, "I don't know how that woman raised that bunch."

Enter Joe Pollock, twenty years older than Keith. Pollock took the boy under his wing, teaching him to ride and rope and string fence. Pollock's spread was way out down the Hole-in-the-Rock Trail, on the plateau southeast of Davis Gulch.

His harsh childhood took its toll on Riddle, and he later developed a drinking problem. "He was pretty handy on a horse and all," remembered DeLane Griffin. "When he got out of the service, he drank, and he was meaner'n strychnine when he was drunk."

Nearly everyone in Escalante agreed that Pollock and Riddle rustled. "Joe made a living stealing cattle," said Della Christianson, who had also seen Everett come through town. "He'd go down in the Desert, run cows off a ledge or shoot 'em, then take the calves. And Joe taught Keith how to steal."

In Panguitch I found documents from 1922 and 1930 bringing Joe Pollock to trial for rustling, but both times he was acquitted. Though I failed to find any record of the case, everybody in Escalante remembered that Pollock had finally been convicted around 1938, and served time in prison. Della Christianson recalled the sting that trapped the cowboy. "The Cattlemen's Association took a calf, cut a slit in its hide, and sewed a silver dollar into it. They found the calf with Joe Pollock's brand on it. The sheriff produced the silver dollar." Gail Bailey, coincidentally, was the president of the Cattlemen's Association.

According to Della Christianson, "Keith became a recluse later in life. If you came to his home, he'd go in the bedroom and hide."

At the time Everett disappeared, Keith Riddle was nineteen years old, Joe Pollock thirty-nine. Riddle died in 1984, at the age of sixty-eight; Pollock twenty years earlier, at the same age. The recurrent scenario that bits of Escalante gossip outlined was that Everett had stumbled upon some rustlers far out on the Escalante Desert. As I had earlier learned, to put a scare into the likes of Pollock and Riddle, the Cattlemen's Association had circulated the false rumor that a government agent was coming to Escalante to investigate. Caught red-handed slaughtering a cow, completely unaware of the advent of a twenty-year-old artist in the country, the rustlers assumed Everett was that government agent. One or both of them had killed the young man to cover up their crime.

I could not dismiss the possibility that Riddle's "confession" was after all a drunken boast, or even that Norm Christensen had made up the story. In Fredonia, Arizona, I managed to track down Loy Riddle, one of Keith's sons. Born in 1950, Loy could have known about the Ruess matter only from tales his father had told him more than twenty years after the fact. Loy, of course, had heard the rumors implicating his father. Over the phone, he told me, "On my father's deathbed, I said, 'Dad, if you killed the little guy, let me know where he's at, 'cause there's still a $10,000 reward out on him. Tell me and I'll collect.' Dad said, 'Hell, I never even met the guy.' " Loy believed that it was Gail Bailey who had fingered his father and Joe Pollock.

Another persistent motif in the gossip of the old-timers nagged at me. From four different sources I had heard the imputation, always repeated in the exact same phrase, that Everett's killers "had throwed his body in the river." Clearly the river implied was the Colorado, as its tributary, the Escalante, dwindles to a trickle in November. As Norm Christensen said to me, "There's so many places out there to dispose of a body—tie a couple of rocks on him, throw him in the river. After three-four months of catfish and carp feedin' on him, there wouldn't be much left."

Had Everett run into Keith Riddle and Joe Pollock out on their winter range, he must have left Davis Gulch on a hike to the southeast. Perhaps he had climbed the single line of Moqui steps that attacked that side of the canyon, though I had blanched at the thought as I had stood at the foot of that hand-and-toe trail. But the Pollock range embraced a large quadrangle bordered by the Hole-in-the-Rock, Kaiparowits Plateau, Davis Gulch, and the Escalante River. Where in that featureless badlands might the fateful encounter have taken place?

Melvin Alvey had given me another fugitive clue. He said that a long-dead rancher who had participated in the 1935 search had told him that somebody had found unexplained footprints in the mud at Jackass Bar, on the Colorado. But where was Jackass Bar, and how did you get there? There was no such name on the 1987 USGS topo map, for the sandbar had long since been flooded under the waters of Lake Powell.

No one in Escalante seemed to remember where Jackass Bar was. More than forty years before, they had turned their backs on the farthest reaches of the Escalante Desert. Joe Pollock's range languished unused, its topography forgotten. As DeLane Griffin told me, "All the guys who knew that country're in the cemetery today."

But McKay Bailey, Gail's son, had a vague memory of Jackass Bar. "Joe Pollock used to put cows down on the bar," he drawled. "Probably Joe built the stock trail down to it. It's right there, right below this old spring—Joe Perdence's seep, named for an old Spanish guy, lived out that way a long time." Bailey took my map and drew a crooked line on it.

I had thought I had wrapped up my research at the beginning of June. Like Bud Rusho, I would not solve the mystery of Everett's demise. But now, in early July, I was seized with a feverish obsession at least to retrace what might have been the vagabond's last trail.

The temperature was in the high nineties when I got out of my rental four-by-four, not far from the top of the Hole-in-the-Rock cleft, and started rim-walking northeast. McKay Bailey's line on the map was evidently off by a mile or two, for when I came to the place where he thought Joe Pollock's livestock trail headed down to the river, I stood on the edge of a sheer cliff.

I pushed on through a maze of sandstone billows, ridges, and cirques, backing off dead-end chutes, as I threaded a route that few, I guessed, had ever walked. I never did find Joe Perdence's seep. But after a couple of hours, growing dizzy in the brutal, windless heat, I found the first cairn, a two-foot pillar of stacked rocks. A hundred yards beyond it I found another, then another. With mounting excitement I traced the old livestock trail, marveling at the route-finding skill of its architect, as it took the only line among the slickrock domes and prows that livestock could negotiate. Just above Lake Powell I found the broad steps, hacked with axes out of the bedrock, coated with the brown patina of the decades, of a classic Western stock trail.

Standing on the lake shore, I stared into the opaque water, trying to see down to Jackass Bar, drowned under two hundred feet of reservoir and silt. By the time I started back, the temperature was over 100 degrees, and I was down to one quart of water.

On the rim again, I took a slightly different route back to my vehicle, following cairns I had missed on the way out. As I passed behind a small butte, I saw two logs lying on the ground, bleached white by the sun, but showing plainly the cuts of the ax-blows that had hewn them to size. Beyond the logs, I spotted a rusted can. It had a pair of tiny holes gouged in the lid, beside two PUNCH HERE legends embossed in the metal.

Clearly the place had been an overnight camp, the can tossed aside by its long-ago visitors, the logs never burned in the fire. (I took the can with me, then returned it to the site months later. To my wonderment, an expert in such matters confidently dated the can to 1935, plus or minus a year or two.)

All the way down the livestock trail, I had pictured the killers hauling Everett's inert body on horseback before they dumped it in the river. Could this have been the same men's camp, coming or going? On the verge of heading on toward my car, I noticed a strange pile of rocks not far from the discarded logs. The more I stared at it, the more I was convinced that the mound was man-made. Two feet high, six feet across, the pile was plainly old, for a gnarled sagebrush grew out of it. It looked like the kind of pile of flat rocks you might build to cover something.

A wild surmise seized my thoughts. I saw Everett, having escaped Davis Gulch to explore the plateau to the southeast, stumbling into his fatal encounter with the rustlers. I pictured them loading his body on horseback to carry it to the Colorado. Then, weary with their bloody toil, or caught short by the early night of late November, they stopped here to camp.

It seemed improbable that the mound before me could be Everett's grave: surely if his killers had decided to hide his body, they would not have interred it smack on the trail. But what if the mound hid some of his belongings, paraphernalia the criminals did not want to trust to the river? What if the 1934 diary lay buried here?

The skeptic in me demurred. The mound could be merely the grave of some old cowboy's dead dog; it could be flat rocks piled up to smother an old campfire; it could even be an odd but natural scattering of stones. And yet . . .

There was only one way to find out. I knelt beside the pile and seized the topmost stone. But just as I started to dig through the dirt below, an old instinct stopped me. What first gave me pause was the

ethic I had learned in Anasazi sites: never disturb a ruin. The Antiqui-
ties Act, moreover, protected not only seven-hundred-year-old dwellings but a sixty-three-year-old grave, or even a historic cache.

Yet as I stood over the mound and wiped my hands on my shorts,
as if to rub away the itch that had tempted me to dig, I realized it
wasn't the pile of rocks that I most wanted to leave undisturbed—it
was the mystery of Everett Ruess. And I felt an odd elation, for no
one else had ever had the chance to stand here, stare at the mound,
and wonder *What if?*

I drank the last of my water, hoisted my pack, and started on.
Turning for a last look at the old campsite, I was struck by a tantalizing thought. If that mound was Everett's grave, then, as he had
predicted to Waldo, he had indeed found the wildest, loneliest, most
desolate spot in which to die.

Comb Ridge

W HEN MY ARTICLE ABOUT EVERETT was published in the
Spring 1999 issue of *National Geographic Adventure,* Bud
Rusho took it as a personal challenge. Over the phone, I gave him
detailed directions to the old campsite on the trail to Jackass Bar. Immediately he set out with three companions to investigate the place.

Rusho found the site, then, with no compunctions about the An-
tiquities Act, started digging. As he later wrote,

> Convinced that the mound could not be a grave, we ten-
> tatively began discarding rocks and loose sand. But within
> twenty minutes of digging to a depth of about eighteen
> inches, we found only sandstone bedrock! Apparently the
> mound had been formed by a natural disintegration of a
> small sandstone hoodoo, leaving sand covered by broken
> slabs of rock. It was not a grave; neither was it a repository
> for Everett's journal and camp gear.

I reacted to Rusho's debunking mission with relative equanimity.
My hunch about the mound, I had always known, was a long shot.

And the fact that the protuberance in the earth turned out to be a natural bulge did not disprove the possibility that the trail to Jackass Bar
had been the route taken by Everett's killer or killers on their way to
dumping his body in the Colorado River. The campsite itself, dated by
the tin can to around 1935, could very well have been the overnight
stopping place of the ranchers who might have perpetrated the crime.

On the other hand, nothing I had discovered in 1998 and early
1999 really proved anything definite about Everett's fate. All I had
to go on was Keith Riddle's confession to Norm Christensen, and
the persistent Escalante rumor about rustlers murdering the vagabond
and throwing his body into the Colorado River.

For the next nine years I kept Everett Ruess on my personal back
burner, even as I made many further hiking and backpacking trips
into the Escalante canyons. During that time I never returned to Davis
Gulch. But in 2002, I spent a blissful week exploring the top of Kaiparowits Plateau. As preparation for that outing, I once more interviewed Escalante old-timers, especially DeLane Griffin, who knew
Fifty-Mile Mountain (as the locals call it) better than any other man
or woman alive. During my prowls atop Kaiparowits, I kept an eye
cocked for any vestige of a sign that Everett might have explored the
remote mesa, but, as I expected, I found nothing of that kind.

Throughout those nine years, I hiked the canyons of Utah and
Arizona every chance I could get with Vaughn Hadenfeldt, the wilderness guide who had shared my research forays in 1998 in quest
of Everett. In 2004, Vaughn, our mutual friend Greg Child, and
I made what was apparently the first complete traverse of Comb
Ridge, 125 miles over eighteen days, as we started just east of Kayenta, Arizona, and ended northwest of Blanding, Utah. Following
the crest of that dramatic sandstone escarpment day after day, we
also looped low on its eastern flanks to explore Anasazi ruins and
rock art, as well as Navajo petroglyph panels dating back as far as
the end of the nineteenth century, along with the occasional ruined

sweat lodge where Diné sheepherders had long ago cleansed their bodies and souls.

Two thirds of our journey crossed the Navajo reservation. In camp several nights, as Vaughn cooked up tasty dinners, he told Greg and me about his friend Denny Bellson, a Navajo who lived just east of Comb Ridge in a house he had built for himself in 1993. Denny's favorite pastime was to explore the nooks and crannies of the Comb, as well as the benches of Chinle Wash, which carves a sinuous gorge through the escarpment as it makes its erratic journey north toward its junction with the San Juan River. Never having met Denny, I imagined him, I suppose, as a bit of a kook, for the primary goal of his sleuthing was to find old Spanish treasure—this despite the fact that there is little or no evidence that the conquistadors of the sixteenth through eighteenth centuries ever reached the Comb. But Denny was all the same a repository of local lore. He had told Vaughn, for instance, that in more than twenty years of exploring Chinle Wash, he had never found its silt-laden current clean enough to drink, even after filtering a potful and letting it stand for hours to settle.

One day in May 2008, Vaughn called me up at my home in Cambridge, Massachusetts. Out of the blue, he said, "Denny thinks he may have found Everett Ruess."

I could not suppress a derisive snort. "Yeah, you bet," I rejoined. "Tell him to keep looking."

"Shut up and listen a minute," Vaughn countered. Then he told me an extraordinary story.

*   *   *

Denny's grandfather was a man named Aneth Nez. Born in 1899, Aneth was a tall, well-built, stern-faced man who wore his hair tied back in the traditional Navajo ponytail, kept in place with a tight bandanna. His hogan, the six-sided house in which he had grown up, stood only a few miles east of Comb Ridge.

One thing that Aneth did for hours at a time was to sit on the crest of the Comb and survey the country beneath him. Sometimes those vigils were practical, for he was a sheepherder tending the flocks that grazed below him on the willows and tamarisks fringing Chinle Wash, or on the grasses stubbling the rocky slopes. But sometimes Aneth's outings were simply idle and contemplative. Like all traditional Navajos, he had a deep connection with the land. It spoke to him in ways no white man or woman could understand.

One day in the 1930s, Aneth's eye had been caught by a novel and unexpected phenomenon. Some three hundred feet below his airy perch, a young man was traveling along the wash. The intruder was an Anglo. He had two pack animals, one that he rode and one that was packed with gear dangling from the saddlebags. Aneth saw a frying pan, a coffeepot, and other items that suggested the youth was on a camping trip. But he moved with an urgent purposefulness, as if searching for something.

In the 1930s, the presence of white strangers in such a remote corner of the Navajo reservation was an unusual event. It was all the more surprising that this traveler was so young, and that he was there by himself. Aneth stayed out of sight: the youth never realized that he was being watched. Where had he come from, Aneth wondered. Where was he going? What was he looking for?

During the next several days, Aneth spotted the young traveler again. But on the third or fourth occasion that he caught sight of the wanderer, Aneth realized immediately that something was desperately wrong. The young man was yelling and riding as fast as he could. And the men who were chasing him were Utes.

Traditional enemies of the Navajo, the Utes are an entirely unrelated people. In the 1930s, the band of Utes nearest the Navajo reservation resided near Blanding, Utah. Aneth had grown up afraid of the Ute ruffians who had routinely robbed and beaten up his older brother, who as a teenager had been hired by white ranchers near

Monticello, north of Blanding, to tend their sheep. But south of the San Juan River, on the reservation, Aneth felt safe, for Utes seldom ventured anymore into the homeland of their ancient foes.

As Aneth watched, the Utes caught up with the young man, hit him in the head, and knocked him off his pack animal. Then they stole all his belongings, took the pack animals, and rode away north.

After the Utes were gone, Aneth climbed down from the crest of the Comb to the bottom of Chinle Wash. The young man was dead by the time Aneth got to him. Rather than look for a burial site in the sandy stream bank, the Navajo man carried the body up to the rim, probably slung across the saddle of his horse. In the process, he most likely was smeared with the victim's blood. In a rock crevice on the crest of the Comb, Aneth buried the young stranger.

* * *

For at least three and a half decades, Aneth told nobody about what had happened that day in Chinle Wash. Only in 1971 did he feel compelled to share his dark secret with his granddaughter, Daisey Johnson. Thirteen years older than her brother, Denny Bellson, Daisey waited another thirty-seven years to tell Denny the story.

A few weeks before Vaughn had called me in May 2008, Daisey had come from her home in Farmington, New Mexico, to Bluff, Utah, to visit relatives, including Denny. A dispute over sheep grazing rights was the ostensible reason for the rendezvous. But, as Daisey later recalled, "One of the grandkids asked us how the Utes used to treat us." So she told the tale that Denny had never heard before—about Aneth Nez, the Comb Ridge, and the young Anglo riding away from his pursuers on the bench beside Chinle Wash.

Fifty-six years old in May 2008, Daisey was a troubled woman. A year and a half earlier she had been diagnosed with ovarian cancer. She had undergone a round of chemotherapy that nauseated her and caused her hair to fall out. But the cancer had gone away. Now, just in the last few weeks, it had come back. This time Daisey went to a medicine man.

"He asked me, 'Have you been messing with the dead?' " Daisey would later explain to me. "So I told him about Grandpa."

In Bluff, Denny listened to his sister's story in electrified silence. In 1971, at the age of seventy-two, Aneth himself had fallen ill with cancer. He had paid a medicine man to diagnose his trouble. Either Aneth had told the medicine man about witnessing the murder on the Comb, or the man had divined it. "He said," Daisey narrated, " 'You had no business messing around with that body.' " To her relatives, Daisey added, "When Grandpa carried the boy up to the grave, he must have got a lot of blood on him—that's what made him get sick later."

The medicine man told Aneth that the only way he could cure his cancer would be to retrieve a lock of hair from the head of the young man he had buried decades earlier, then use it in a five-day Enemy Way curing ceremony. "I was nineteen," Daisey said. "I was home for the summer. I heard Grandpa and Grandma arguing about something. Grandma said, 'You should have left him alone! Left him be!'

"So I asked Grandpa, 'What are you talking about?' He said, 'I'm going to tell you this story, and I'm only going to tell you once.' That was the first time I ever heard anything about the young dude the Utes had killed down there in Chinle Wash."

Daisey drove her grandfather, who had never learned to operate a motor vehicle, out toward the Comb in the family pickup. She waited in the cab for two hours. "He came back," Daisey recalled, "and said, 'He's still there.' "

A few days later, Aneth drove out to the Comb again with another medicine man. This time he retrieved a lock of hair from the grave.

In the curing ceremony, Daisey explained, the medicine man dusted the lock of hair with ash—"so it will never bother the patient again." On the fifth day, "The medicine man said a prayer, thanking the spirits for making the patient well again. Somebody yelled, 'It's ready now!' The medicine man put ash on the lock of hair, then shot it with a gun, to destroy it completely.

"And then Grandpa got better."

According to the medicine man whom Daisey consulted in 2008, it was not her role in 1971 as driver for Aneth Nez that was the sole cause of her own cancer. A far more grievous event had occurred ten years after the pickup ride. "Grandpa got sick again in 1981," Daisey reminded her relatives in Bluff. "He was eighty-two years old. I told Grandma to take him to the hospital in Cortez [Colorado]. The night he was admitted, we all went over there, my mom and my aunts and all. We asked the doctor what was wrong with him. The doctor said he had stomach cancer, and that they couldn't do anything for him.

"Two weeks later, I went to Cortez to drop in on Grandpa. There was a nurse coming out of his room. She said, 'I just took his temperature. You can visit him, but he's not talking much.'

"I went in, but Grandpa had already passed. His mouth was open. I started shaking him. He was already gone, but I kept shaking him, and saying, 'Grandpa! Grandpa!' He didn't answer."

Daisey paused in her storytelling and took a deep breath. "This year, when I went to the medicine man, I told him about shaking Grandpa in the hospital and calling out to him. He said, 'That would have done it. You don't ever touch the dead or talk to the dead. You don't mess with death.' "

Denny Bellson lives on the Navajo Reservation, just off U.S. Highway 191 south of Bluff, not far from where both he and Daisey had grown up, and where Aneth Nez had lived. As he listened to his sister's story, Denny realized that the grave must lie somewhere near the house in which he had resided for the last fifteen years. Throughout his adult life, Denny kept a close bond with the land on which he grew up, as he prowled around Comb Ridge and Chinle Wash, looking for hidden treasure. Now Denny was seized with a passion to find the grave where Aneth had buried the young man back in the 1930s.

For several days, Denny spent the time he had off from his carpentry and craftsman jobs out hiking Comb Ridge, looking into every corner and cranny along the rim. Then he returned to Bluff to visit Daisey again. This time he brought with him a USGS topo map, annotated with penciled-in landmarks—the hogans and grazing pastures of the neighbors and relatives with whom he and his sister had grown up.

"I tried to get her to show me where she'd parked the pickup with our grandpa," Denny later told me. "When I showed her the map, she recognized a Y in the road near Colored Rock Woman's house. She gave me real good directions."

It was May 25, 2008. Denny rushed back out to the Comb, while Daisey drove home to Farmington. In less than two hours of searching, in an obscure crevice just under the crest of the Comb, Denny found what he was looking for. And he saw at once that the person whose bones lay in that unlikely tomb had been buried in haste, and perhaps in great fear.

When Daisey got home, the phone was ringing. It was Denny on the line. He blurted out four words: "I found the grave."

Neither Denny nor Daisey, nor anyone in their family, had ever heard of Everett Ruess. Shortly after first listening to his sister's story about their grandfather, Denny had summarized the tale to a friend in Bluff, Michael Peed, a retired art professor originally from Montana. At once Peed remarked, "Gosh, that sounds a lot like Everett Ruess." Peed wrote down the vagabond's name.

Denny got on a computer, Googled the name, and learned the basic outlines of the story of the artist and poet who had vanished near Davis Gulch in 1934. Later, Peed lent Denny a copy of Rusho's *A Vagabond for Beauty.*

A few days after he found the grave, Denny took Vaughn Haden-feldt out to the site. Denny showed Vaughn how, rounding a corner on a ledge, he had stumbled across a few stringy pieces of black, desic-cated leather, then the wooden framework of an old saddle, and then a single wooden stirrup. All these objects were lying open to the air, in plain sight, yet in a remarkably obscure location. Just beyond the stir-rup a narrow crevice gaped in the bedrock, beneath an eight-foot-high cliff. From a distance, Denny thought he could see bones in the dim recesses of the crack. He approached, verified that the bones were human, but touched nothing. As a traditional Navajo, Denny scrupu-lously observed the taboo about not coming in contact with the dead. Now, on his second visit with Vaughn, the strips of leather, the saddle, and the stirrup lay just as Denny had found them, as did the jumble of bones in the crevice.

That evening, Vaughn telephoned me. Listening to my friend's syn-opsis of the bizarre story about Aneth, Daisey, and Denny, I clung to my skepticism. "It's a coincidence," I told Vaughn. "Everett's burros were found in Davis Gulch. How'd they get over to Chinle Wash?"

"Yeah, that's a problem," Vaughn acknowledged. But he went on, "The grave could be a Navajo crevice burial, but there's something pretty weird about it. Denny says if it was a Navajo grave, they'd have buried the saddle and the other stuff with the dead man. And it doesn't look like the guy was carefully laid out in the crevice. It looks like he was jammed in there in a hurry."

Vaughn sent me a few digital photos he had snapped at the site. One was a good shot of the stirrup. I got out *Vagabond for Beauty.* In a couple of photos of Everett on burro-back, the stirrups looked very much like the artifact Denny had found. But for all I knew, stir-rups in the 1930s in the Southwest were all of a single make. To take another photo, Vaughn had leaned into the opening of the crevice and shot straight down. The upper half of a smooth white skull protruded intact from the dirt. Beside it was a leather belt decorated with metal studs, buckled closed in a twisted loop.

The photos intrigued me, but it took another call from Vaughn to plant the hook. "Hey, David," he said over the phone, "I think you ought to take this seriously. What if it really could be Everett?"

I pondered the wild improbability. What did I have to lose? "Okay," I said to Vaughn. "It's worth a trip out there, I guess. Ask Denny if he's willing to take me to the site."

I called my editors at *National Geographic Adventure* to see if they were interested in this possibly new wrinkle about Everett Ruess. Guarded but curious, they agreed to finance my junket to Bluff.

Before I could get to Utah, however, Denny called the FBI in Monticello. If by some remote chance the grave was that of Everett Ruess—or of some other Anglo who had been killed by Utes—it was thus a crime scene. Fearful of violating legal sanctions, Denny felt it his duty to call the authorities.

I called up Rachel Boisselle, special agent in the Monticello office. Over the phone, she seemed friendly. She, too, had never heard of Everett Ruess, so I filled her in on the seventy-four-year-old saga. Boisselle was planning to head out to the site with Denny in a few days. But she was plainly skeptical. "Denny's already dragged us out to another place down near Poncho House where he found bones coming out of the ground," she told me. "When we got there, we could see right away that it was an Anasazi mother and child. We covered the bones back up."

The Ruess story plainly intrigued Boisselle, however. "You can be sure we'll treat this new burial with the utmost respect," she told me just before we hung up. "We won't disturb a thing."

I had my misgivings. I called Greg Child, who lives in Castle Valley, Utah—only 120 miles north of Bluff—to tell him what was going on. Greg was as intrigued by the developing enigma as Vaughn and I were. Now *Adventure* commissioned Greg to photograph the strange crevice burial.

Greg drove down to Bluff and found Denny, who took him out on the Comb. "At the grave, Denny didn't touch a thing," Greg told me later. "And on the way back, he made me wash my hands in this spring he knew about. I had to wash them over and over again before Denny would let me get into his truck."

At the site, Greg spent an hour photographing the burial—not only the "artifacts" (saddle, strips of leather, stirrup) lying on the ledge, but the top of the skull protruding from the dirt inside the crevice and the buckled belt beside it.

Greg's photos, it turned out, would provide the only careful documentation of the burial site before the FBI team came in and trashed it completely.

*   *   *

In Bluff on July 7, I met Denny Bellson. Forty-three years old in the summer of 2008, he had a quiet demeanor but, I sensed at once, an alertness that took in every nuance of his surroundings. Of medium build, with dark hair flecked with gray and a mustache drooping past the corners of his mouth, he squinted through rimless spectacles that a professor might have worn.

With Vaughn, we drove south on Highway 191, then turned west on a gravel road. At the wheel, Denny took one fork after another, as the branching trails petered out in vestigial slickrock tracks. "When I was a kid," Denny said, "I asked my dad, 'Do people live out there?' " He pointed through the windshield at the stark plateau ahead of our truck. "Dad said, 'Nope. You go out there and it just drops off into a big canyon.' I thought it was like the end of the world."

Finally we parked the truck and started hiking. It was 96 degrees and windless, and within minutes my face and chest were covered with sweat.

I noticed that Denny was toting a .357 Magnum in a holster strapped to his belt. "Why do you carry that gun?" I asked.

"Might step on another bobcat." On a search for the grave back in May, Denny explained, he had put his weight on a rock beneath which a bobcat was crouching. "Spooked him bad," Denny said. "Bobcats can be vicious."

We came to the rim. Just below us, I recognized the shelf Vaughn, Greg, and I had hiked in 2004 on our traverse of the Comb. We had passed within a hundred yards of the grave site, I would soon realize, without suspecting there was anything interesting just above us on the right. Now Denny dropped one level, scuttled around a few corners, then stopped before a cranny so nondescript I wouldn't even have bothered to search it for potsherds.

"Who piled up those rocks?" Vaughn asked, pointing at an assemblage that covered some six feet of crevice.

"FBI," Denny answered.

As we pulled the camouflaging stones away from the grave, Vaughn groaned, and I cursed out loud, for I had seen Greg's photos of the site before the feds had gotten here. "What the hell did they do?" I asked.

In a deadpan voice, Denny narrated his outing a week before with the FBI. The team had consisted of Rachel Boisselle from the Monticello office, two Navajo criminal investigators, and the San Juan county sheriff, who had invited his three sons along. "One of the CIs tried to lift up the skull," Denny recounted, "and it broke into pieces. The FBI lady decided right off that it was a Navajo crevice burial. They acted like I was wasting their time."

I was staring at the desecrated grave. The heavy saddle, the stirrup, and other odds and ends that Denny had originally found on the ledge in front of the crevice had been jammed into the tight space, further damaging the skeleton. When they were done, the whole team had covered up their work by piling stones to hide the grave.

"Sounds like they thought they were out on a fucking picnic," I muttered.

Denny smiled. "It kinda was."

"You just sat there and let them do it?"

"Wasn't up to me. They're the FBI."

The three of us sat on boulders, surveying the wreckage. I wiped my brow with a bandanna. "I can smell those bones," Denny said. I couldn't, but Vaughn nodded. Denny added, "I could smell 'em when I got here the first time."

"How did you find the grave?" I asked.

"Came around that corner there." Denny pointed north. "I saw part of the saddle. That led me to the crevice."

"Was it exciting?"

"No. Spooky."

Daisey's story about Aneth Nez was dancing in my head. "Why did your grandfather haul the body up here?"

Denny shrugged. "Dunno. Preserve it, maybe. Use it later."

"For medicine?" I was out of my Navajo depth.

"For his ceremony."

From the rim we could see Chinle Wash stretching north into the distance. Denny pointed to a pair of tall cottonwood trees three hundred feet below and a mile away. "They call that place the Standing Tree. I think that's where the kid was killed by the Utes."

At Vaughn's urging, we scrambled down to the wash. None of us expected to find anything from the 1930s—flash floods over the decades would have scoured clean the creekbed and its banks. Vaughn, Greg, and I had backpacked this very stretch of the Chinle in 2004. But now the hike down from the rim and back up gave us a visceral sense of the effort Aneth Nez must have undertaken to bury the young man in the high crevice.

Back at the grave site, I asked Denny, "You think the saddle was Aneth's?"

He nodded. "It would've been contaminated."

"Why did Daisey wait thirty-seven years to tell you your grandfather's story?"

"Dunno. You'll have to ask her."

I hestitated before posing what felt like an intrusive question. "Denny, is it dangerous for you to come here?"

"It is," he answered right away. "Doesn't matter if this guy is white, Mexican, or Navajo. It will probably affect me later."

I thought about that. "Why are you willing to take Vaughn and me here?"

"I want to find out who this guy is." Denny stared at the crevice. "Well, he sure picked the loneliest place to die."

I was impressed. Denny had been doing his homework.

The next day I drove to Farmington to talk to Daisey Johnson. We met for lunch at the International House of Pancakes, her favorite restaurant. She had dressed up for the occasion, wearing a bright red blouse and a brooch made of concentric rings of turquoise stones. Her wavy auburn hair seemed to belie her age—but after a moment I realized that it was probably a wig, for I knew the chemotherapy had caused her hair to fall out. Now Daisey's face bore a frown of anguish—the residue of her months of suffering from a cancer that would not go away.

A week earlier, over the telephone, Daisey had told me a brief version of Aneth Nez's story. Now she recounted her grandfather's saga in much greater detail.

"When Grandpa brought back the lock of hair, it was in a plastic bag," Daisey explained. "I saw it later for just a second. Maybe I wasn't supposed to see it. Maybe I wasn't supposed to know what Grandpa did with that white man."

Daisey retold the story of the five-day Enemy Way curing ceremony her grandfather had undergone, culminating with the covering of the lock of hair with ash, then shooting it with a gun. "After that,"

Daisey said, "once the ceremony was done, I didn't hear anything more about the guy down there in Chinle Wash. But I kept thinking about him. He must have family somewhere. I kept thinking if my son was laying out there somewhere, I would want somebody to tell me where he was. Plus, what was even more shocking was that the guy was only twenty years old."

There was a long pause. I asked, "Do you have any interest in going out to the grave site?"

"No." Daisey's answer was emphatic.

"Because it would be harmful for you?"

Daisey sighed. "The medicine man warned me just last week not to hang around the dead, not even to go to any funerals."

"Denny told me," I said, "that he thinks having found the grave site is dangerous for him."

"It is. I don't know why he's doing it. I hope he puts ash on himself every time he goes out there."

There was another long silence. Daisey had ordered dessert, but the pie and ice cream sat untouched on her plate. "How do you feel about the possibility this could be Everett Ruess?" I asked.

"I hope it is," she answered. "I hope they solve it. He was such a young guy. What was he doing out here all alone? I hope they take him back to wherever he came from. He's got family there."

*   *   *

Before I had gone out to Utah in July 2008, I had telephoned Brian Ruess, who lives in Portland, Oregon. One of four children of Waldo Ruess and his wife, Conchita, Brian and his three siblings were Everett's closest living relatives, though all four had been born too late to have met their vagabond uncle. Waldo had died in 2007, the day after his ninety-eighth birthday. During his last years, the lifelong quest Waldo had pursued to solve the great mystery of his brother's fate had been redoubled by his four children. But after decades of fielding leads and hints and theories that had never panned out, the family had become skeptical that any new evidence would ever surface.

After my long phone conversation with Brian, however, he instantly e-mailed his siblings. "How is this for weird?" his missive began. He deftly summarized the story of Denny, Daisey, and Aneth Nez. Brian closed, "Pretty fascinating!"

By now I had another assignment from *National Geographic Adventure*. For its tenth anniversary issue, in April–May 2009, the magazine would run a second story about Everett Ruess, a decade after my report on the mystery in the premiere issue.

Was there any way, I wondered, to prove or disprove whether the bones Denny had discovered in the Comb Ridge crevice could possibly be Everett's? What about DNA?

The same day that I called Brian, I got in touch with Bennett Greenspan, president of Family Tree DNA, a Texas-based firm that has done consulting work for the National Geographic Society for many years. Once more I related the haunting story Daisey had told me over the phone. After a pause, Greenspan gave me an answer. It was a long shot—a very long shot. But with the right pair of samples and the most sophisticated sort of lab work, Family Tree might just be able to demonstrate a match. Or prove a mismatch.

But if we were ever to probe the mystery deeper, by retrieving a DNA sample from the Comb Ridge skeleton, that was a business that had to be done with the utmost delicacy and through proper channels. On our various visits to the site, Vaughn, Greg Child, Denny, and I had not so much as touched a single bone. If "messing with death" was a dire Navajo taboo, it would be flagrant desecration for white folks to disturb what might well be a Native American burial.

Before heading out to Utah, I had also gotten in touch with Ron Maldonado, the supervisory archaeologist in the Navajo Nation Historic Preservation Department, based in Window Rock, Arizona. Maldonado was instantly intrigued by the unfolding saga—and instantly cautious. He agreed, however, to go out to the site with us and have a look around. Though a Hispanic, Maldonado, I soon learned, was married to a Navajo woman. He also had vast experience with crevice burials on the reservation.

Several days after my first visit to the grave, Vaughn, Denny, and I met Maldonado at the café-cum-convenience store that amounts to the town of Mexican Water. The archaeologist was a hefty fellow in his early fifties, with hippie-length salt-and-pepper hair and a Burl Ives beard and mustache. He spoke in a soft, thoughtful voice, often after long pauses.

With Denny leading the way, we drove three vehicles through the maze of dirt roads west of Highway 191 out onto the slickrock plateau, then hiked to the rim of Comb Ridge. The day was as hot as on our previous foray, and my tongue was parched long before we arrived.

Rachel Boisselle had called Maldonado before the FBI had headed out to the Comb, and I had forwarded to him Greg's photos of the grave as it looked when Denny had found it. Now, as soon as Maldonado peered into the crevice, he sucked in his breath. "Rachel promised me they wouldn't move anything," he complained. "I'm just really ticked off at what they did." Gently he removed the saddle and the other "artifacts" from the crevice. "In a crime scene," he said, "you don't just shove the goods into the grave."

For the next hour, lying awkwardly on his side, sweating profusely, Maldonado reached into the crevice and deftly wielded a trowel to pick the dirt away from the bones. He, too, avoided touching any part of the skeleton. Instead, he studied its layout. As he had two days before, Denny sat about ten yards away, watching and saying little.

After a while, Maldonado commented, "It's definitely a full-sized skull. But it's still growing. It looks like a guy in his twenties." Many minutes later: "He's not facing east. As far as I can tell, he's facing to the southwest. If it was a Navajo burial, he'd be facing east."

Later still: "It just doesn't look like a Navajo burial. They would have put the saddle in the crevice with him."

Denny spoke up: "They would have killed the horse, too. Hit it with an ax, and left the ax handle in the grave."

Still later, Denny asked, "Smell the bones?"

Maldonado sat up, trowel in hand. "Yeah. You can smell them even when they're a thousand years old. It gets into the dirt. It's a smell I can never forget. This guy I used to work with calls it 'people grease.'"

We took a break to sit in the shade and eat lunch. Maldonado mused out loud, "Look at that crevice. It's not a likely place to bury somebody. You could make a much better burial right over there, or there." He pointed to a pair of ample slots in the rimrock cliff just behind us. "He may have been trying to hide the body in a hurry," Maldonado went on, referring to Aneth Nez. "Just stuff him in there, then maneuver him around. He had to get him in the ground before sunset.

"It all makes sense. The 1930s were a really volatile time on the reservation. The government had started wholesale livestock reduction, killing thousands of Navajo sheep and cattle. They were hauling the kids off to boarding schools. Here's a Navajo guy who witnesses a murder. Your grandpa"—Maldonado nodded at Denny—"doesn't want the remains just lying out on the ground. In the thirties, if a white guy gets killed on the rez, they call out the cavalry. Round up a bunch of Navajos, pick a suspect, and lock him in jail. I can see why your grandpa would have tried to hide the guy. And then I can see why he wouldn't tell anybody about it for thirty-some years."

After lunch, Maldonado went back to work. Finally, toward late afternoon, we sat in the shade again. The archaeologist lowered his head and wiped his brow as he pondered, silent for so long that he seemed to be meditating. Finally he spoke: "It just doesn't look like a Navajo burial. Who else lives in this area?"

"Nobody," said Denny.

"Who else could be buried out here?"

Denny shook his head. He had asked his neighbors. There were no old stories of grave sites on this part of the Comb. "Mom and Dad," Denny added, "always told us to stay away from here. They never told us why."

"According to Navajo Nation policy," Maldonado said, "we're supposed to protect graves, whether Native American or not. But we're also supposed to try to find the lineal descendants, if there's an unidentified body." He turned to me. "Who's the relative you talked to?"

"Brian Ruess. He's Everett's nephew."

"Ask him to request a DNA sample." It was obvious that Maldonado's decision had not come easily to him. He stood up and hoisted his fanny pack. "Out here," he said, "Navajo oral tradition is pretty accurate. Based on that tradition, I think there's a good chance this is Everett Ruess."

*   *   *

For the grave that Denny had discovered on the crest of the Comb Ridge to be Everett's, a couple of logical puzzles would have to be solved. The most troublesome was what I had started calling "the burro problem." According to Aneth's story, the young Anglo who was chased and killed by the Utes in the 1930s had been riding one animal and leading another. Yet in 1982 Bud Rusho had been told by the surviving search party members that they had found Everett's burros ranging inside the open corral in Davis Gulch.

But if, as the old-timers told me in 1998, Gail Bailey had indeed found the animals on his own, before the March 1935 search had been launched, and had taken the animals up on "the mountain," where they were never seen again, how could we credit the truth of any Escalante testimony about the burros? Rusho's *Vagabond for*

Beauty reprinted a photo of the searchers on horseback leading what looks like a pair of burros up a livestock trail. Could they be different beasts from Everett's Cockleburrs and Chocolatero?

If one supposes that Everett had left his burros in Davis Gulch while he explored eastward, another logical snag immediately presents itself. Chinle Wash lies sixty miles as the crow flies east of Davis Gulch, maybe ninety miles as a hiker might wend his way. In his three years of exploring the Southwest, Everett had never been known to stray far from his burros or horses. After his first foray into Yosemite in 1930, when he had struggled with the burden of a fifty-pound pack, Everett had sworn always to use pack animals in the future.

It seems highly unlikely that in November 1934, Everett might have left Cockleburrs and Chocolatero in Davis Gulch, then covered the ninety rugged miles to Chinle Wash carrying his belongings on his back. It is doubtful that he even had a pack large enough to hold camping gear, food, clothing, and painting kit for an extended journey.

What eventually seemed the most logical solution to the burro problem came to me after another old Southwestern crony, Fred Blackburn, commented, "The hardest thing to do with a pack animal is to get it to cross a big river." Fred owns and trains horses, and has led many a wilderness outing with those animals, as well as other treks with mules, burros, and llamas. His remark reminded me of the passage from Everett's last letter to his parents, in which he described the extreme difficulty he had had coaxing Chocolatero to cross the Colorado on a sturdy suspension bridge, solved only when "a packer dragged him across behind his mule, and he left a bloody track all the way across."

In the same letter, Everett had anticipated crossing the Colorado during the days to come, noting, "The water is very low this year." In fact, Bureau of Reclamation records that go back to the first decade of the twentieth century reveal that the Colorado was flowing at 2,400 cubic feet per second in early November 1934, and that that level was as meager a flow as was ever recorded in the 105 years from 1906 to the present. It is possible, then, that at a place such as Hole-in-the-Rock, Everett could have waded the Colorado rather than having to swim it.

The parsimonious solution, to my mind, was that after all his troubles with Chocolatero and river fords, Everett had decided temporarily to leave behind or even to abandon his burros in Davis Gulch, cross the river with his camping gear and personal equipment, make contact with Indians on the east side, and buy or trade for new pack animals so that he could explore farther to the east. In previous years he had sometimes bargained with Navajos for burros. And as he had left Escalante, he wrote his parents, he had "more money than I need."

With Denny's discovery of the burial on Comb Ridge, the NEMO carved on the granary in Grand Gulch and the Music Note panel inked on the sandstone wall upstream took on a heightened significance. Grand Gulch lies almost exactly halfway between Davis Gulch and Chinle Wash, smack on the most logical trail between those two canyons. Since Everett had started signing himself NEMO only in late 1934, did the Grand Gulch inscriptions mark his midway passage from one place to the other?

To solidify the authenticity of the NEMO in Grand Gulch, Vaughn and I took Fred Blackburn in to see it in April 2009. Despite having served for several years in the 1970s as a ranger in Grand Gulch, Fred had never found the inscription. But if Vaughn was an expert at deciphering historic signatures scrawled on rock walls and ruins, Fred was a genius of the craft. Sometime schoolteacher, rancher, writer, and historian living in Cortez, Colorado, Fred had received numerous government grants to record the Kilroy-was-here's of early Anglo and Hispanic visitors to such places as Cliff Palace on Mesa Verde and Inscription House in Navajo National Monument. There, using one trick of vision after another, he had teased out scores of badly faded signatures that no one had ever been able to read before.

We reached the granary just before noon. During the eleven years since Vaughn's and my 1998 visit, the NEMO inscription had faded even more, or perhaps been further obliterated by some do-gooder who disapproved of graffiti, no matter how old. Fred couldn't find it until Vaughn pointed out where the four letters made a downward tilt in the mud on the left side of the granary. I doubted that Vaughn himself could have seen it had this been his first attempt.

Suddenly Fred grew animated, narrating his excitement out loud. "N, E, M, O—that's what it says!" he blurted. "And I really doubt it's a copycat. It's a weird place to put it on a wall. If you'd put up a copycat, you'd pick a sucker like Bannister, right on the trail." Bannister Ruin, one of the most prominent in the Gulch, lies several miles upstream from the obscure granary on the ledge where we peered at the fugitive characters.

Photography is useless for such faint inscriptions. For the next hour, using a physician's magnifying glass to amplify his vision, Fred laboriously sketched the signature in pencil in a large notebook he carries with him wherever he documents historic writing in the wilderness.

"Somebody's obviously tried to rub it out," Vaughn said.

"It just takes one more asshole," Fred added, "and it's gone."

As Fred sketched the faint letters, I stared over the winding canyon to the south. A cottonwood downstream blazed with young green leaves, and the opposite wall rose in a smooth, ruddy parabola. For all its defensiveness, the granary site had a lordly command of its surroundings. "It's a real Everett kind of place," I murmured.

"Yeah," said both Vaughn and Fred simultaneously.

It had been years since Fred had looked at Rusho's *Vagabond for Beauty*. Back at the trailhead late that afternoon, I got out a copy and opened it to the photo of the charcoal inscription in Davis Gulch.

Fred's voice rose to a gloating screech. "Damn right!" he declared. "That's it! It's the same! The 'O' is more oval, the 'M' is short-cropped at the top, the 'E' is slanted."

"It sure does look similar," said Vaughn.

"The same damn guy wrote it, that's why!" Fred crowed.

*   *   *

After I telephoned Brian Ruess, he consulted his three siblings. They agreed to request the DNA sample. On the advice of Bennett Greenspan of Family Tree DNA, I helped Brian and his sister Michèle determine which family specimen the Texas lab might test. Greenspan was bent on looking for mitochondrial DNA, which is carried only in the maternal line, so samples from Waldo's four children could not be used as a match for the bones in the crevice. But there was no living person related to Everett by a strictly maternal connection. Waldo would have been the ideal source for mitochondrial DNA, but he had died the previous year.

Michèle Ruess came up with a clever possible solution. After Waldo's death, his wife, Conchita, had kept her husband's favorite hairbrush, which still had fragments of his hair tangled in the bristles. Hair itself contains no DNA, except in the follicles attached to the roots. Here was the long shot—but Greenspan was willing to give it a try. Michèle carefully wrapped the hairbrush and sent it to the lab in Texas.

On July 22, Ron Maldonado went back out to the site with Denny and Greg Child. I would have given much to be along on this outing, but by then I had left Utah and gone home. Greenspan had briefed Maldonado on how to recover human remains without contaminating them with one's own DNA. A molar tooth, he counseled, would be the very best thing to find.

At the site, Maldonado started excavating in as gingerly a fashion as he could. Lying loose in a cranny in front of the crevice was a

1912 Liberty dime that had been converted into a button. Maldonado retrieved it so that Greg could photograph it. The thing struck all three men as a very Navajo kind of relic (antique Navajo belts made of silver dollars fetch high prices in today's Southwestern gift shops). But we also knew that Everett loved to wear Indian jewelry. In any event, the button gave us a *terminus ad quem:* the burial could not have taken place before 1912.

Almost at once, to his relief, just inches below the surface Maldonado came across two loose molar teeth. With great care, he removed and packaged them. There would be no more digging that day.

As soon as he got back to Window Rock, Maldonado e-mailed me about a bizarre event that had occurred as the men returned to their truck:

> A dust devil (whirlwind) started at or near me violently sending dust into the area. It seemed that it visited each of us individually and slowly meandered down the road, lingering, appearing to die out, then starting again. It is all very strange and definitely associated with the burial. Denny stated that it was Mister Ruess. Such things are associated with the dead and should be avoided at all costs. It has been a strange day.

We all hoped for a quick answer from Family Tree, but in the end, the testing would take many weeks and involve stranger twists and turns than any of us, including Greenspan, could have anticipated. When the verdict came down, it left all of us baffled, confused, and in a sense, back at square one.

*   *   *

Family Tree eventually admitted that somehow one of their own lab technicians had accidentally contaminated the sample. After sorting out the consequences of this glitch, on September 30, Greenspan finally sent me an official report. Most of it was couched in technical jargon, but the conclusion was unmistakable. Greenspan wrote: "It is clear that the mtDNA from the root of the tooth and the DNA from the hair brush do not contain the same signature, and that both are European in origin and not Native American."

Later, over the telephone, Greenspan admitted to me that he was not at all happy with the hairbrush. The DNA from Waldo's hair was "degenerated," and it might have been contaminated by being handled by others. On the other hand, he was one hundred percent certain that the molar DNA was Caucasian. It was not only not Navajo—it belonged to no Native American.

So the body in the crevice on Comb Ridge was most likely not that of Everett Ruess. It was instead that of some other young white man.

But who the hell was he?

Between 1912 and, say, 1940, there were very few white men of any kind wandering about the Navajo reservation. And in southeastern Utah during that era, if an Anglo vanished in the wilderness, pretty much everybody knew about it. For weeks after getting Greenspan's DNA report, I sought out regional historians and old-timers to ask them if they knew of any tales of Anglos disappearing on the rez in the 1920s or 1930s. The best informed scholars told me that nothing in Aneth Nez's story rang even the faintest bell.

Despite the lingering reservations we all harbored about the soundness of Family Tree's findings, Ron Maldonado decided to complete the excavation, in hopes of coming up with further clues to the young man's identity. A few days before our return to the Comb, I was in Boulder, Colorado, having dinner with my friend Steve Lekson. Of all the Southwestern archaeologists I had met, I considered Lekson the most brilliant.

Now I told Steve about our Comb Ridge quest. He didn't know much about Everett Ruess, but his eyes lit up. "You can do a lot more than just DNA," he said, when I had finished my recital. "A physical anthropogist can tell all kinds of things from bones. What kind of bones have you got?" At the end of the evening, Steve gave me the e-mail address of his colleague at the University of Colorado, Dennis Van Gerven.

On November 23, I was back on the rim of the Comb with Maldonado, Denny, Greg, and Vaughn. The blazing heat of July had given way to a late autumnal glory: soft, low-angled light, cool in the shade, balmy in the sun. Maldonado unpacked his tool bag, then lay in an awkward position on his side, as he reached into the crevice and excavated with trowel and brush. He kept up a running commentary. "Water's been comin' through here," he said. "There's a lot of disturbance, but I think it's natural. . . . Seems like a jumble of bones. Not like a crevice burial—just stuff the body in any way you can. . . .

"Holy smokes, what's going on in here? That looks like a tooth way over here, by the lower leg. . . . He's definitely been crunched in here tight."

Maldonado's labor confirmed our initial suspicion that the crevice was almost too shallow to hold a human body. Everything about the confused muddle of the bones bespoke haste, concealment, and a desperate forcing of the body into a rock coffin into which it did not really fit. After two hours of steady work, Maldonado completed his excavation.

I was disappointed that we had found not a single scrap of apparel, but Vaughn said, "I'm not surprised. Leather and cloth just rot away, or the varmints get it. It's prime stuff for pack rats to build their nests with."

The only "artifacts" Ron's troweling had revealed were a couple of old metal buttons and about twenty-five beads—yellow, orange, red, and green, made apparently of glass and turquoise. Some were so tiny that I could not imagine how an artisan had drilled holes through them. "Probably a necklace," Maldonado ventured, "that he had

hanging around his neck. The cord they were strung on is long gone."
To all of us, it was disconcerting to find an ornament that seemed so
Native American in style. But I remembered Everett's pride in the Navajo bracelet he had bought—"whose three turquoises gleam in the
firelight," he wrote in his last letter to Waldo.

At the end of the excavation, Maldonado had said, "I think we've
found his lower jaw." Now the mandible rested on the surface of a
nearby boulder as we studied it. Most of the teeth were still in their
sockets. Two of the left front incisors overlapped, indicating a severe
overbite. Maldonado soliloquized: "No fillings. But the teeth aren't
ground down, either. He had a crooked smile, that's for sure. Definitely an adult, not a child. He had a kind of pointy chin."

"What do you want to do with it?" I asked.

"Give me a minute. I've got to think." As he had in July, Maldonado seemed to retreat into a trance. I realized that he was weighing
all kinds of moral considerations on his mental scales, including, as he
had said the previous summer, the desire to give "solace and closure"
not only to the Ruess family, but to Daisey Johnson. Perhaps fifteen
minutes passed before he spoke again, and when he did, it was as if
he had prepared a speech.

"On the rez," he said, "when you come across a Navajo burial,
you can almost always find somebody who knows who it was. In
this case, there's nothing of that sort around. I've never had anybody
claim affiliation to a burial when there wasn't someone really there in
the ground. Especially the older people—they don't make up stories.
They don't have any reason to make up a story.

"But on the other hand, I've never before found an Anglo buried
in a crevice." Maldonado paused as he looked around at each of us.
"It's okay with me to recover this mandible and get it to the guy at
CU. As long as we all pledge to return it to the grave after he's finished
analyzing it. Everybody on board with this?" We all murmured our
assent.

Maldonado wrapped the mandible in tissue, then inserted it in a plastic bag. I put it in my day pack and carried it out to the car, where I returned it to the archaeologist. "I'll get in touch with Van Gerven, and have him talk to you."

Maldonado held the package in his hands. "I have no idea what we'll learn from this," he said. "Maybe nothing."

*   *   *

Dennis Van Gerven ignored my first two e-mails. Later he admitted he was doing his best to stiff-arm my inquiries, since he tended to get bombarded with pleas from nut cases who had watched too many episodes of *CSI*. His first communiqué had annoyance written all over it, as he signed off, "In short a study of the mandible from my point of view would be quite pointless."

I persisted. "Would there not be some chance you might see something the DNA test couldn't tell us?" He e-mailed back, still annoyed, "I seriously doubt it but Paul and I would be willing to look at it." Around New Year's Day, Maldonado shipped the mandible to Paul Sandberg, Van Gerven's grad-student assistant.

Meanwhile on the Internet I had found the report of one of Van Gerven's cardinal triumphs. In the "Hillmon case," Van Gerven had solved a riddle of faked identity that had vexed experts since 1879, and that had been important enough twice to reach the Supreme Court. The man's modus operandi had been to superimpose photos of an excavated skull onto historic photographs of living men, to ascertain the best match. Reading the report, I realized that Van Gerven knew his way around a skeleton.

I hammered away, e-mailing a detailed account of Everett Ruess, Aneth Nez, Daisey Johnson, Denny Bellson, and our efforts so far on Comb Ridge. And I promised to scour the Internet for all the photos of Everett I could find and forward them. Slowly, Van Gerven warmed to the challenge. On January 6 he e-mailed me, "Dig up everything that you can. We may be able to do something interesting." By "dig up" I assumed he meant "find photos," not return to the grave with shovel in hand.

The case had caught Van Gerven's fancy. "The money shot is the profile," he e-mailed on January 10, referring to a side photo of Everett taken by Dorothea Lange in 1933. Already, Van Gerven had noticed a striking similarity between the mandible and the deep jaw in the Lange photo. But the anthropologist was frustrated. "Is the portion of the mandible," he queried me on January 12, "the entirety of the material recovered?"

"Forgot to mention," I wrote the next day, "the upper part of the skull was intact when we first saw the site, but the FBI team managed to destroy it when they tried to yank it out of the ground! Would a picture of it pre-FBI help?"

Within an hour, Van Gerven e-mailed back, "Yes yes yes. Do you have the pieces??? God, get them and send them. . . . Get us the photos and try for each and every piece of skeleton. Man, let me know." A full-blown fever had evidently seized the former skeptic.

Greg Child's photos from before the FBI outing and mine from after pushed Van Gerven over the edge. I thought my snapshots of the saddle crammed on top of the smashed cranium would dismay anyone who saw them, but Van Gerven was jazzed. "God there is a skull!" he e-mailed back. "If it is still just that complete or even if not we will take the ID to a whole new level. The best stuff is still there!!!!" If someone could retrieve—or even simply measure in situ—other parts of the skull, Van Gerven told me over the phone, he might be able to reconstruct the whole head and compare it to the photos of Everett Ruess.

The upshot was that Van Gerven and Sandberg decided to drop everything at the beginning of a hectic spring term at CU and head down to southeast Utah. I got in touch with Maldonado, Denny, and Vaughn to arrange yet another rendezvous. On January 23 the two scholars drove all the way from Boulder to Bluff, an eleven-hour journey, their four-by-four packed with tools. And the next day the five men headed out to the grave site. For Denny, it would be the eighth visit since he had first stumbled upon the lonely grave the previous May.

On January 24, Van Gerven, Sandberg, Denny, Vaughn, and Ron Maldonado went out to the site. As I sat stewing in Cambridge, wondering what magic this team might pull off, they went to work in the rock crevice. It had rained for several days in southeast Utah, and the dirt roads were slick as they drove the plateau toward the crest of the Comb, but as soon as the men reached the hidden cranny, the sky cleared and a benevolent sun shone down upon them.

Maldonado turned the excavating over to Van Gerven and his doctoral student. In the first few minutes they made a startling deduction from the bones: these were unmistakably the remains of a male between the ages of late teens and early twenties. Piece by piece, the physical anthropologists retrieved one rib and vertebra and toe bone and tooth after another; they also salvaged many scraps of the young man's skull. Digging deeper than even Maldonado had in November into the farthest recesses of the crevice, they found many more glass and turquoise beads, as well as a turquoise pendant. Each bone and artifact was gently handled and wrapped for removal to a CU lab. From new molar teeth, Van Gerven thought a colleague of his might retrieve another DNA signature.

There were some surprises. "I think whoever killed him stole his shoes," Van Gerven told me two days later.

"Why do you think that?"

"The guy wasn't out there walking barefoot. And Denny agreed, if a Navajo buries somebody, he leaves his shoes on him."

"Vaughn thought a varmint might have taken the shoes."

"Nope," Van Gerven responded. "If a predator gets his teeth into the shoe, he pulls the foot loose with it. We've got a heel bone. We've got big toes, for Christ's sake!

"The wonderful thing," Van Gerven went on, "is that we have diagnostic bones from the lower face. The nasal region is pivotal—where the bridge of your glasses sits. If we can put all the pieces of skull together, and if the contours fit the photographs of Everett, then we've got a hell of a case."

At the very end of the day, wedging himself as deep inside the crevice as he could, Vaughn found the most provocative artifact yet. It was a metal button, embossed with the logo MOUNTAINEER curving around the rim above an X, in the vertices of which the numerals 0–1–2–3 were tucked. At once Vaughn thought of Everett's rambles in the Sierra Nevada in 1933. There the vagabond had befriended Park Service rangers and Sierra Club hikers. Was the button a vestige of some such association?

A friend of Vaughn's who was an expert in buttons (yes, archaeology has become that specialized!) eventually e-mailed him an analysis:

> [The button] probably came from a pair of Mountaineer overalls made by ZCMI in Salt Lake City. They began manufacturing Mountaineer overalls in 1872 and they were still available in the 1930s and for who knows how much later. ZCMI is the Mormon Church's Zions Cooperative Mercantile Institution. It started to manufacture all sorts of goods by Mormons for Mormons so that the Utah economy was stimulated and insulated from leakage to the outside world. We have found work clothes buttons marked ZCMI, so the Mountaineer button may be a later version.

This information, however, did not prove that the overalls in question had belonged to an Anglo, for in the early decades of the twentieth century, Indians in Utah regularly bought and traded for Mormon-made clothing.

Back in Boulder, Van Gerven and Sandberg's first task was to stabilize the very fragile pieces of bone—especially skull fragments—they had retrieved from the crevice. Many of the bones were sun-bleached and eroded after decades of exposure to the elements. But the anthropologists were heartened to find, as Sandberg wrote me in late February, that "three fragments of the face, two of them with teeth still in place, were tightly embedded and protected in the dirt, and we had a nearly complete mandible. It seems as though a previous attempt to force the skull out of the dirt [i.e., by the FBI] had left much of the face intact under the surface."

From the very start, Van Gerven and Sandberg were able to make what they called a "biological profile" of the victim. "The shape of the pelvis told us that the individual was male," Sandberg explained. "The degree of developmental maturity of the bones told us that he was between the ages of nineteen and twenty-two, and measurement of the femur gave us a stature estimate of five feet eight, give or take a couple of inches."

The facial fragments were critical to reconstructing the dead man's physiognomy. Molding the stabilized bones in place with clay representing the missing parts, the scientists painstakingly rebuilt a partial model of the head. For comparison, they had two of the splendid portraits of Ruess that Dorothea Lange had shot in 1933, one face-on, one in profile. As Sandberg explained,

> Using Adobe Photoshop CS, we blended images of Ruess and the bones together. This technique is good at excluding people, almost too good because it can easily exclude the right person due to distortions that arise in photography. You've got to take the photo of the bones in the same manner as the portrait. Once we got the two photos superimposed, we aligned two anatomical points that were the easiest to establish on the bones and the portrait. In the profile portrait, they were the top of the nose and the bottom of the mandible. In the front view portrait, they were the edges

of the teeth. Now the question becomes, do the other anatomical landmarks line up? They do. Everything matches.

"I'd be just as happy to disprove the match as I would to prove it," Van Gerven had warned me as the two men had started their work. But day by day he grew more animated. "I have a really good feeling about this," he told me in early February. A few days later: "So far, there's nothing exclusionary."

Finally, at the end of February, Van Gerven phoned me with his verdict. "All the lines of evidence converge," he said. "This guy was male. Everett was male. This guy was about twenty years old. Everett was twenty years old. This guy was about five foot eight. Everett was about five eight.

"Everett had unique facial features, including a really large, deep chin. This guy had the same features. And the bones match the photos in every last detail, even down to the spacing between the teeth. The odds are astronomically small that this could be a coincidence."

Van Gerven paused. "If I had to take it to court, I'd say that it matches Everett Ruess with reasonable professional certainty."

*   *   *

Van Gerven and Sandberg wanted further corroboration of their find, however, so they enlisted Kenneth Krauter, a colleague at the University of Colorado, who is a professor of molecular, cellular, and developmental biology and a leading expert on DNA. Krauter and his assistant, Helen Marshall, agreed to perform a new DNA test on the bones. From one of the femurs Marshall cut a cross-section disk, used an ultrasonic method to clean it of all possible contaminants, then pulverized and dissolved it to extract the DNA at the core.

Meanwhile, the four Ruess nieces and nephews all sent saliva samples to Krauter's lab. The aim was to compare the DNA in those samples with the DNA extracted from the femur. A nephew or niece would be expected to share about 25 percent of the DNA of his or her uncle.

Using state-of-the-art hardware and software from Affymetrix, an industry leader in gene technology, Krauter and Marshall compared no fewer than 600,000 DNA markers. (CODIS, the protocol used in most criminal forensic cases, is capable of comparing only from fifteen to eighteen markers.)

To Krauter and Marshall's surprise and delight, the comparison with the saliva samples yielded an overlap very close to 25 percent of the markers for all four nieces and nephews. To double-check their results, the scientists compared the femur DNA to a database of fifty random strangers. The overlap with all fifty was infinitesimal—only tiny fractions of one percent at most. Further checking their results against possible errors, Krauter forwarded his analysis to colleagues at Harvard, who vouched for its integrity.

In April 2009, Krauter announced, "The combination of forensic analysis and genetic analysis makes it an open-and-shut case. I believe it would hold up in any court in the country."

On April 30, 2009, with my article in *Adventure* just out, the National Geographic Society held a nationwide teleconference to announce our discovery. In a motel room in Farmington, New Mexico, Denny, Daisey, and I shared a telephone, as did Ken Krauter and Dennis Van Gerven from an office at the University of Colorado in Boulder; also on the line were Ron Maldonado in Window Rock, Brian Ruess in Portland, and Michèle Ruess in Seattle. Asking us questions from their assorted venues were reporters ranging from the *New York Times* to the *Los Angeles Times* and the Associated Press, as well as regional correspondents in Denver, Boulder, Durango, Salt Lake City, Tucson, and other Western cities and towns.

The media response was electric. "A Mystery of the West Is Solved," read the *New York Times* headline. "Enigma Unraveled," announced the online InsideOutsideMag.com. "The Mystery of Everett Ruess' Disappearance Is Solved," declared the *Los Angeles Times*. Other publications hailed Everett more poetically, as "Kerouac of the Canyonlands" (*Tucson Weekly*) and "Man-Child in the Promised Land" (*American Spectator*). The furor reached an international audience, as publications in the United Kingdom, Germany, and even Russia picked up the story. The Russian clipping, titled "In the United States found the remains of the missing 75 years ago poet," contained some pithy poeticizing of its own, as rendered by Google's automated translation service:

> Discovers bone Denny Bellson, a resident at the Utah Navajo Indian reservations. According to Bellsona, his late grandfather in 1934 saw Ruessa beaten to death and robbed, and hid the body in the cleft of the coyote and the vultures.

The news brought the bloggers out of the woodwork. Many of the comments were simply appreciative: "Kind of sounds like a Tony Hillerman novel," wrote one commentator, and another, "Very fascinating story, it makes me want to go wander around the Chinle area too and see the same sites that Ruess did." Others were downright weird, like the post of a blogger calling himself "Toy": "I guess there's only one thing left to do . . . is have an uprising against the UTE. Its the only way we can remain safe in the West. . . . Take away their casinos!!!"

Around Escalante, the locals reaped a grim satisfaction from the discovery. A woman identifying herself as the daughter of Joe Pollock and niece of Keith Riddle e-mailed the Ogden *Standard-Examiner:* "TO THOSE PEOPLE WHO MADE A VIDEO [presumably Diane Orr's *Lost Forever*] AND WROTE THE STORY OF EVERTT [my 1999 article in *Adventure*], I THINK YOU DID A VERY BIASED

VERSION OF WHAT YOU HEARD FROM OTHERS. . . . WE AS
A FAMILY HAS BEEN HURT BY WHAT WAS WRITTEN ABOUT
JOE AND KEITH AND NO ONE WHO KNEW MY DAD AND
UNCLE BELIEVED ANY THING THAT WAS WRITTEN." An-
other relative gloated (also in capital letters), "UNCLE JOE AND
UNCLE KEITH ARE GRINNING AT THE FICTION WRITERS
AND STORY TELLERS ABOUT NOW."

A number of commentators wondered out loud whether Aneth
Nez himself had committed the murder, conveniently blaming it on
Utes. That thought had in fact occurred to Vaughn Hadenfeldt and
me early on, but it was not the sort of speculation we were eager to
share with Denny Bellson or Daisey Johnson.

On June 22, I moderated a panel discussion sponsored by the Glen
Canyon Institute in the packed Orson Spencer Hall auditorium at the
University of Utah in Salt Lake City. Brian and Michèle Ruess had
come from the West Coast to share their insights into the uncle they
revered but had never met. Others speaking from the lectern included
Denny, Vaughn, Greg Child, and Bud Rusho, who had reluctantly
been won over to the Comb Ridge discovery. The audience was fervent and enthusiastic, and hung on every word that Denny, Brian,
and Michèle spoke. The cult of Everett Ruess seemed to me to pulsate
through the auditorium. But in the Q&A period after the discussion,
two or three skeptics rose to voice their doubts about our solution to
the mystery. One of them was Kevin Jones, the Utah state archaeologist. It puzzled me that Jones seemed not only to resist our findings,
but to be angry that we had dared to announce them. In the coming
months he would play the critical role in a slowly rising tide of doubt
about the Comb Ridge find.

Although we had exchanged months' worth of e-mails, I had never
met Brian and Michèle before we came together in Salt Lake City. A
few days before the June 22 panel, Michèle, her husband, Mark Trav-

ers, and I drove from Salt Lake City three hundred miles south to Bluff. Michèle wanted to visit the grave.

For weeks, Michèle and Daisey Johnson had been e-mailing each other, and they had had a sympathetic telephone conversation. Now Daisey, who was visiting her sisters in White Rock Point, a small trailer park on the reservation south of Bluff, agreed to go out to the site with us, though she had decided not to come within three hundred yards of the grave itself. As soon as the two women met for the first time, they threw open their arms and hugged. Michèle murmured, "Daisey! Thank you for coming."

Daisey's cancer had gotten worse. It took a painful effort for her to make her way a hundred yards from our vehicles to a rock bench from which she had a commanding view of Chinle Wash meandering off to the north. She was content to sit there and wait while the rest of us—Vaughn, Ron Maldonado, his colleague John Stein, Denny, Michèle, Mark, and I—ambled down the now-familiar route through the ledges to the crevice from which the bones had been excavated.

A few weeks before, Maldonado and Van Gerven had shipped all the bones and "artifacts" (beads, buttons, buckled belt, and the like) to Christella Campbell, Michèle and Brian's sister, who lived in Santa Barbara, California. It was the plan of Waldo's four adult children to have the remains cremated, then scatter the ashes over the Pacific Ocean, in a family tradition more than a century old. (In 1909, Christopher and Stella had strewn the ashes of Christella, their firstborn, who had died of spina bifida at the age of six weeks, across the waters of San Francisco Bay near the Golden Gate.)

At the grave site, Michèle sat on a boulder, pulled out a piece of paper, and recited "My Soul Set Free," a poem Everett had written in 1930, at the age of sixteen, in which he imagines his soul floating over cliffs and forests and out to the Pacific. Its last stanza:

Where seagull shadows fall across the waves,
And high above, the sky is blue and wide,
Content, my soul drifts out alone to sea,
Upon the surging, restless, rhythmic tide.

When she was finished, Michèle addressed the rest of us with tears in her eyes: "That's where we're bringing him. That's where his parents, his brother, his sister, his uncle, and his maternal grandparents are—with the sea and the waves."

Back at the bench where Daisey waited, we took photos of each other in various groupings. The mood was almost that of a family reunion. Abruptly, Michèle unpinned a piece of antique jewelry from her blouse and gave it to Daisey. It was a tiny pin made of silver, with a small turquoise sphere in the center, shaped like a bird or perhaps an angel. It had belonged to Stella, Michèle's grandmother, Everett's mother. Deeply moved, Daisey attached it to her own blouse.

An hour later we assembled in the trailer home of one of Daisey's sisters in White Rock Point, as she and another sister fixed us all a lunch of Navajo tacos. Sitting at the kitchen table, I asked Daisey why she had been unwilling to approach the crevice grave.

"It was an enemy thing," she answered. "It's twice as dangerous."

Denny elaborated, "It's like a lightning strike."

"Grandpa should have buried him there, down in the canyon," Daisey added. "Not carried him up to the ridge."

A few minutes later, Daisey turned to her sisters, working over the stove only a few feet away. She was fingering the pin Michèle had given her. "I want this buried with me when I go," she said. "Not this." Her hand moved to the brooch with the ring of turquoise stones, the same ornament she had worn during our first meeting in Farmington eleven months earlier.

Shocked and upset, Daisey's sisters turned away, refusing to answer or even meet her gaze. "I know I don't got long," Daisey said to me, but loud enough so her sisters could hear. "I spent so much time on the other side, it's not so bad. I'm not afraid of it." She nodded her head toward her sisters, who had edged even farther toward the other end of the kitchen. "They don't want to hear me talk about it. They don't want to hear about death."

* * *

Through the summer of 2009, an undercurrent of backlash against our Comb Ridge discovery simmered across the Southwest. Some of it was merely romantic, the knee-jerk reaction of Ruess partisans who, after seventy-five years, simply didn't want the mystery to be solved. And some of it was downright nasty, attacking me and the National Geographic Society for making such a public splash of our find.

But some of it was thoughtful, and came from sources I respected, veteran explorers of the canyon country who had themselves pondered long and hard about Everett's fate. A fellow named Chuck LaRue, based in Flagstaff, Arizona, sent me a long e-mail laying out his arguments against what he was calling "Comb Ridge Man" being Everett, despite the apparently conclusive DNA result obtained by Ken Krauter and Helen Marshall. Among LaRue's arguments:

> ER would never in a million years [have] left his burros in Davis Gulch. These were his lifeline and he would have been very strongly bonded with them. He would not have abandoned them. . . .
>
> ER's pattern wherever he went was to go into towns and hang out awhile. For him to get to Chinle Wash/Comb Ridge he would have either gone through Kayenta or into Bluff where the people would have noted him and remembered him. To go straight to Chinle Wash would have been an aberration of his previous patterns.

Another Flagstaff native who was skeptical was the writer Scott Thybony. I had never met the man, but had read him for years, admiring such books as his *Burntwater,* a collection of sly, slender meditations on the Southwest. He was also far more of an expert on Navajo culture than I was. Vaughn knew Thybony well, and put him in touch with me. By e-mail, Thybony argued,

> Aneth's story doesn't fit the pattern of what I'd expect from a traditional Navajo in the 1930s. If he witnessed Utes killing a white man, I can't see any reason why he wouldn't report it to the trader or Indian agent and a number of reasons why he would. The tribal police and the feds were active on the rez and investigated other murders. And I've seen how Navajo react around a body. For him to mess with the remains of an outsider who died violently, a life cut short, is hard to imagine.

A few weeks later, Thybony added,

> The fact that no one reported seeing ER between Soda Gulch and Chinle Wash is a problem. That was big, remote country and essentially roadless with nobody permanently living there, but lots of people passed through—cowboys, trappers, outlaws, Indians, a few prospectors. The Ruess family did a good job of getting the word out to the traders, ranchers, rangers, and other government types. Nothing, no sightings.

The most strident objections focused, curiously enough, on a single digital photo I had taken of the mandible we had removed from the crevice in November 2008. *National Geographic Adventure* had put the photo online. It was clear that the teeth still fixed in the mandible showed no trace of dental fillings. Among the files archived at the University of Utah were two pages of Everett's dental records. These had been mailed to Stella on July 16, 1935, from the College of Dentistry at the University of Southern California. At the time, Stella and Christopher had been alerted to the discovery of the burned corpse near Gallup, New Mexico, and it was these records that had ruled out the possibility that the victim could have been Everett.

The records documented two inlays and one gold foil, work performed in December 1932 and January 1933, while Everett was home in Los Angeles between his second Southwest expedition and his upcoming jaunt into the high Sierras. The tooth chart, however, was at best ambiguous—the squiggles on certain molars might indicate where the fillings had been placed, or they might identify problem areas for future work. Further complicating the evidence was the fact that the records had been drawn up not at the time that Everett had visited the USC dentist(s), but only two and a half years later, in response to the parents' plea. Who knew how reliably the School of Dentistry had kept track of routine office visits that had occurred thirty months earlier?

Nonetheless, the more vehement of the naysayers seized upon these records to discredit our discovery. Dennis Van Gerven was inclined to dismiss such canards, for, as he pointed out, from the complete assemblage of bones he and Paul Sandberg had removed from the crevice, no fewer than thirteen teeth were missing.

My photo of the mandible created other problems, however. It was here that Kevin Jones, the Utah state archaeologist, entered the fray. At our Salt Lake City panel discussion, Jones had come up to Greg Child at the end of the evening, fixed him with a glare, and whispered, "It's not Everett."

In June, on the Utah State History website, Jones published an online paper titled "Everett Ruess—A Suggestion to Take Another Look." Although Jones had never examined the University of Colorado scientists' work firsthand, nor actually seen the mandible, his broadside poked holes from every direction in the chains of reasoning that had led first Van Gerven and then Krauter to declare that the Comb Ridge skeleton was Everett's.

Vexed by the fact that Jones had not sent his critical article to me, Ron Maldonado, or any of the CU scientists, I called him up when I was in Salt Lake City and asked if we could meet. Instead, he insisted on a phone call that lasted, as it turned out, more than an hour. The barely suppressed anger in his voice disconcerted me, as Jones derided the CU experts (none of whom he knew personally) for being completely out of their professional depth.

Why, I wondered, was Kevin Jones, whom I had liked when I'd interviewed him for other articles, so pissed off? I suspected that he was miffed that because the grave lay on the Navajo Reservation, it was entirely out of his own jurisdiction as state archaeologist. Yet Jones never called Maldonado to ask the Navajo Nation archaeologist about his decision to excavate.

In his paper, Jones laid out a dozen sources of doubt about the identification of the Comb Ridge skeleton. But over the phone, he focused on the mandible. "I know a Native American jaw when I see it," he told me. The incisors, he went on, were "shovel-shaped," possessing marginal ridges on the inner or tongue side that resulted in a scooped-out surface. The trait is very common in Asian and Native American populations, but rare in Caucasians. In addition, Jones went on, all the teeth in the mandible looked heavily worn, most likely as the result of decades of grinding by sand in the typical Native American diet.

Since Jones seemed reluctant to convey his doubts directly to the CU scientists, I passed on his criticisms to Van Gerven, who responded,

> A great fuss is made about the skeleton having shovel-shaped incisors. There was a time when anthropologists viewed such traits as proof of racial identity—racial typology.

Sadly, some still do. The fact is that no race possesses any
trait exclusive to itself. In the case of shovel-shaping some
8% of Euro-Americans and 12% of Afro-Americans pos-
sess the trait while 10% of Native Americans lack the trait
entirely.

Van Gerven and his assistant, Paul Sandberg, also pointed out
that shovel-shaped incisors are found almost exclusively on the max-
illary teeth—those of the upper jaw—not on those in the mandible.
As Sandberg later wrote me, "People don't talk about shoveled lower
incisors. It's not a trait that is typically scored and recorded. I don't
even think there are any data on the frequency of shoveling in lower
incisors in human populations."

About the grinding down of the teeth, Van Gerven stated,

> The wear is absolutely consistent with the kind of diet that
> Ruess is likely to have had out in that sandy environment
> as well as preparing and cooking food in an environment
> where sand and grit gets into everything. So nothing there
> is at all surprising. Indeed given Everett's many years in the
> deserts of Utah and Arizona, I would be puzzled if there
> was no wear! On a personal level, back in my 20's I spent 6
> months in the Sahara Desert [in the Sudan] and lost almost
> as much enamel as the Ruess skeleton! That didn't make me
> a Nubian and it didn't make me 70 years old.

Had the naysayers been confined to armchair second-guessers, Michèle and Brian and their two siblings might well have ignored them
and gone ahead to cremate the remains. All of us had been alarmed
by the looming possibility that the crevice on the Comb might become a pilgrimage site, like the bus on the Stampede Trail in Alaska
in which Chris McCandless had died. The last thing the Navajo Na-

tion needed was a stream of Ruess cultists illegally traipsing across
the rez to leave their mementos strewn about the grave site, like the
graffiti and kitschy treasures that litter Jim Morrison's grave in Père
Lachaise cemetery in Paris. Already, in fact, Denny Bellson had fielded
and turned down numerous requests from strangers who wanted to
be guided to the crevice. Not only in print but in conversation, Greg
Child and Vaughn Hadenfeldt and Ron Maldonado and I had been as
vague as possible about the precise location of the site.

And given the fanaticism of the more ardent fans of Everett Ruess,
it was even conceivable that someone might try to steal some of the
bones. During the week or two between our NGS teleconference
and Van Gerven's shipping the bones to Christella Campbell, he had
fended off several bizarre inquiries from total strangers demanding to
see, photograph, handle, and even X-ray the "evidence."

But criticisms from someone with Kevin Jones's undeniable credentials gave the Ruess family pause. Instead of cremating the remains,
they decided to heed Jones's request for another—a third—DNA test.
In Boulder, Ken Krauter welcomed the decision, so certain was he that
a third test would corroborate his findings.

And at this point the four siblings took charge of the business,
leaving Jones, Maldonado, Van Gerven, Krauter, Denny Bellson,
Daisey Johnson, and me out of the loop. Already the Ruesses had
been stung by accusations that the NGS, to score a publicity coup,
had orchestrated the whole shebang, putting pressure on the family to
go along with a sensational detective story that the *Adventure* writer
(me), perhaps in cahoots with Denny and even Daisey, had concocted
out of whole cloth.

At this point, Kevin Ruess, who lives in Virginia, and who so far
had been the sibling least caught up in the controversy, appealed to
his professional contacts to find the best possible DNA lab to undertake the third test. So as to fend off any hints of complicity, the family
did not even tell any of us which lab they had chosen.

*   *   *

More weeks passed, then months. On August 25, 2009, Daisey Johnson died, succumbing at last to the ovarian cancer she had first contracted in 2006. She had turned fifty-seven two weeks earlier. At a burial service on August 29, her relatives gathered at her mother's house to mourn and remember her. A memorial pamphlet the family printed up captured their grief: "When we think of your beautiful face it all seems so wrong. You had so much to look forward to and so much left to do." Yet her sisters had honored the wish she had expressed in June in the trailer at White Rock Point. The eulogy continued, "Jewelry you loved and now you have new accessories, a pair of Angel's wings. The world has lost a wonderful girl, a true and amazing individual."

The pamphlet also reproduced two pictures of Daisey with Michèle Ruess on Comb Ridge, a painting and a woodcut of Everett's, and the famous stanza from his "Wilderness Song": "Say that I starved; that I was lost and weary. . . ."

In September, Brian Ruess telephoned me. The news he blurted out shocked me. "It's not Everett," Brian said. "In fact, even worse, it's a Native American."

At first I refused to believe it. Of course, I did not *want* to believe it. How did we know this new lab hadn't made a mistake, like the one that Family Tree DNA had apparently stumbled over in 2008? But Brian revealed that the new test had been performed by the Armed Forces DNA Identification Laboratory (AFDIL), in Rockville, Maryland, a government-affiliated institution with vast experience in identifying victims such as soldiers on battlefields and a comparably vast DNA database, as well as the stored blood samples from thousands of veterans who have served in the armed forces.

AFDIL took an entirely different approach from Krauter and Marshall's. Instead of comparing DNA extracted from the skeleton's femur with that in the saliva samples from all four of Everett's nieces and nephews and using Affymetrix software to compare as many as 600,000 markers, the government lab did a Y-chromosomal test of DNA from two skeletal samples, a tooth and another piece of femur. Because the Y chromosome that is crucial to this test is passed down solely in the male line, AFDIL compared the skeletal DNA with a sample only from Kevin Ruess.

Had Everett's nephew been related to the person buried in the crevice grave, all seventeen key markers in the Y chromosome should have matched. Instead, AFDIL found only one matching marker. Scanning their database of Y-chromosomal types from all over the United States, the lab did not find any exact match. It did, however, find close matches with three individuals. All three were Native Americans.

The brief summary an AFDIL scientist finally e-mailed me was full of technical terms such as "Y-STR profile" and "mtDNA sequence" and "Y-haplogroup," and was thus beyond my comprehension. But the work seemed sound enough to convince the family. Brian had prepared a press release announcing our collective mistake to the world, as well as the family's intention to return the bones to Ron Maldonado for reburial on the Navajo reservation. But several of us persuaded Brian and his siblings to hold off long enough for Ken Krauter and the AFDIL technicians to make a thorough comparison of notes.

Months later, Krauter told me his initial reaction to the AFDIL finding. "I was in a state of total disbelief. At first I wanted to deny it."

More weeks passed. Mike Coble, the AFDIL scientist in charge of the analysis, generously rolled up his sleeves to go over Krauter's test data, as well as AFDIL's, with a fine-toothed comb. Despite the potential for animosity between the experts, Coble and Krauter collaborated in a truly disinterested and collegial reexamination of the two tests. As Krauter later said, "This is how science is done."

And at last Krauter found the fly in the ointment. It was not, as some had speculated, a problem of contamination of the DNA samples in the CU lab. Nor could it be chalked up to sloppy work on his and Marshall's part. The glitch came as a result of Krauter's application of Affymetrix GeneChip technology. Though widely considered the industry's gold standard for DNA research analysis, Affymetrix remains unproven for this type of forensic work. Krauter saw the Ruess case as an opportunity to break new ground, and he was encouraged to do so by Affymetrix. Unbeknownst to anyone, however—including Affymetrix itself—the firm's software can produce a false reading (what Krauter calls "noise") when amounts of DNA that are too small are used in tests.

When my editors at *Adventure* tried to get the Affymetrix company, which is based in Santa Clara, California, to comment on this apparent problem, which promised to have huge repercussions for hundreds or even thousands of other DNA analyses being conducted around the world, the firm retreated like a turtle into its shell. A company spokesman maintained that its software was never intended for forensic use. But at the time the Affymetrix website contained the following claim: "Analysis of mitochondrial mutations [with GeneChip technology] is informative for a variety of applications from disease genetics to forensic identification." The firm's public-relations spokesman authorized only a single bland boilerplate statement for publication: "Professor Krauter is a valued customer of Affymetrix. We are happy to assist him with the review of his study, as and when he needs our help."

What the "noise" in the software meant was that it produced a gene identification that appeared to be legitimate when it was really highly suspect. Even worse, when Krauter's computer analyzed the bone samples alongside the data from the Ruess nieces and nephews, it biased the results in favor of the Ruess family members, yielding a partial similarity between the "noise" and the family's DNA at a frequency of 25 percent—exactly the expected value if the skeleton were Everett's.

Krauter refused to blame Affymetrix. For our follow-up *nostra culpa* in *Adventure,* he insisted, "We screwed up by relying on the technology too much. Fortunately, the error uncovered how the extreme sensitivity can be misleading if a researcher takes its output at face value. We will definitely reexamine how that software can be optimized, and when alternative methods should be used." Privately, he told me, "It was a real bummer. It made me fear that all our data from all our recent work was wrong." Also privately, Helen Marshall admitted that she was even more upset than her mentor. "It was an innocent mistake," she told me, "but it was devastating. It involved real people and real emotions. I'll never get over this."

For his part, Dennis Van Gerven was dumbfounded. If the AFDIL disproof was solid, it meant that a purely coincidental match between the face and teeth of the Comb Ridge skeleton and those of Everett had happened. The likelihood of such a match was infinitesimal. For *Adventure,* Van Gerven said, "I will go to my grave believing that we could not exclude [the match] based on the best anatomical evidence. A random skeleton was found that by chance alone matched sex, age, and stature. That in itself is remarkable." To Ron Maldonado in November, he e-mailed, "I still think it's Everett. But I don't know how."

*   *   *

On October 22, 2009, Brian Ruess issued the press release, titled "Ruess Family Accepts Comb Ridge Remains Are Not Those of Everett Ruess." The bones and "artifacts" were shipped back to Maldonado. Without telling anyone when or where he was going, Maldonado later went out alone with the remains and reburied them—not in the same crevice from which they had been extracted, but in a safe, obscure location that he felt would suit the dignity of an unidentified Native American.

The newspapers seized upon the collapse of our discovery. The Associated Press headline read, "Family: Remains Found in Utah Not Poet Ruess." National Public Radio chimed in: "Mystery Endures: Remains Found Not Those of Artist." Kevin Jones refrained from uttering I-told-you-so's, at least publicly. A single piece in *High Country News* stuck it to all of us who had collaborated in the apparent find on Comb Ridge. Titled "Skeletons in the Closet," it celebrated Jones's detective work by way of a profile of his varied career ("aspiring novelist," bluegrass mandolin player, dedicated pursuer of grave-robbing criminals around Blanding, Utah). The photo showed Jones squinting at an arrowhead as he held it up to the light. The subhead: "Utah State Archaeologist Kevin Jones Knows His Bones."

Back in May 2008, when Denny Bellson had first taken him out to the Comb Ridge site, Vaughn Hadenfeldt had knelt before the crevice, peered inside it, and gently touched the top of the protruding skull with his index finger. "Is that you, Everett?" Vaughn had whispered.

Now we knew the answer.

HAPPY JOURNEYS

GIBBS SMITH, THE PUBLISHER of so many books about Everett Ruess, may be right: it is not the mystery of Everett's disappearance and final fate that makes him so interesting, but his achievements by the age of twenty. As a precocious artist, a writer of promise, a romantic visionary verging on the mystical, a bold and resourceful solo explorer of the wilderness, and in some sense the first true celebrator of the beauty of the Southwest for its own sake, Everett traces a unique and meteoric path across the American landscape. The cult that has accreted around him since he headed into Davis Gulch serves as the ultimate proof of how Everett's wild quest captivates the minds and hearts of his legions of admirers.

Yet it is impossible to disentangle Everett's vanishing from the legend that clings to him. By latest count, at least eighteen books have been published that claim to solve the mystery of Amelia Earhart's disappearance in 1937 somewhere near Howland Island in the Pacific. None of the theories, however, has come close to winning the day. Had Earhart crash-landed on Howland, been rescued by Japanese or American sailors, returned home to write a book about her adventure, flown for another decade or two before giving up the cockpit, and died peacefully in her bed at a respectable age, she would still be acclaimed as one of America's pioneering aviators, but hardly as the mythic figure she has become. Earhart is fixed in the amber of time, forever androgynously beautiful as she looked at the age of thirty-nine, in fearless pursuit of her bravest challenge—to be the first woman to fly around the world. Everett, too, is fixed in that amber, as captured by Dorothea Lange's splendid portraits of him at age nineteen.

In the aftermath of the AFDIL DNA result that disproved our identification of the skeleton on Comb Ridge, all of us involved in the discovery suffered a crushing sense of letdown and disappointment. And we all wondered if our desire to solve a long-standing mystery had run away with our better judgment. During our several visits to the crevice, as we kept finding beads and pendants and Liberty dime buttons, but no patently Anglo belongings, Vaughn Hadenfeldt and I had shared recurring doubts. "It sure does look like a Navajo grave," Vaughn said more than once. Even after Van Gerven and Sandberg had so perfectly matched the facial features of the skull with the Lange photographs, I still expected Krauter and Marshall's DNA test to disprove the identification. When their result seemed to clinch the case, I was as stunned—and of course exhilarated—as anyone.

Now, beneath the disappointment, and far deeper, those of us involved in the Comb Ridge find shared a profound sense of shame. In our zeal to solve the mystery, we had dug up a Native American, probably a Navajo. Any way you looked at it, that was a terrible desecration. Maldonado's reburying the bones elsewhere on the reservation would never repair the harm we had done.

I felt bad, too, for Michèle and Brian Ruess and their siblings, Christella Campbell and Kevin Ruess. The roller-coaster of hope followed by disappointment on which I had bought them a year-and-a-half-long ride, in the process thrusting them into the public eye, now seemed a cruel tribulation, no matter how sincere my efforts may have been. And it meant that the eternal campaign to solve the mystery of Everett's disappearance and fate had once more taken its toll on the family. Christopher and Stella had spent the rest of their lives trying to find out what had happened to Everett, as had Waldo after his parents' deaths. Now the ordeal had revisited the third generation, Waldo's children, like some inexorable Aeschylean curse.

The grave site and the skeleton on Comb Ridge nonetheless raised other dark questions. No one but Kevin Jones had disputed Van Gerven and Sandberg's finding that the person interred in the crevice had been male, about twenty years old, and around five feet eight inches tall. And all of us who had seen the site, as well as Van Gerven and Sandberg when they examined the bones, agreed that the victim had suffered severe perimortem trauma. Whether or not he was a Navajo, the man may well have been murdered and buried in desperate haste. Here, perhaps, was evidence of a cold-case homicide every bit as vexing and intractable as the puzzle of Everett's fate.

With the collapse of our discovery, the possible explanations for Everett's demise reverted to something like the four hypotheses that had stayed current ever since 1935. These included the scenario that he was killed by rustlers who then dumped his body in the Colorado River. Despite the triumphant blog-posts of folks from Escalante, perhaps Keith Riddle and Joe Pollock were not off the hook after all.

In March 2010, a beguiling tribute to the power of Everett's legend emerged. Back in 2004, Vaughn Hadenfeldt's good friend Joe Pachak had been hiking in the narrow canyon beneath an Anasazi ruin called Eagle Nest. The site lies on Comb Ridge, less than a dozen miles north of the San Juan River. Vaughn, Greg Child, and I had been there a few years earlier, as we figured out a way to climb into the beautiful but vertiginous ruin, and mused over a rich petroglyph panel at the base of the cliff. But we missed what Pachak saw—dinosaur bones emerging from the Navajo sandstone of the cliff.

Keeping his find close to the vest, Pachak turned the work over to a team of paleontologists from the University of Utah. It took them five years to excavate, preserve, and analyze the bones, but when they were finished, they realized they had the nearly complete skeleton of a hitherto unknown species of dinosaur. The herbivorous sauropod had weighed some two hundred pounds, was between ten and fifteen feet long, and could walk on its hind legs. It had flourished about 185 million years ago. The scientists speculated that the creature had been trapped in the sudden collapse of a sand dune, which hardened into cliff over the eons thereafter. They also speculated that the Anasazi who had built and lived in Eagle Nest must have been well aware of the strange bones, which, seven hundred years before Pachak's discovery, had most likely been far more visible than they were in 2004. The fossilized animal may well have contributed to the spiritual numen of the eerie redoubt engineered in a natural cubbyhole 200 feet up the nearly vertical cliff.

With no pressure from Pachak, and certainly not from any of us involved with our own discovery on the Comb, the University of Utah team named the new species *Seitaad ruessi*. *Seit'aad* is the Diné name for a sand-desert monster in the creation myth that devoured its prey. *Ruessi,* obviously, was a tip of the paleontological cap to the lost vagabond. Whatever the truth of Everett's demise, he is now linked eternally by scientific nomenclature to Comb Ridge.

* * *

When he had called me in September 2009 to tell me about the AFDIL result, Brian Ruess had confided that he believed that Aneth Nez's strange tale about witnessing the murder of a young white man in Chinle Wash was in all likelihood a true story about Everett's death—it was just, Brian mused, that Denny Bellson had found the wrong body. Ron Maldonado agreed.

It was not, of course, Aneth Nez who had found the wrong body in 1971. With his precise memory of the burial he had carried out in the 1930s, Aneth would not have made the same mistake that Denny did. Thus it is almost certain that a grave of an Anglo victim lies on the crest of the Comb, still undiscovered, perhaps not far from the one Denny located in May 2008.

In any event, the scuttlebutt around Bluff by November 2009 was that Denny was already poking around on Comb Ridge as he looked for other graves.

Brian Ruess's hunch that Aneth's story was actually about Everett hinges on the following reasoning. The story Aneth told Daisey Johnson in 1971 was too specific in its details and too unusual for him to have made up. And since no one in Aneth's, Daisey's, and Denny's extended family had ever heard of Everett Ruess before 2008, there is no way any of them could have tailored a fabricated story to fit Everett's disappearance. Moreover, there would have been no reason for Aneth to have concocted the tale, and no reason, if he had, to keep it a secret for more than three decades. The five-day Enemy Way ceremony Aneth had had performed for him in 1971, in hopes of curing his cancer, was a deeply serious business. It required a lock of hair from the body Aneth said he had buried in the crevice on Comb Ridge in the 1930s. And to be efficacious, that lock of hair had to belong to a white man, or at least to a non-Navajo.

If Aneth did in fact see a young white man murdered in Chinle Wash, but it was someone other than Everett, it seems strange that months of inquiry on my part about other Anglos going missing on the reservation in the 1930s produced not a hint of a story that dovetailed with Aneth's account.

The NEMO inscription on the granary in Grand Gulch, discovered by Ken Sleight in the late 1960s and verified by Fred Blackburn in 2009, seems authentic, carved in the mud by Everett, not by some later copycat. And since that site lies midway between Davis Gulch and Chinle Wash, right on the most logical route between the two canyons, it remains a powerful argument for the scenario that sometime after November 1934, Everett made his way east from the Escalante toward Monument Valley or Canyon de Chelly—or Chinle Wash.

During the months I spent in 2008 and 2009 puzzling over Everett's fate, three new pieces of evidence fell into my lap. The first came indirectly, via Fred Blackburn, who in November 2009 had received a visit from Eric Atene, a Navajo working for the Bureau of Land Management out of Moab. Formerly a guide, Atene had horse-packed supplies into a remote "base camp" for Jon Krakauer and me in 1994, as we launched a probe of a slot canyon in the wilderness northwest of Navajo Mountain that we thought might be unexplored. Hiking in with Atene to the site of our gear depot, I realized that few natives knew this backcountry labyrinth better than he did.

Fifteen years later, visiting Fred, Eric brought up Everett Ruess. "You know," he said almost casually, "he had a name—Hosteen _____." Fred failed to catch the Diné pronunciation of the name, but Eric glossed it for him: "The man who walks with burros.

"He came through here," Eric added, indicating not Cortez, where he was visiting Fred, but the Navajo Mountain area. "Came across the [Colorado] river and down Navajo Canyon. He wouldn't stay with the Navajos, but he had a tree he'd camp under. They'd see his tracks and know he was back."

From the start of my inquiry, I had wondered what kinds of oral stories the Navajos might have preserved about Everett. But I also knew you didn't just drop by an old-timer's hogan and interview him. A well-guarded fragment of lore such as the one Eric was sharing with Fred had to be freely given, not asked for—and only after years of friendship and trust.

The second odd piece of evidence came shortly after my *Adventure* piece was published, when a stranger named Greg Funseth sent me a provocative e-mail. On my next visit to Salt Lake City, I had lunch with Funseth. A fifty-one-year-old computer software engineer, Greg was a rock climber, a desert hiker, and a passionate fan of Everett Ruess. Now he had a compelling story to tell me.

In 2001 he had made a solo backpacking trip into Davis Gulch, partly to commune with the spirit of Everett, but partly in hopes of discovering something new about the way the vagabond had met his end. For two days Greg explored every inch of the gulch, which he had to himself in early June. "I'm in one of the most inhospitable, remote places in the U.S.," he wrote in his diary. "I love this place!" At times he would stop and shout to the surrounding walls, "Are you here, Everett?"

On the third day, Greg found an obscure and difficult route out of the gulch on the opposite side from the old livestock trail by which he had entered. It was, apparently, an Anasazi hand-and-toe trail that I had missed in 1998. Then Greg wandered aimlessly across the slick-rock plateau that stretched beyond. Beneath a short sandstone cliff, he stopped for lunch. It was only after an hour at this site that he stood up, glanced at the cliff behind him—and froze in astonishment. There, neatly etched on the ruddy stone, he saw

NEMO
1934

For various reasons, Greg told no one except his wife about the discovery for the next eight years. Nor did he return to Davis Gulch. I felt extraordinarily privileged that he had chosen to share his find with me.

In October 2009, Greg met writer Scott Thybony and me on the Hole-in-the-Rock Road, near the head of Davis Gulch. It was a serene autumnal day as we set off across the billowing domes and sandy hollows of the mazelike plateau that stretched ahead of us. An easy place to get lost, if you didn't keep track of your bearings.

Greg led us unerringly to the wall with the inscription. As soon as I saw it, I knew that it was Everett who had carved it. The orthography—the down-slanting E, the short-cropped M, the oval O—exactly matched the Davis Gulch inscriptions that had been found by the searchers in 1935. And if I thought the Grand Gulch granary lay in an obscure place—well, this nondescript wall in the middle of nowhere was beyond obscure.

In all likelihood, Greg had been the first person ever to discover this NEMO. And Thybony and I were probably the second and third people to see it. A dazzling find in its own right, it also could be marshaled to support the idea that sometime in late 1934, Everett had left Davis Gulch to head east toward the Colorado River, perhaps crossing it at the Hole-in-the-Rock gash in the towering cliffs.

The third tantalizing clue came from Thybony, who was working on a book part of which told the story of another young desert explorer named Dan Thrapp. After working for a year at the American Museum of Natural History in New York City, Thrapp set off on a mission to explore the desert, even though it was his first trip ever to the Southwest. Setting off from Green River, Utah, in November 1934, he told friends he expected to be gone for three weeks. Instead, he was on his own for three months. A search was launched for Thrapp during the same months that the searches for Everett were under way; several newspapers ran stories about both lost wanderers in the same issue.

When Thrapp resurfaced in Bluff in the spring of 1935, he wondered crankily what all the fuss was about. He had gotten along fine by himself, pairing up with a series of strangers, some of them known outlaws. Thrapp would go on to craft a distinguished career as a Southwest historian, one of the leading experts on Apaches.

Now Thybony told me that on the Emigrant Trail (the continuation of the Hole-in-the-Rock Trail east of the Colorado River, the route by which the Mormon pioneers had reached the San Juan in

1880), somewhere just east of Grand Gulch, sometime in February 1935, Thrapp and his companions had lost the trail in a snowstorm. They had ridden in a circle to re-find the route, and as soon as they did, they discovered the fresh tracks of a man and two pack animals—tracks that had not been there an hour earlier. But Thrapp's party never made contact with this stranger.

Now Scott and I both wondered: Had Dan Thrapp come within minutes of running into Everett Ruess, as Ruess headed east beyond Grand Gulch? A few weeks after Scott first told me this haunting anecdote, I was prowling around the Clay Hills Divide, looking for anything that could be linked to Everett. That low pass on the Emigrant Trail is a half-day's journey on foot west of Grand Gulch. Instead of traces of Everett, however, I discovered a different inscription on the mud wall of an Anasazi structure inside a cozy alcove:

> DAN THRAPP
>   NYC
> Feb. 20th
>   1935

Scott had not found the inscription himself, nor was he aware of Thrapp ever having left his "Kilroy was here" anywhere else on his marathon journey. After making his own visit to the ruin, Scott wryly e-mailed me, "Thanks for passing on that find. I owe you a NEMO."

There is no proof, of course, that the fresh prints in the snowstorm on the Emigrant Trail had been left by Everett and his burros. But the possibility is tantalizing, and if it happens to be true, Thrapp's inscription on the wall of the Anasazi structure would give the last possible date for Ruess's wanderings in the winter of 1934–35.

All this, of course, may be mere wishful thinking. There is a chance that Aneth Nez saw Everett murdered, and that the poet-artist's body still lies out there somewhere, on Comb Ridge or in Chinle Wash. But there is an equal chance that Aneth's story was about someone else. The mystery of the vagabond who vanished near Davis Gulch in November 1934 endures.

As Brian Ruess told me, "Everett just doesn't want to be found."

ACKNOWLEDGMENTS

Everett Ruess first piqued my interest when I read Bud Rusho's *A Vagabond for Beauty* in the late 1980s. What put me on his trail in earnest, however, was a decision in 1998 by John Rasmus, who plucked a query about Everett from a small pile of story ideas I'd offered him for the start-up issue of *National Geographic Adventure*. Ten years later, Rasmus again turned me loose in the field, after I told him about Denny Bellson's startling discovery on Comb Ridge.

John has been my editor since 1979 at three different magazines. He remains the single editor for whom I have the most respect and admiration, among the scores for whom I have written articles during three decades of freelancing. Without his expression of interest in Everett Ruess, this book would not have happened.

At *Adventure* in 2009, features editor Mike Benoist plunged into the complex story that spiraled out of the Comb with a dedication and passion that impressed me, even while I'd come to expect it as Mike's default setting during the five years he'd served as my hands-on text editor. Equally committed to getting the best out of the story were photo editors Sabine Meyer and Caroline Hirsch, assistant editor Ryan Bradley, associate editor Mary Anne Potts, communications director Caryn Davidson, and photographer Dawn Kish.

Back in 1998, when I first researched the disappearance of Everett sixty-four years earlier, a number of old-timers in Escalante, Utah, shared with me their priceless memories of the twenty-year-old's brief visit in November 1934, as well as insider gossip from subsequent years about what might have happened to the wanderer. Not all of these men and women are still living, but I retain a lasting gratitude for the help given me by Melvin Alvey, Norm Christensen, Della Christianson, DeLane Griffin, McKay Bailey, Arnold Alvey, Jerry Roundy, Loy Riddle, Dan Pollock, and Doyle Cottam.

In Salt Lake City, Bud Rusho generously shared the research that had gone into his own book about Everett, which by 1998 had become a cult classic, even while he sensed that some of my conclusions were likely to contradict his. The staff at the Utah State Historical Society gave me full access to the important collection of papers by Harry Aleson, who more vigorously than anyone else from the late 1940s until his death in 1972 had tried to solve the riddle of Everett's fate. At his Pack Creek Ranch near Moab, Aleson's younger crony and fellow river guide Ken Sleight shared his own ruminations about the puzzle, and gave me directions to the NEMO inscription in Grand Gulch that he had found in the late 1960s. Historian Gary James Bergera outlined for me the careful reasoning that would go into his essay " 'The Murderous Pain of Living,' " arguing that Everett might have committed suicide.

Through much of my time in the field in 1998 and early 1999, I was accompanied by Vaughn Hadenfeldt, who runs his wilderness guide service Far Out Expeditions out of Bluff, Utah. Since I'd first hiked on Cedar Mesa with Vaughn in 1994, he'd become one of my favorite and most regular companions on strolls into the Southwest backcountry. Among all the friends I've ever hiked with, Vaughn has the best eye for the artifact in the dirt, the obscure petroglyph high on a sandstone wall. It was he who relocated the NEMO inscription on the Anasazi granary in Grand Gulch, far fainter by 1998 than when Ken Sleight had first found it. Vaughn shared my prowlings into Davis Gulch and out toward the Hole-in-the-Rock cleft above the Colorado River, when I thought I might be on the trail of the men who could have murdered Everett. Vaughn's congenital skepticism served as a much-needed check to my runaway enthusiasm.

In 2008, it was Vaughn who alerted me to Denny Bellson's discovery of the grave site on Comb Ridge that might dovetail with the strange story told by Denny's grandfather, Aneth Nez, about watching a young Anglo wander alone with two pack animals up and down Chinle Wash sometime in the 1930s, until one day he was chased down and killed by Utes. And Vaughn overcame my own skepticism, persuading me to look into the Comb Ridge enigma further.

Joining Denny Bellson on the Comb, and listening to his stories, were critical to opening the apparently new chapter in the mystery of Everett Ruess. Through Denny, I met and befriended his sister, Daisey Johnson, who was the sole primary source for Aneth Nez's story. Daisey's courage in trying to plumb the depths of the mystery, even as she was suffering from terminal cancer, and her heartfelt compassion for the Ruess family, moved me deeply.

Once I was fully "on board" with what seemed to be a possible new resolution of the mystery of Everett's fate, I enlisted a host of friends and strangers over the course of a year and a half, in an effort to settle beyond a reasonable doubt the identity of the person interred in the Comb Ridge grave. Greg Child, a frequent companion of Vaughn and me on excursions in search of Anasazi ruins and rock art, got involved early, taking the only good photos of the grave site before it was irrevocably disturbed by the FBI team. Ron Maldonado, the only official who could authorize excavation of the site, took a keen interest in the Comb discovery, counterbalanced by a profoundly thoughtful weighing of the pros and cons of proceeding further.

I got in touch with Brian Ruess, Everett's nephew, one of his four closest living relatives. Brian and his sister, Michèle Ruess, threw themselves into the investigation, supplying me time and again with information and insights only the Ruess family were privy to. Michèle, in particular, got caught up in the search, and I cannot thank her enough for the scores of kindnesses she showered on the rest of us, as well as for her seemingly limitless fund of knowledge about everything having to do with the uncle she had never met. Although less passionately invested in our quest, Brian and Michèle's siblings,

Christella Campbell and Kevin Ruess, played vital roles in the unfolding drama. The help of the whole family was something I could hardly have taken for granted, for Everett's nieces and nephews, like their father and their grandparents, had tracked down one false lead and imaginary sighting after another over the decades. They could well have spurned me from the start as another mad inventor of a solution to Everett's fate.

Once we realized we needed DNA tests to clinch an identification, Bennett Greenspan of Family Tree DNA agreed to take on the project. His generosity in trying to help us solve the case is not vitiated by the ambiguity of Family Tree's results. Through my friend Steve Lekson, a brilliant Southwestern archaeologist at the University of Colorado, I made contact with five fine CU researchers who, without receiving a single dime in compensation, took the mystery on as their own project, spending countless hours rigorously trying to determine the truth of the case. Those five are physical anthropologists Dennis Van Gerven and Paul Sandberg, molecular biologists and DNA experts Kenneth Krauter and Helen Marshall, and statistician Matt McQueen. On several visits to Boulder, I got to like all five of these scholars, and to understand the complexity of their scientific art. When the results they were initially confident of proved erroneous, all five were devastated. In the public press, they were sometimes accused of shoddy and even corrupt work by critics who knew absolutely nothing about their science. The false result had come about not because of any pivotal errors on their part, but thanks to a glitch in a software program the company that had produced it was unaware of, and thanks to an almost infinitely unlikely match in the cranial structure of two different individuals. I am grateful to all five for their magnanimity in never blaming me for dragging them into a morass they could not have foreseen, and for staying in cordial contact long after the last thuds had been registered in the Everett Ruess blogosphere.

Mike Coble, of the Armed Forces DNA Identification Laboratory, which finally proved that the body in the crevice on the Comb was not Everett's, exhibited the spirit of disinterested science at its finest, as he helped Krauter reexamine every step of his research on the case. Coble later went out of his way to explain to me the intricacies of his own DNA protocol.

As the buzz mounted over our apparent solving of the Ruess mystery, all kinds of interested observers added their momentum to our push toward clarity. I am lastingly grateful to old friend Fred Blackburn, the best decipherer of historic inscriptions I have ever met, who also got emotionally involved in the search; to Richard Ingebretsen, who organized a well-attended Salt Lake City symposium about our find; to his tech assistant Justin Coles, who put together a stunning PowerPoint show; to Steve Roberts, who implanted a Ruess conference in the annual Escalante Days festival; to publisher Gibbs Smith, who shared his long thoughts about Everett; to bookseller Ken Sanders, who did likewise; to AP writer Paul Foy, who sent a number of tips my way; to Nathan Thompson, whose master's thesis on Everett supplied valuable tidbits; to Maldonado's colleague in the field, John Stein, who pointed out a prehistoric road just below the grave on the Comb that Vaughn and I had stared at numerous times without seeing; and to Steve Jerman, licenser in charge of Everett's blockprints, who aided my grasp of the young man's artistic genius. Equally valuable were several skeptics who never believed that "Comb Ridge Man" (as one of them dubbed the skeleton Bellson had found) was Everett, but who so cogently shared the fruits of their years of wondering about what had happened to the lost wanderer after November 1934. The two most lucid were Chuck LaRue and Scott Thybony, both residents of Flagstaff, Arizona, desert rats with impeccable credentials, and deep probers of the Ruess mystery.

Out of the blue, Salt Lake City software engineer Greg Funseth contacted me and told me about an amazing find he had made eight years earlier—of a NEMO inscription perhaps no one else had ever seen since Everett had carved it in late 1934. A few months later, Funseth guided Thybony and me to the obscure site. It made for one of the most enthralling days I have ever spent in the Utah wilderness.

Once my quest to solve the riddle of Everett's disappearance had expanded into an effort to write a full-fledged biography of the young man, I spent many days in the J. Willard Marriott Library at the University of Utah, where the Ruess Family Papers collection is housed. Archivist Elizabeth Rogers was a shining model of helpfulness during the hours I spent sifting through reams of letters and old documents, and her own fascination with Everett and his family gave me insights I could never have come up with on my own. I have never had a smoother, more congenial, or more professionally scrupulous working relationship with an archivist or librarian in decades of carrying out comparable research. Among Elizabeth's colleagues, photo curator Lorraine Crouse and multimedia archivist Roy Webb were also friendly and helpful.

At Broadway Books, my editor, Charlie Conrad, "got it" from the start. His own involvement with the saga of Everett, his many novel and provocative suggestions, his superb job of editing on matters both large and small, and his championing of the work through the inevitable pitfalls of publishing in such perilous times, renewed my faith in the worth of trying to write a book that people might actually want to read. Jenna Ciongoli, Charlie's tireless assistant, promptly answered a hundred of my fussy little questions, and shot back at me another fifty I would have blithely overlooked had I been left to my own devices. Random House lawyer Matthew Martin sagely vetted the book, damping down some of my grumpier cheap shots but standing shoulder-to-shoulder with me when a fusillade was really needed.

This is my tenth book shepherded from proposal to hardback on the shelves by my diligent and clever agent, Stuart Krichevsky. By now I've come to count on Stuart's care and enthusiasm, and though he may not realize that I appreciate it, I also admire his integrity in bluntly telling me what won't work in print as well as his sharp eye at ferreting out what might. I don't think, however, that I had ever seen Stuart get so caught up in the day-by-day roller-coaster of my research. He even laid out a dragnet on the Web, and every few days he would forward me, under the electrifying heading "Google Alert—Everett Ruess," a choice morsel of congratulation or diatribe from the farthest precincts of the cult republic made up of Ruess devotees.

Stuart's colleague Shana Cohen was equally engaged, handling many of the logistical and legal tangles that flourish in the realm where mortal writers fear to tread. Although I've come to depend on her intelligence and her skill at cutting to the chase, I'm no less grateful to Shana for those talents this time around.

Finally, I owe a deep debt of thanks to my wife, Sharon Roberts, and to my longtime climbing buddy, Jon Krakauer, who kindly volunteered to write the foreword to this book. As they have been doing with my manuscripts for years now, both Jon and Sharon read *Finding Everett Ruess* in an early draft, and their critiques helped reshape the book for the better. For the *much* better, I believe. They remain not only my first but my shrewdest readers, and if either of them has gotten sick of my writing style, they've been gentle enough not to let me know it.

NOTE ON SOURCES

The vast bulk of the surviving manuscripts of original writings by Everett Ruess is archived in the Ruess Family Papers collection in the J. Willard Marriott Library at the University of Utah. That collection also contains many writings by and documents pertaining to other members of the Ruess family, especially Everett's brother, Waldo. And the collection holds the original copies of the richly detailed 1932 and 1933 diaries that Everett kept during his long journeys through the Southwest and California. However, the diaries from his 1930 and 1931 excursions have gone missing, perhaps forever. And the 1934 diary—which Waldo believed would contain the fullest and most mature of all his brother's musings on life—disappeared with the wanderer after November 1934.

On Desert Trails with Everett Ruess, first published in 1940 and still in print in a slightly different format, gathers together a miscellany of excerpts from Everett's essays, letters, and diaries, as well as reproductions of some of his best watercolor paintings and blockprints. The 2000 commemorative edition adds a thoughtful epilogue by W. L. (Bud) Rusho, titled "Everett Ruess and His Footprints," as well as a provocative essay by Gary James Bergera, titled " 'The Murderous Pain of Living': Thoughts on the Death of Everett Ruess."

Until now, the best source for Everett's writings, as well as the book that launched the Ruess cult, was Rusho's 1983 compendium, *Everett Ruess: A Vagabond for Beauty.* In 1998 Rusho published *Wilderness Journals of Everett Ruess,* which transcribes the 1932 and 1933 diaries. In 2002, Rusho brought out a combined edition of *Vagabond* and *Wilderness Journals* that also printed many hitherto unknown photographs of Everett and his family, ranging from his childhood through his last year. And in 2010, Rusho republished the combined edition under a new title, *The Mystery of Everett Ruess,* appending to the previous texts a short afterword covering the controversy aroused by our findings at the grave site on Comb Ridge.

Rusho's books, however, are vitiated by his practice of silently omitting passages, some of them fairly lengthy, from both the letters and the diaries, a practice he has never publicly explained. Even more maddeningly, through no fault of Rusho's, some of the letters he had at hand in 1983 and published in *Vagabond* have since gone missing. No one in the family or involved in the publishing of the books seems to know what may have happened to such important documents as the letters to Frances, possibly the only love of Everett's short life.

There is no doubt that many original works by Everett lie in private hands today, but whether they will ever find their way to museums or libraries remains very much in doubt. The doleful history of the Larry Kellner "collection" recounted in this book is only the most egregious example of such unacknowledged hoarding.

The Utah State Historical Society contains the extensive papers of Harry LeRoy Aleson, one of the most dogged sleuths who ever tried to solve the mystery of Everett's fate. Wallace Stegner's early and perceptive essay about Everett, "Artist in Residence," is found in the pages of his *Mormon Country.* Edward Abbey's sonnet mystically evoking Everett as "hunter, brother, companion of our days" appears as an afterword to Rusho's *Vagabond.* Copies of some of Everett's best blockprints, as well as other memorabilia, can be purchased through Steve Jerman at the website *http://everettruess.net/.* Nathan Thompson's unpublished master's thesis linking Everett with the Southern Utah Wilderness Alliance (SUWA) was submitted to the faculty of the Department of Communications at Brigham Young University in 2003.

My own pair of articles about Everett appeared in the Spring 1999 and the April/May 2009 issues of *National Geographic Adventure*. In addition, my short explanation of how the DNA testing at the University of Colorado produced an erroneous result can be found online at *ngadventure.com*.

Much of the research I conducted for this book was in the form of personal interviews and e-mail correspondence. (The acknowledgments name most of my sources for such insights and information.) For the background of the town of Escalante in the 1930s, I relied on a number of privately printed and rather obscure local history books, including Jerry C. Roundy's *"Advised Them to Call the Place Escalante,"* Fay L. Alvey's *"Damn Silliness,"* Nethella Griffin Woolsey's *The Escalante Story*, and DeLane Griffin's priceless personal scrapbook of his life as a rancher on the Escalante Desert and Kaiparowits Plateau. For documents about cattle rustling in the Escalante area, I consulted records kept at the Garfield County courthouse in Panguitch, Utah.

Ultimately, the most important source for this book was the landscape itself. The countless hours I spent hunting on the ground for clues to Everett's demise, or retracing segments of his journeys on foot, gave me at least as visceral an understanding of his passion for the wilderness as the equivalent amount of time I spent poking through books and libraries. On canyon rims and desert plateaus, I felt that I had come as close as I ever could to finding Everett Ruess.

INDEX

ABOUT THE AUTHOR

DAVID ROBERTS is the author of more than twenty books on mountaineering, adventure, and history, including *No Shortcuts to the Top, K2,* and *The Will to Climb,* which he cowrote with Ed Viesturs, as well as the memoir *On a Ridge Between Life and Death.* He has written for *National Geographic, National Geographic Adventure,* and *Smithsonian.* Roberts lives in Massachusetts.